MASTERPIECES OF 20TH-CENTURY AMERICAN DRAMA

Recent Titles in
Greenwood Introduces Literary Masterpieces

Masterpieces of French Literature
Marilyn S. Severson

Masterpieces of Modern British and Irish Drama
Sanford Sternlicht

MASTERPIECES OF 20TH-CENTURY AMERICAN DRAMA

Susan C. W. Abbotson

Greenwood Introduces Literary Masterpieces

GREENWOOD PRESS
Westport, Connecticut • London

11-05

Library of Congress Cataloging-in-Publication Data

Abbotson, Susan C.W., 1961–
    Masterpieces of 20th-century American drama / Susan C.W. Abbotson.
       p. cm. — (Greenwood introduces literary masterpieces, ISSN 1545–6285)
    Includes bibliographical references and index.
    ISBN 0–313–33223–1 (alk. paper)
    1. American drama—20th century—History and criticism. I. Title. II. Series.
PS350.A23 2005
812′.509—dc22   2005014520

British Library Cataloguing in Publication Data is available.

Copyright © 2005 by Susan C. W. Abbotson

Library of Congress Catalog Card Number: 2005014520
ISBN: 0–313–33223–1
ISSN: 1545–6285

First published in 2005

Greenwood Press, 88 Post Road West, Westport, CT 06881
An imprint of Greenwood Publishing Group, Inc.
www.greenwood.com

Printed in the United States of America

The paper used in this book complies with the
Permanent Paper Standard issued by the National
Information Standards Organization (Z39.48–1984).

10 9 8 7 6 5 4 3 2 1

To my darling children,
Rachel, Harry, and Brenda,
who sacrificed a lot of "Mummy time"
so I could get this written.

Contents

Introduction

Any attempt to explicate twentieth-century American drama within a single chapter becomes an exercise in compromise. Although certain theatrical movements, productions, and playwrights must be covered, there are numerous others, many influenced by the former, whose contributions are worthy but must go unmentioned for brevity's sake. This chapter is an introduction only and does not purport to tell the whole story; it merely shares the highlights. Serious drama has been privileged over comedy and musical theater because of its more profound ability to affect its audience. The focus is also on drama rather than theater, even though the two are often inextricable, which means that the primary focus is on plays and playwrights rather than their means of production.

To set a context for twentieth-century American drama, it helps to briefly outline what has come before. The first master American dramatist to achieve a worldwide reputation was Eugene O'Neill, who did not begin writing until 1913, but it would be a mistake to think he had sprung to life from a barren stage. Live professional drama had been produced on American shores since the eighteenth century by both touring companies and theaters in many of the larger cities, and although many early productions were from European scripts, American writers made contributions from these early days to help build the foundation on which twentieth-century American dramatists would build.

The first professionally produced play written by an American, nonetheless, was highly derivative of Shakespeare; a historical melodrama in verse, *The Prince of Parthia* (1767), by Thomas Godfrey, was so unremarkable that it closed after a single performance. The next hundred years saw only minor improvements, despite the efforts of playwrights like Royall Tyler, William Dunlap, and Susanna Rowson. Tyler first introduced Americans as a theatrical subject in *The Contrast* (1787), a social comedy in the style of English Restoration comedies, which explored the differences between Americans and the British. Dunlap, often referred to as "the father of American drama," was the first American able to live from the proceeds of his dramatic writing. Author of more than 50 plays, he is best known for comedies including *The Father; or, American Shandyism* (1789) and romantic, historical verse drama such as *André* (1798), both of which can be seen as attempts to define the "American" character for the national audience. Rowson, also an actress, wrote patriotic melodramas, like *Slaves in Algiers* (1794), about Americans escaping from captivity in Algiers. Most American-written plays during this period, and well into the nineteenth century, were either farces, romantic tragedies, or sentimental melodramas. They were strongly derivative of better-known European playwrights, and few had lasting merit.

Plays that could be conceived as developments were ones that dealt in native subjects, including James Nelson Barker's *The Indian Princess* (1808) and John Augustus Stone's *Metamora; or, the Last of the Wampanoags* (1829), which had American Indian protagonists (albeit Eurocentric stereotypes) and sparked interest in frontier melodrama. The nationalistic sagas of western expansion portrayed by playwrights like Mordecai Noah and Louisa Medina appealed to American patriotism and helped develop American stock characters such as the Yankee and the frontiersman. Other plays by Denman Thompson and Bronson Howard, respectively, were set in New England and the South. Realism had yet to be fully accepted, but Augustin Daly presaged it with plays like *Under the Gaslight* (1867), with its fairly authentic portrait of a one-armed Civil War veteran surviving in New York.

African American drama was also present in these early days, with William Henry Brown's *The Drama of King Shotaway* (1823). It was performed at his own short-lived African Grove Theater in New York and was the first professional play by an African American. Brown's theater was sadly closed due to racist pressure, fearing the loss of African American patronage in the restricted seating offered in mainstream theaters. The play that sparked the most interest in African Americans and had the largest cultural impact was the slavery saga *Uncle Tom's Cabin* (1852), adapted from Harriet Beecher Stowe's book by George L. Aiken. This was the most popular American play of the nineteenth century and was repeatedly performed across the country. Its depictions of African Americans were, however, sentimental at best and the cause of much resentment by later African American playwrights.

The close of the century was a period of great dynamism in American theater, but more in terms of transition than creativity. Known as the Gilded Age, this period referred to changes in the way theaters were organized and the number being built rather than to any great changes in artistic style. New York developed as a center, with the creation of a group of theaters that became known as Broadway. Shows continued to be more spectacle than substance, and few "modern" plays gained production in an increasingly syndicated arena that promoted touring companies around popular shows. This was the period during which James O'Neill, father of Eugene O'Neill, became trapped in the role of Edmund Danté in a touring production of *The Count of Monte Cristo* (1883), which ran for 29 years. Public preference was for vaudeville, black musicals, and the melodramatic musical extravaganza of shows like *The Black Crook* (1866), a version of the Faust story with a dancing female chorus line, which marked the beginnings of the burlesque style. But there were signs of higher-minded developments, strongly influenced by Norwegian playwright Henrik Ibsen's social realism.

James A. Herne's tale of marital infidelity, *Margaret Fleming* (1890), is considered the first American realistic play, with its restrained dialogue and well-drawn characters, and foreshadows the main direction of serious twentieth-century American drama to come. Though some found its subject matter distasteful, it inspired others, like Edward Sheldon, to embrace realism. Sheldon contributed a number of realistic portrayals of the American working class in plays like *The Nigger* (1910), an early, honest depiction of racial antipathy, and *Salvation Nell* (1908), with its revelation of the sordid life of tenement dwellers that Eugene O'Neill would find inspirational, and to which he pays homage in *The Iceman Cometh* (1946). Such dramas opened up new subject areas and a more socially engaged style of writing for American playwrights. Other important writers from this period include Clyde Fitch and Rachel Crothers. Fitch wrote more than 50 plays—predominantly incisive satires of materialism and upper-class hypocrisy—culminating in *The City* (1909), which shocked audiences with an onstage morphine injection and depiction of an incestuous marriage. Crothers wrote more than 30 plays from the early success of *The Three of Us* (1906) to *Susan and God* (1937), highlighting gender issues as she explored the nation's double standards and the state of "modern" marriage.

The prosperity of the next few decades drew many immigrants to American shores and saw the growth of industry and urban centers, the onset of American consumerism, and a growing prospective audience for plays both old and new. Nineteenth-century theatrical values were being increasingly challenged by modernist ideas, affected by political upheavals around the globe, and scientific theories from Charles Darwin to Carl Jung, which vastly complicated concepts of humanity. There was a growing dissatisfaction with the predictability of commercial theater and the inauthentic characterizations so often presented. In 1912 Equity was formed to allow actors greater power, and other theater workers were also becoming unionized; the costs of putting on large shows were becoming unfeasible. As movies grew in popularity, costly touring shows could not compete, and alternatives were needed to keep theater alive.

The growth of the Little Theater movement in the 1910s and the onset of groups like the Washington Square Players and the Provincetown Players, with their focus on artistic merit rather than box-office potential, offered new artistic freedom and possibility. The Provincetown Players, founded in 1915 by fledgling performers and playwrights under the leadership of George Cram Cook, gave Eugene O'Neill his chance to be heard, alongside Edna St. Vincent Millay, Edna Ferber, Susan Glaspell, and many others. Through them, Glaspell produced *Trifles* (1916), one of the earliest examples of American feminist drama, and Millay her expressionistic pacifist satire *Aria Da Capo* (1919). The group began in a makeshift theater on an old wharf in Provincetown but soon moved to a small theater in Greenwich Village. Resolutely experimental, their growing reputation for innovation in both staging and material drew much critical attention.

By the 1920s, the Provincetown Players had become professionally oriented. They continued to produce O'Neill's work and had other successes, including Paul Green's *In Abraham's Bosom* (1926), which won a Pulitzer and transferred to Broadway. Green's play marked white interest in presenting African Americans less sentimentally and more realistically onstage, in his depiction of an African American idealist's attempts to improve his rural community; but the viewpoint was white and seen as unrealistic by writers of the Harlem Renaissance, just as they had been disturbed by the exotic/primitive portrayal of their race in O'Neill's *The Emperor Jones* (1920), another influential play that also promoted German expressionism on the American stage. African American drama of this period was plentiful, but not usually produced in mainstream theaters and rarely published, so most fell beneath the critical radar.

Influential contributions to early black theater were Angelina Weld Grimké's *Rachel* (1916), about the effect of lynching on a middle-class African American family, which influenced other African American women to write about injustice. In 1923, African American drama also broke through to Broadway with Willis Richardson's one-act folk drama, *The Chip Woman's Fortune* (1922), followed two years later by the full-length *Appearances* (1925), by Garland Anderson, about the trial of an honest bellhop unjustly accused of raping a white woman. Yiddish theater was also flourishing, and playwrights including Sholom Asch, David Pinsky, and Halper Leivick strove to create something beyond the usual sentimental melodrama or slapstick, taking on serious social topics. They would influence later Jewish playwrights writing in English, such as Clifford Odets and Arthur Miller. Latin American and Chinese theater also existed in this period but were not producing plays in English.

Despite the innovative efforts of small theater groups, popular nonmusical theater in the early part of the century remained dominated by sentimental melodramatic blockbusters, including Anne Nichols's *Abie's Irish Rose* (1922) and Jack Kirkland's adaptation of Erskine Caldwell's *Tobacco Road* (1933). The former ran for over 2,500 performances and the latter more than 3,000. However, there was a new breed of critic looking for something more exciting, coupled with a demand for theatrical entertainment of all kinds and fed by talented new playwrights who were given opportunities to experiment with the Little Theater groups. New, serious American drama had both its champions and its outlets. It provided an arena in which a controversial play like Sidney Howard's *The Silver Cord* (1926) could win acclaim with its Freudian depiction of the smothering aspects of mother love and advance the concept of realistic modern problem-drama. Although Howard was influential, it was O'Neill who dominated American drama from the 1920s into the 1930s as he graduated from the Little Theater groups to Broadway with *Beyond the Horizon* (1920), a naturalistic rural tragedy that won a Pulitzer and ran for an entire season, stunning audiences with its visceral presentation of how people's own misguided choices can ruin lives.

O'Neill's plays display a restless search for fundamental meanings of life and death while exploring what he saw as the sickness of the society around him. Both highly innovative and willing to explore the possibilities of realism, symbolism, and expressionism, alongside techniques that include stream of consciousness, asides, chorus, and masks, O'Neill would try anything to effectively convey his message. Though his output can be seen as uneven, his popularity ensured his dramatic experiments would be emulated. In 1936 he was awarded the Nobel Prize for his great contribution to drama. O'Neill also won three more Pulitzers, including one for the posthumously produced *Long Day's Journey into Night* (1956), O'Neill's magnum opus, which draws together his commonest themes and concerns, and presents some of his most complex characterizations.

In 1919, the Theatre Guild, re-formed from the remaining talents of the since disbanded Washington Square Players, began presenting a variety of

serious plays produced to a high standard of artistry. They would become one
of the most influential producing organizations in America. Other works by
O'Neill were successfully produced, along with premier plays by rising talents Elmer Rice and Maxwell Anderson. Rice is best known for his daringly
expressionistic *The Adding Machine* (1923), which relates the life, afterlife,
and return to earth of a dehumanized office drone, Mr. Zero, representative of
modern man. This was typical of the new symbolistic drama, with its abstract
staging, distorted dreamlike sequences, and stark social message, showing
audiences and playwrights the potential of such techniques. Rice also offered
graphic, naturalistic works, like his Pulitzer-winning *Street Scene* (1929), set
in a New York tenement.

Anderson was just as varied, but his biggest contributions were to the
development of realism and dramatic blank verse. In the 1930s he produced
more than 30 plays, including the imaginative verse comedy *High Tor* (1936),
historical verse tragedies like *Elizabeth the Queen* (1930) and *Mary of Scotland*
(1933), and the more contemporary verse tragedy *Winterset* (1935), which
explored questions of truth and justice in its hypothetical consideration
of the effects of new exculpatory evidence coming to light in the Sacco-
Vanzetti case. This is considered by many to be his best play. One of his last
plays, *The Bad Seed* (1954), a prose dramatization of William March's novel,
caused controversy with its forthright depiction of an evil, murderous child,
challenging beliefs in children's innocence.

Despite all of this productivity, during the Depression years into the
1940s, the theater suffered financially. The Federal Theater Project (FTP)
was initiated in 1935 to try and tide things over, creating jobs for out-of-
work theatrical people, from stagehands to writers and actors. Though shut
down by Congress only four years later out of fear for its socialist politics and
supposed immorality, the FTP presented over 63,000 performances of over
1,000 productions to over 30 million people during its reign. It also developed some innovative theatrical practices through sponsored units, including
the Negro Theater and the Living Newspaper. Landmark productions of the
Negro Theater were its controversial "voodoo" *Macbeth* (1936), created by
Orson Welles and John Houseman and which was set in Haiti, and William
Du Bois' *Haiti* (1938), a play about Haitian politics; both depicted influential
images of black nationhood. Living Newspaper offered agitprop, documen-
tary-style pieces that examined current social issues—for example, Arthur
Arent's *Triple-A Plowed Under* (1936), about the difficulties caused by the
Agricultural Adjustment Administration.

Another significant producing group from this period was the Group
Theatre, founded by Lee Strasberg, Cheryl Crawford, and Harold Clurman,

with its emphasis on ensemble production and socially conscious drama. Influenced by the Moscow Art Theater, it also pioneered the naturalistic method-acting philosophies of Constantin Stanislavsky. Sidney Kingsley gave the Group its biggest hit, and some financial security, with his meticulously researched and intensely real hospital drama, *Men in White* (1933). The Group also brought Clifford Odets to public attention with his agitprop drama *Waiting for Lefty* (1935). Agitprop was a style of theater designed to incite its audience to political action, reflective of the social unrest of the era. Its language and situation were simplistic, designed to highlight social abuse. The Group's aims, however, were more artistic than political. Odets adopted but also elevated this style to produce America's best-known play about workers' rights. The play's dialogue was innovative for its time in its attempt to re-create working-class cadences. Odets's forceful realistic drama about a struggling Jewish family in the Depression, *Awake and Sing* (1935), was produced that same year and showed a subtler side to his writing.

In contrast to the downcast social pictures offered by Odets and Kingsley, and to help counteract the gloom of the Depression years, a number of worthwhile comedies were produced in this period. Playwrights such as George S. Kaufman and Moss Hart collaborated on a string of hits; Clare Booth wrote witty, psychologically insightful exposés of marriage and the socialite life; and Philip Barry's equally insightful *The Philadelphia Story* (1939) struck a firm chord as a distinctively American social comedy, and its success temporarily rescued the Theatre Guild from financial ruin, allowing it to continue to support new artists. Howard Lindsay and Russel Crouse's nostalgic domestic comedy, *Life with Father* (1939), became the longest-running drama in the history of Broadway with over 3,200 performances. Such plays were not profound; they gently addressed social issues but contributed little in the way of dramatic innovation.

Thornton Wilder managed to blend comedy with a more serious undercurrent and new techniques that rejected old-style realism in his Pulitzer-winning plays *Our Town* (1938) and *The Skin of Our Teeth* (1942). *Our Town*, on the surface a simple story of the lives of two families in the early twentieth century, was ingeniously staged without scenery and presented directly to the audience by the Stage Manager. Its subtle understanding without sentimentality spoke to a nation nostalgic for a simpler past. It has become an American folk classic, frequently produced in America and abroad. The innovative, antirealistic *Skin of Our Teeth* is a farce by design but serious in intent, as it offers an optimistic vision of humanity's survival from the Ice Age to its contemporary troubled era overshadowed by World War II.

Inspired by the realism of Sidney Howard, with his compact construction, sharply drawn characters, and precise dialogue, Robert Emmett Sherwood and Lillian Hellman would also make important contributions from the 1930s onward. Sherwood began writing comedy but found greater success with his realistic problem-dramas. He won Pulitzers for *Idiot's Delight* (1936), a complex combination of comedy, drama, and music that attacked war profiteering; the inspiring historical saga of Abraham Lincoln's early years, *Abe Lincoln in Illinois* (1938); and *There Shall Be No Night* (1940), a call to arms against totalitarian aggression. Hellman's plays, despite their occasional resort to melodramatic contrivances, were mostly well-crafted realistic pieces that offered distinct characters and strong plots that unflinchingly explored issues of evil, failure, and the power of money. She shocked Broadway audiences with her frank treatment of lesbianism in *The Children's Hour* (1934) and fascinated them with the cruelty of the Hubbards in *Little Foxes* (1939). *Watch on the Rhine* (1941) was another early antifascist drama, and *Toys in the Attic* (1960) an insightful exploration of the overpossessive, destructive love of the Bernier siblings.

Radical social change had profoundly affected the American viewpoint that had survived the Roaring Twenties, the Crash, and the Depression, followed by the impact of the Russian Revolution and World War II, alongside a surge of interest in the psychology of Sigmund Freud. The darker side of people had been revealed, and the nation faced moral, social, and religious crises as traditional values appeared to collapse. By the middle 1940s we see the emergence of two major American dramatists—Tennessee Williams and Arthur Miller—who would respond to the nation's growing feelings of disillusionment and unrest. While Williams would explore psychological realism, Miller would expand the field of American social drama.

Williams's *The Glass Menagerie* (1945) did much to establish his reputation and theatrical voice. Many of his innovations in staging, such as the use of screen devices and musical themes, were set aside, but the poeticism of his writing, followed up by the sensitively created, psychologically haunting characters in *A Streetcar Named Desire* (1947), became a cry that others heard. It was voted the most important play of the twentieth century by the American Theatre Critics Association and represents Williams at his best. Miller credits the vitality and the lyricism of *Streetcar* as liberating him to experiment more freely in his own work. Williams went on to have a string of successes throughout the 1950s into the 1960s, all exploring similar concerns regarding the nature of success and failure in a variety of social contexts, many of which were also made into highly successful movies to bring them to an even wider audience.

Although inspired by Williams, Arthur Miller's work sharply contrasts with his contemporary in both vision and style; whereas Williams focuses on the disconnection between individuals and their society, Miller is concerned with their connection. Miller's first Broadway play flopped, but his second, *All My Sons*, ran for 325 performances and brought him to critical attention. He followed this with what is possibly the best-known American play world-wide, *Death of a Salesman* (1949). It won numerous awards, showed an amazing endurance with its frequent popular revivals, and, by current publishers' estimates, still sells around 200,000 copies a year, not including the acting edition. Searingly honest and innovative in form in the way Willy Loman's consciousness is displayed, *Salesman*'s impact has been emotional and dramatic as well as sparking a major debate concerning the nature of tragedy.

The compassion and understanding that so strongly affected audiences watching Willy Loman's demise grew to chilling anger in Miller's retelling of the 1692 Salem witch trials in *The Crucible* (1953). Miller wanted to show the connection between those trials and the dangerous injustice and rigid ideology behind the Communist hunts of the 1950s run by the House Committee on Un-American Activities (HUAC), led by Senator Joseph McCarthy. Thus, his play becomes not only a powerful piece of human drama but an indirect reminder of an era that profoundly affected American theater when many of its participants were blacklisted or felt threatened into silence. While *The Crucible* sells 50,000 fewer copies a year than *Salesman*, it is the most performed of Miller's more than two dozen plays.

During the 1950s, William Inge was often ranked alongside Williams and Miller and was clearly influenced by the former in his focus on lonely people seeking love. His plays, like *Come Back, Little Sheba* (1950), with its depiction of the tensions in an arid marriage, and *Bus Stop* (1955), with its ensemble cast stranded at a diner during a snowstorm while they work out their issues, were generally more conventional, and so, ultimately, less influential. Because his plays were predominantly set in the heartland states, Inge has been seen as a spokesperson for the Midwest, bringing its worries, concerns, and way of life to mainstream view, as best illustrated in his Pulitzer-winning *Picnic* (1953), about a vagabond's impact on a variety of women in a rural backwater.

The World War II economy had injected much-needed cash into American theater, but it now had to combat the rise of the far more accessible television. By 1949 there were around 2 million television sets in the United States, and by 1950, 85 percent of the population claimed to regularly watch them. In the 1950s the theater needed to reestablish a cultural foothold, partly through the development of cheaper alternatives to Broadway to keep theatergoing within financial reach of the majority. Thus Off-Broadway and later Off-Off-Broadway were born in New York and helped to feed grassroots theaters in other major cities.

Off-Broadway consisted of a variety of inspirational theatrical groups, including Living Theater and Circle-in-the-Square. Living Theater had been founded in 1947 by Julian Beck and Judith Malina and was dedicated to experimental works. It would produce Jack Gelber's chillingly realistic exploration of heroin addiction, *The Connection* (1958), which invoked controversy by its depiction of addicts content with their way of life. Kenneth Brown's *The Brig* (1963), set in a nightmarish Marine Corps prison, helped cement its reputation of producing hard-edged, innovative works. In 1951, under the leadership of Theodore Mann and José Quintero, Circle-in-the-Square began presenting new plays and revivals of plays that they felt needed a second chance, in a more intimate arena-type stage, which generally used little in the way of sets or props. Their focus on the actor attracted much talent, including George C. Scott, Dustin Hoffman, James Earl Jones, Geraldine Page, and George Segal. Through two changes of premises they continue to challenge audiences with their original and intelligent productions.

Another important alternative venue was Joseph Papp's Public Theater, which began with the New York Shakespeare Festival in the mid-1950s but successfully diversified to premier plays previously unproduced in New York, such as Paul Zindel's testament to human resiliency, *The Effect of Gamma Rays on Man-in-the-Moon Marigolds* (1970). Also included were new American plays such as Charles Gordone's *No Place to Be Somebody* (1969), the first play by an African American to win a Pulitzer; David Rabe's *Sticks and Stones* (1971), about the impact of Vietnam; and Jason Miller's exploration of the masculine psyche in *That Championship Season* (1972). Papp has long been a big champion for emerging ethnic writers and theater practitioners, initiating the Festival Latino in the 1980s and working with many Asian American and African American artists.

Administered by the *Village Voice* to theaters beyond Broadway that had fewer than 300 seats, Obie Awards have been presented to the best Off-Broadway plays since 1956. These awards have become as prized as the more established New York Drama Critics' Circle Awards, which began in 1936. However, growing success led to greater economic costs, and by the close of the 1950s, new, cheaper producing groups began to form, eventually becoming known as Off-Off-Broadway. The trend began in a coffeehouse called Caffe Cino, owned by Joe Cino, in Greenwich Village. In 1959 he started presenting a variety of plays, including the first works of such later important dramatists as John Guare and Lanford Wilson. This inspired other groups looking for a freer dramatic outlet, such as Reverend Al Carmines's Judson Poets' Theater, Ralph Cook's Theatre Genesis, and Ellen Stewart's Café La MaMa (later renamed La MaMa ETC [Experimental Theater Club]), which has helped promote the work of numerous artists, producing virtually a play a week in its first five years of operation.

In the 1966–67 season Off-Off-Broadway mounted 300 productions, double that of Off-Broadway and Broadway combined for the same period. These Off-Off-Broadway groups were particularly useful in fostering and promoting the work of ethnic minorities, women, gays, and lesbians. A number of new nonprofit theater groups and university theater departments had also been founded in other major cities around America, bringing important new artists and topics to light. For example, Megan Terry came to attention through Omaha Magic Theater, and August Wilson through Yale Repertory Theater, which premiered a series of his plays in the 1980s. A number of these groups, such as San Francisco Mime Troupe (which has dealt with gender and class issues since the 1950s in an adapted form of commedia dell'arte), Free Southern Theater (supporting civil rights through docudrama and integrated companies from 1963 to 1980), and the Bread and Puppet Theatre (exploring puppetry and mime since 1961) were founded to forward sociopolitical issues. El Teatro Campesino, created with and in support of local farmworkers, brought leading Chicano playwright Luis Valdez to light, and inspired other Latino theater groups in California and beyond.

Advances were also being made in African American theater, partly sparked by the growing civil rights movement, but also by the groundbreaking Broadway success of Lorraine Hansberry's *A Raisin in the Sun* (1959), the first play by an African American woman to be produced on Broadway. The play, in the social drama tradition of Arthur Miller, depicts a middle-class African American family trying to advance itself in American society, and it anticipated many of the mounting concerns for African Americans and women of its day. It was one of the first widely seen plays to humanize the victims of racism in America and was the first play by an African American to win the New York Drama Critics' Circle Award for best play of its season.

Hansberry's success may also have helped bring more attention to other notable African American women playwrights, such as Alice Childress, Adrienne Kennedy, Ntozake Shange, and Suzan-Lori Parks. Writing at the same time as Hansberry, Childress wrote a number of powerful dramas, including *Trouble in Mind* (1955) and *Wedding Band* (1966), addressing race relations and female roles. Coming later, Kennedy found her voice Off-Broadway in dramas like *Funnyhouse of a Negro* (1964), which explores similar issues to Childress but in a more surreal format. Shange, meanwhile, created a theatrical expression more closely related to African performance in her conception of the "choreopoem," with its ritualistic movement, dance, and mix of poetry and prose, which she displayed in *for colored girls who have considered suicide/when the rainbow is enuf* (1976) and subsequent works. Parks inventively explores issues of race, gender, and identity using historical characters, surrealism, and satire to produce such controversial works as *Imperceptible Mutabilities in the Third Kingdom* (1989) and the Pulitzer winner *Top Dog/Underdog* (2001).

Black theater, of the 1960s in particular, presented the public with vehemently militant, as well as sensitive, portrayals of African Americans and their role in American society and history. Le Roi Jones (who renamed himself Amiri Baraka in 1968) had a large impact with highly creative but implicitly angry plays including *Dutchman* (1964) and *Slave Ship* (1967), which virulently attacked what he saw as racist issues and institutions. His work inspired other African American playwrights, such as Ed Bullins, Lonne Elder III, and Douglas Turner Ward, to explore in a variety of forms their outrage at white prejudice and issues of black pride. The Black Arts Movement (BAM), in which Baraka was a central figure, assisted in the development of African American theater as well as other artistic forms in order to build a sense of community and bring to light the concerns of African Americans around the country.

Although there were a number of individually successful plays during the 1950s, beyond Williams, Miller, and Inge, no particular playwrights made their mark on mainstream drama, and the 1960s were even leaner, dominated by just two major playwrights: Edward Albee and Neil Simon. Simon started out writing sketches for television and the occasional stage revue but came to public attention with the likeable comedy *Come Blow Your Horn* (1961), with its tale of an aging playboy deciding to settle down. Using believable characters and everyday dilemmas, Simon's string of Broadway successes continued well into the 1970s. In the 1980s he gained more critical credibility with his bittersweet autobiographical trilogy, which included a Pulitzer for *Lost in Yonkers* (1991). He is the most commercially successful American playwright of the century. Though a proficient and highly entertaining writer, Simon has not stretched the boundaries of drama so much as capitalized on them.

Like Simon, Albee's work is entertaining but also more challenging and critically exciting in its powerful exploration of metaphysical problems and troubling human relationships. In many ways, Albee can be seen as a generational equivalent to O'Neill—writing innovative, experimental drama within a milieu that was highly responsive to such productions—with 1960s

Off-Broadway and Off-Off-Broadway paralleling the Little Theater movement that had helped bring O'Neill to light in the 1920s. Albee began by writing short plays in the absurdist tradition, such as *Zoo Story* (1959), *The Sandbox* (1960), and *The American Dream* (1961), which caused a major sensation with their Off-Broadway productions.

The Theatre of the Absurd had grown as a response to what many saw as a collapse of moral and social values in the twentieth century. The primary aim of its plays was to point out the absurdity of life. Albee was clearly influenced by European playwrights Samuel Beckett, Eugene Ionesco, and Harold Pinter, and his early efforts were initially produced in Europe, but after their American productions in 1960 and 1961, the possibilities and the impact of this new type of theater would echo throughout American dramatic circles. Albee's first full-length play, *Who's Afraid of Virginia Woolf?* (1962), which explores the intricate relationships of two married couples, brought him fame and critical adulation. Although it has a realistic veneer, its surreal nature is never far from the surface, and it was an unusual and brave choice for a Broadway opening. It won a New York Drama Critics' Circle Award, and Albee has since been awarded three Pulitzers for other works; however, *Who's Afraid?* remains his most memorable and best-known work.

Meanwhile, during the 1960s, theaters beyond Broadway were experimenting not just with Theatre of the Absurd but also the Theatre of Cruelty (which forced audiences to become active participants in the play's experience), nudity onstage, and anything that would reflect the general rebelliousness of the time. An offshoot from Living Theater, Joseph Chaikin's Open Theater, founded in 1963, emerged as the most influential avant-garde theater of the 1960s and drew much acclaim. Using improvisation in its explorations of alternatives to psychological realism, the Open Theater developed a distinctive, physical style and worked closely with its playwrights. They produced Megan Terry's *Viet Rock* (1966), one of the first plays to protest the Vietnam War, and Chaikin collaborated with Sam Shepard on a number of his later works. Also, the National Endowment for the Arts (NEA) and the National Endowment for the Humanities (NEH), both formed in the mid-1960s, helped to fund much new art.

In 1967 Richard Schechner created an influential experimental approach that he called "environmental theater," which used nontheatrical venues for the performance space and, similar to the Theatre of Cruelty, would break down the supposed barriers between audience and actor. His Performance Group took classic texts and turned them into new performance pieces by adding contemporary references, linking them to aboriginal rituals, and altering the texts' environment. The collective exploration of violence,

Commune (1970), patched together literary and historical accounts from the Mayflower to Vietnam and was related by actors representing members of Charles Manson's notorious commune. While Schechner dissolved the company to pursue his studies, Elizabeth Le Compte and Spalding Gray continued his work, with the Wooster Group, founded in 1975.

The Wooster Group's first production, *Sakonnet Point* (1977), was an improvisation based on Gray's childhood in Rhode Island, but later plays mix Gray's memory with other texts such as *Point Judith* (1980), with its scenes from *Long Day's Journey into Night*. The Wooster Group's style evolved, including dancelike movement and surreal visual images to provocatively deconstruct classic American plays. *Route 1 & 9* (1981) controversially juxtaposed *Our Town* with a bawdy burlesque performance in blackface to expose what they felt was the false idyll created by Wilder's original text. Further controversy was stirred by efforts to mix *The Crucible* with a speech on drugs by hippie guru Timothy Leary in *L.S.D. (. . . Just the Highpoints)* (1984). Though known as a liberal, Miller forced them to remove scenes from his play.

America's avant-garde theater has had a number of influential contributors, but the most notable are Robert Wilson and Richard Foreman, who both came to notice in the 1970s and remain active today. Wilson has produced a series of increasingly lengthy epic pieces, including *The Life and Times of Josef Stalin* (1973), which ran for 12 hours, in which he rejects narrative structure and presents a collage of words and images from multiple sources to create a complex web of the symbolic, the fantastic, and the familiar. Such pieces typically utilize a variety of visual and audio media. Foreman's postmodern performance pieces, such as *Total Recall* (1970) or *Pearls for Pigs* (1997), try to emulate the shifting human consciousness, using constantly changing symbolic stage sets filled with enigmatic characters to provoke thought in their audiences.

American Indian drama found its voice during the 1970s in the plays of Hanay Geiogamah, including *Body Indian* (1972) and *49* (1975), as well as in the work of groups like the Spiderwoman Theater Collective. Meanwhile, the same period saw both Latin American and Asian American theater gaining recognition, although prominent Latino and Latina playwrights, including Carlos Morton, Eduardo Machado, Nilo Cruz, Maria Irene Fornés, and Cherríe Moraga, and Asian Americans Frank Chin, Elizabeth Wong, Velina Hasu Houston, and Philip Kan Gotanda achieved notice in theaters mostly outside of New York. Luis Valdez managed to get his expressionistic documentary-style rendition of Chicano life, *Zoot Suit* (1978), on Broadway for a brief run, but only David Henry Hwang, best known for the clever exploration of Eastern/Western cultures in his deconstruction of a Puccini opera in M. *Butterfly* (1988), had any marked success on the Broadway stage during the twentieth century. In most cases, these playwrights were motivated by a dual desire to correct stereotypes of their culture held by the mainstream and to explore the conflicts of their hyphenated identities. These burgeoning talents offer much hope for the continued growth and diversity of the next century of American theater.

Since the 1970s Broadway's economic structure has discouraged untested new plays, especially anything nonrealistic, and most critically interesting American drama has evolved elsewhere, though sometimes transferring to Broadway once established. One of the best-known and inventive playwrights from the 1970s to emerge beyond Broadway is Sam Shepard. He established his career in the 1960s through Off-Off-Broadway with a string of provocative, experimental dramas produced by Theatre Genesis, La MaMa, and Caffe Cino. The Pulitzer-winning *Buried Child* (1978) brought him national acclaim, which he has since cemented with a string of powerful plays that deconstruct much of American culture and include *True West* (1980), *Fool for Love* (1983), *A Lie of the Mind* (1985), and *States of Shock* (1991). Often criticized for his obscurity, Shepard continues to blend the real and the surreal, offering innovative dramas that may frustrate as much as offer insight to his audiences, but refuse to be complacent. In 1996 the Chicago-based Steppenwolf Theatre mounted a revival of *Buried Child,* which transferred to Broadway and became Shepard's first Broadway production.

Several female playwrights also came to notice during the latter part of the century, mostly through regional or Off-Broadway theaters. A number of these were rewarded with Pulitzer Prizes acknowledging their work, including Beth Henley's *Crimes of the Heart* (1981), Marsha Norman's *'Night Mother* (1983), Wendy Wasserstein's *The Heidi Chronicles* (1988), Paula Vogel's *How I Learned to Drive* (1998), and Margaret Edson's *Wit* (1999). Though most of these deal with gender issues, they are more than the feminist tracts that dominated earlier women's theater, offering wider explorations of politics, illness, social abuse, and power.

Other influential works were Mart Crowley's *Boys in the Band* (1968), which introduced a sympathetic, naturalized presentation of homosexuals to mainstream theater and prepared the way for plays by Terrence McNally, Larry Kramer, and Tony Kushner. Kushner's two-part *Angels of America* (1990–91), which explored AIDS in both actual and metaphorical terms, was a dazzling work full of ingenuity and provoking ideas. It reaffirmed the possibility of successful experimental drama on Broadway, as well as drawing attention to the lives and status of American homosexuals.

The 1980s were marked by the ascendancy of one prominent African American playwright, August Wilson, who asserted his intention to write a play that described the African American experience for each decade of the twentieth century. By the century's end he had completed all but two, and the cycle was completed in 2005 with *Radio Golf*. Two of the "history" plays gained Pulitzers: *Fences* (1985), set in the 1950s, and *The Piano Lesson* (1987), set in the 1930s, and all enjoyed considerable success on Broadway, although they premiered elsewhere. Wilson acknowledges the radical plays of Ed Bullins as an inspiration, but his style is very different, displaying an innovative use of music and metaphor while remaining predominantly realistic. Wilson's central concern regarding the need for African Americans to both honor the past and move confidently to the future are nowhere more clearly illustrated than in *The Piano Lesson,* which was filmed for CBS-TV's Hallmark Hall of Fame television series in 1995.

Postmodern experimental theater practitioners, building on the work of Robert Wilson and Robert Foreman and including Lee Breuer, Philip Glass, Ping Chong, and Laurie Anderson, privilege "performance" over more concrete productions, and are marked by their inclusion of visual images produced by a variety of media, prerecorded voices, rock music, unusual props and settings, and the use of dance. The 1980s and 1990s saw a steady increase of solo "performances." Some were monologues recalling personal experience to help the actor comment on wider social issues, such as Spalding Gray's *Swimming to Cambodia* (1985) or Rachel Rosenthal's pieces. Others were based on original sketches in which a single actor plays a variety of characters, such as Anna Deveare Smith's performances based on interviews following race riots in Brooklyn Heights and Los Angeles, *Fires in the Mirror* (1992) and *Twilight: Los Angeles* (1993), or John Leguizamo's satirical exposés of Latino culture, *Mambo Mouth* (1990) and *Spic-O-Rama* (1992).

The latter part of the century also brought to notice David Mamet, who began his theatrical education in Chicago but reached Broadway in 1977 with *American Buffalo* (1976). The play caused a stir with its free use of obscenity, halting repetitive speech patterns that try to capture urban American speech, and its disturbing vision of the dissolution of American culture. His unique ear for language and the brutal power of his writing continue to amaze critics, just as his capacity for symbolism intrigues and delights. Mamet's exposé of American materialism in *Glengarry Glen Ross* (1984) can be viewed as a *Death of a Salesman* for the next generation. It marks a high point in his career, as both a Pulitzer winner and one of his more accessible plays, but others, like the biting Hollywood satire *Speed-the-Plow* (1987) or the controversial battle of the sexes in *Oleanna* (1993), have been equally well received.

The great growth of nonprofit regional theater groups that began in the 1960s tapered off by the 1990s due to a steady decline in contributions, especially those from foundations, and the drastic decline of the NEA and the NEH. Costs had to be cut and ticket prices raised, making professional theater, even outside of New York, an expensive pleasure. The impact of this is yet to be seen; the danger that with an increasingly narrowed audience, the type of plays produced will become equally as narrow is a possibility. However, the end of the century can also be viewed as remarkable for its tremendous diversity, both among playwrights themselves as well as their styles and topics, which should presage a more hopeful scenario for the future of American drama.

The plays chosen for this study were selected on the basis of the strength of their influence socially and culturally as well as dramatically. Since theater is such a community activity it seemed impossible to separate these areas. While it can be argued that a number of other twentieth-century American plays can equally be called masterpieces, the 10 selected here offer a variety that almost spans the century, as well as paying some small tribute to gender and ethnicity; they also arguably happen to be the best plays by America's best-known playwrights.

Each play will be introduced by a biographical background of the author, highlighting the importance of that particular play in the playwright's development and critical standing. After a synopsis of the plot, there will be a thematic analysis, with explanations of the major characters, the play's literary style and devices, its historical background, and a summary of its critical reception. The social, cultural, and theatrical impact and importance of each play will be conveyed to explain why such works have become so canonical and to show how each has helped shape and define American drama. There will be suggestions for further reading at the close of each chapter and a more general bibliography and index at the book's close.

1

Thornton Wilder
Our Town
1938

BIOGRAPHICAL CONTEXT

Thornton Niven Wilder was born to Amos and Isabella Wilder in Madison, Wisconsin, on April 17, 1897, a second son to be followed by three sisters. His father, a doctorate in political science from Yale, was editor, at the time, of the *Wisconsin State Journal*, but nine years later took the family abroad as a U.S. consul. Young Wilder briefly bounced back and forth between the Orient and America and was schooled in Hong Kong, Shanghai, and California, finally graduating from Berkeley High School. While in Berkeley, at the age of 10, he had become interested in Greek drama, offering his services as an extra in the local university performances. Although his parents' marriage was essentially loveless, Wilder was very attached to his siblings and used his later financial success to support many of them. They mostly wrote either fiction, poetry, or essays and were known in some circles as the American Sitwells. Wilder himself never married, although family, and its importance, has always been central to much of his writing. With the royalties he got from his second novel, the best-selling, Pulitzer-winning *The Bridge of San Luis Rey* (1927), he bought a large house for the family in Hamden, Connecticut, although he typically spent over half his time traveling throughout the United States and Europe. His father, keen on education, had been eager to give his sons, especially, as broad an experience as possible and arranged for them to work on farms in various parts of the country during their summer vacations, no doubt encouraging Wilder's wanderlust.

He started his undergraduate career at Oberlin College in Ohio but transferred to Yale, from where he graduated in 1920. After this, he studied archeology in Rome for a year, Italy being a favorite place of his grandmother. This greatly influenced his attitude toward history and the impact of time on the human condition, a common theme in much of his work. On his return, he taught French at the Lawrenceville School in New Jersey for four years and then gained an MA in French literature from Princeton. During this time he also wrote two novels, *The Cabala* (1926), an allegory of Christianity and paganism among a decadent European nobility, and *The Bridge of San Luis Rey*, about an eighteenth-century priest's search for theological meaning after the accidental death of five people. The success of the latter allowed Wilder to subsequently spend the rest of his life as a writer, although he continued to teach occasionally and was a popular lecturer.

Meanwhile, he had begun writing what he called his "Three-minute" plays at Oberlin, influenced by Theodore Dreiser's *Plays of the Natural and the Supernatural* (1916). Many of these were later collected in *"The Angel That Troubled the Waters" and Other Plays* (1928). Although largely unplayable as stage pieces, they nevertheless revealed an interest in religious issues and a refusal to be confined by realism. At Yale he had boldly updated and adapted Ben Jonson's *The Alchemist* (1610) to take place in 1871 New York and turned it into an allegorical treatment of the Second Coming, which was published in the *Yale Literary Magazine* in four installments as *The Trumpet Shall Sound* (1919–20). In 1928 he went abroad with his sister Isabel to study European stage techniques.

His third novel, an exotic exploration of Greek culture and the onset of Christianity, was called *The Woman of Andros* (1930). Marxist critic Michael Gold, who felt that serious literature should address only contemporary social issues, attacked the book as facile escapism. Many critics feel that Gold's public derision may have prompted Wilder to turn his attention to the more American subjects he chose in his next collection of plays. His follow-up novel, *Heaven's My Destination* (1934), parodied facets of American life in the Depression period and was certainly more socially relevant. *"The Long Christmas Dinner" and Other Plays* (1931) became Wilder's first popular dramatic pieces. Influenced by European experimental and nonrealistic theater, the plays in this volume mostly eschew, or at least satirize, the conventions of realism, and a number, including the title play, *Pullman Car Hiawatha*, and *The Happy Journey to Trenton and Camden*, prefigure his later plays in their lack of scenery; use of an onstage stage manager as narrator and formulaic, sometimes allegorical characters; and the way they telescope time. These three plays soon became some of the most frequently performed American one-act plays, causing eager anticipation for his later full-length pieces.

Wilder's first full-length productions, however, were translations: André Obey's *Le Viol de Lucréce* (1932) and Henrik Ibsen's *A Doll's House* (1937). *Lucréce* closed after only 31 performances, and although *A Doll's House* was more successful, it was unremarkable but for its pairing of Wilder with director Jed Harris, who would go on to direct Wilder's first original full-length play. The long-awaited *Our Town* finally appeared in 1938, winning Wilder his second Pulitzer Prize. The idea for the play had come to Wilder in 1935 as a short piece he titled "M Marries N." By 1936 this had expanded into a longer piece called *Our Village* but was completed as *Our Town* the following year. The play had been written while Wilder was traveling to and fro, partly in Europe, and partly at an artists' retreat known as the MacDowell Colony, in Peterborough, New Hampshire, which Wilder often patronized. It was his walking in this area and around Lake Sunapee that had inspired his sense of location.

Wilder's next play, a largely realistic romantic farce called *The Merchant of Yonkers* (1938), was initially unsuccessful but became a major hit in 1954 after being revised and reproduced as *The Matchmaker*. A decade later this was turned into the hit musical *Hello Dolly!*, which financially secured Wilder for the rest of his life. Although *The Skin of Our Teeth* (1942) won Wilder a third Pulitzer, it was not without controversy. Critics virtually accused him of plagiarizing James Joyce's *Finnegans Wake* (1939). Although he later acknowledged an indebtedness to Joyce, Wilder had certainly used similar ideas, character types, and actions in works prior to *Finnegans Wake*, and the debt was one of inspiration rather than theft. The play's optimistic message that civilization will always be rebuilt, whatever the disaster—be it the Ice Age, a biblical flood, or a cataclysmic war, all of which are featured in the play—made it a popular hit among audiences horrified by the destruction of World War II. That same year, 1942, Wilder also wrote the screenplay for Alfred Hitchcock's *Shadow of a Doubt* (1943).

Although by the 1950s Wilder's reputation as a major writer had been firmly established, his later works were less predominantly successful, especially among critics. His novel *The Ides of March* (1948), a fictionalized account of the last days of Julius Caesar, had met only moderate success, and his play *The Alcestiad* (first produced as *A Life in the Sun* in 1955), modeled on Greek drama, and its subsequent accompanying satyr, *The Drunken Sisters* (1957), took him in a very different, less popular direction. The German-language libretto that Wilder wrote for Louise Talma's operatic version of *The Alcestiad* in 1962 was poorly received. A number of the plays he wrote during this period were not produced in his lifetime or had fairly minor productions, some only in Europe. They continued to be experimental, and many showed a darker, more pessimistic side to Wilder's philosophy. His final two completed works were both moderately successful novels: *The Eighth Day* (1968), about an innocent fugitive from justice, which won the National Book Award, and *Theophilus North* (1973), about a young teacher finding his way among the Rhode Island elite.

One of Wilder's greatest strengths was his popularity with the general public; his voice reached far beyond a limited artistic elite. Never setting himself apart, despite his advantages, he served in a Coast Artillery Corps in Rhode Island during World War I, having been turned down from the regular military branches because of his poor eyesight. In World War II he enlisted to advance from captain to lieutenant colonel in the Army Air Force Intelligence, serving in Algeria and Italy, and was decorated for his contributions. He was a keen student of many cultures and periods and a humanist of the highest order. Always boldly experimental throughout his career, he liked to fuse the traditional with the new to create new ways of conveying his ideas, which were often centered on what his nephew Tappan Wilder, speaking on a panel at the 2004 American Literature Association conference, described as the "cosmic in the commonplace."

Friendly during his lifetime with Ernest Hemingway, F. Scott Fitzgerald, Sigmund Freud, and Gertrude Stein, he was, like them, a prolific letter writer and often acted in his own plays, especially during summer theater. Multitalented, he wrote plays, screenplays, novels, essays, and librettos in addition to letters, and was an accomplished teacher, scholar, and translator; he is the only writer to win a Pulitzer for both fiction and drama. Wilder was fluent in four additional languages: Italian, Spanish, French, and German. He is probably one of the most cosmopolitan of American playwrights, and yet, ironically, gained greatest fame from his depiction of small-town American life, in *Our Town*. He died of a heart attack in 1975 while working on a sequel to *Theophilus North*.

PLOT DEVELOPMENT

Our Town offers a slice of small-town America over a period of 12 years, beginning in 1901, and is centered on the neighborly interactions of the Gibbs and the Webb families in Grover's Corners, New Hampshire, amid milk and paper deliveries, town gossip, and news. The play features an omniscient Stage Manager who narrates the drama, jokes with the audience, and implicitly connects the people of Grover's Corners with the whole universe. The Stage Manager leads us through these people's daily lives, sets each scene in detail to bring it alive in our imagination, and instructs various town members to contribute additional information about the town's historical and social background. The courtship, marriage, and loss of young couple George Gibbs and Emily Webb lie at the play's center, from their early school days to Emily's ghostly return after dying in childbirth nine years later.

At the play's start, the audience faces a half-lit, empty stage, without curtains or scenery. The Stage Manager brings out two tables, some chairs, and a bench to represent the houses of the Gibbses and the Webbs, and then the lights go down. Initially speaking into darkness, the Stage Manager tells us about the production, and as the lights rise, introduces us to Grover's Corners, verbally describing the town and introducing some of the main characters. Dr. Gibbs is returning home at dawn after delivering a baby and chats with Joe Crowell, the young paperboy, and Howie Newsome, the milkman. The rest of his family noisily rises for breakfast, as do the Webbs on the other side of the stage, and the children all prepare for school. All chitchat about mundane things: the weather, inconsequential town events, details about the neighbors, complaints or satisfaction about what they are doing. This is less a story than an impression of daily life. Mothers chide their children and neighbors have a friendly gossip as they get on with their normal routines.

The Stage Manager dismisses the actors as he introduces Professor Willard to offer a history lesson on the town, and then Mr. Webb, as the newspaper editor, to report on the town's demographics and political structure. Wilder has actors planted in the audience to ask questions to extend this social picture. We are then returned to the town later that afternoon as the children come home from school, and see Emily and George meet up. George gets Emily to help him with his schoolwork and talks about his prospects as a farmer. She worries about her looks, and the Stage Manager again interrupts, this time to point out the intrinsic similarity of these folk to people from other periods. It is now evening as the church choir practices, the children do their homework, and Dr. Gibbs has a father-son chat with George. As the ladies walk home from choir practice they gossip about Simon Stimson, the choirmaster, and his drinking. Then everyone settles down to bed.

The second act takes up three years later, and things have changed little as the town wakes again. It is the morning of the wedding of Emily and George. The parents, especially, feel a little on edge and recall their own apprehensions when they married, but it is clear that this will be a happy marriage. George flouts superstition by going over to see Emily, but she refuses, and all he gets is some fatherly advice from Mr. Webb. The Stage Manager interrupts to take us back to the beginning of Emily and George's courtship.

It begins with Emily berating George for being too conceited about his base-ball abilities, but George apologizes, they go for a soda, and George decides not to go away to agricultural college so he can stay near Emily. Then we return to the wedding ceremony, led by the Stage Manager, who also phi-losophizes about what marriage actually means. Both Emily and George are nervous; each considers pulling out, but they declare their love for each other and go through with it.

For act 3 the stage has been rearranged to depict a cemetery. The graves are marked by chairs, on which the dead sit. It is now 1913, and the Stage Manager updates us on the few changes that have taken place in the town since the last act. A funeral is about to take place, and we learn it is Emily's, who has died in childbirth. Emily joins the dead on the stage and they help her recognize the difference between the living and the dead and prepare her for eternity. Still feeling her connection, Emily yearns to go back, despite the objections of her fellow dead, and chooses her 12th birthday as a moment she believes she was totally happy. Once there she enters the scene and "plays" her 12-year-old self. She is initially in awe of the past and the sight of those she loves, but this soon turns to frustration as she sees everyone too busy to really notice the details of their lives, and she asks to leave. Grieved that life is apparently being wasted on the living, that they are too distracted by the living of it to truly recognize its wonder, Emily rejoins the dead as they watch George, distraught over his wife's grave. The Stage Manager has the last say, describing the way in which life in Grover's Corners will continue, and wishing the audience a good night.

CHARACTER DEVELOPMENT

In one sense, the play's central protagonist is the town itself, since none of the individual characters truly rise beyond the representative. What we become most familiar with is the general life of a complete town. With no scenery or props, Grover's Corners is vividly brought to life before us, indicat-ing that the true spirit of any community lies in the individuals of whom it is composed. Yet Wilder does not make his individuals complex character-izations, but rather types, allowing Grover's Corners to stand for any small American township.

As a community, everyone knows everyone's name and business, and together the residents of Grover's Corners celebrate the ups and downs of everyday life: the births, the marriages, the deaths. They chat as they eat, string beans, and attend choir practice. The two families of the Webbs and the Gibbses and their interrelationships offer a microcosmic slice of the town as a whole, as each represents a typical middle-class American family. During the first act the Webbs and the Gibbses go through their daily routines of meals, school, chores, choir practice, and homework, to cement our recognition of their essential ordinariness. Although the play gradually narrows in on the central relationship of George Gibbs and Emily Webb, neither becomes more than a cipher of the youthful promise they embody—representing two young people who love, marry, and eventually suffer, as Emily dies in childbirth. For Wilder, this was the bittersweet way in which the world turned.

In Grover's Corners people's dreams are modest, unalloyed by materialism or capitalistic designs. Ninety percent of those born in town end up settling there, even when they go to college. Dr. Gibbs is content with a vacation to visit Civil War battlegrounds every other year; their son, George, wishes to be a farmer. Mrs. Gibbs longs to go to Europe but satisfies herself by making French toast and leaving the money set aside for the trip to her son. Mr. Webb runs the town twice-daily newspaper, his wife spends her time canning vegetables for the winter, and his daughter, Emily, is also content to become a housewife.

Yet, despite the contented surface, there are aspects of Grover's Corners that jar. Simon Stimson, the church organist and director of the choir, is unhappy with small-town life. He drinks and restlessly prowls the streets at night, until he commits suicide. To make him fully representative of that type who is never happy, we do not learn the specifics of his troubles, but he remains bitter even in death. The fact that no one in the town offers him any help indicates a social failure—at times, despite the presence of six churches in this small town, these people are too wrapped up in themselves to show any charity or compassion to others. Wilder does not intend for his town to be an ideal, but grounded in human reality.

While ordinary life is at the play's core, it is not a life unalloyed by sadness and waste, for life is capricious—thus Wallace Webb dies from a burst appendix on a camping trip, and Joe Crowell graduates top of his class at MIT but is soon killed fighting in World War I. As the Stage Manager wryly declares, "All that education for nothing." We also might have seen Emily as a woman with a future; academically gifted, she assists George with his homework. Yet he is the one elected class president and she his secretary/treasurer. This foreshadows her marriage to him straight out of high school to become his helpmate and wife, rather than pursue any career of her own. But this is the start of the twentieth century, and Wilder is not concerned with gender issues but with what he sees as a larger scheme. Mr. Webb jokes about how to treat women, but more for the humor than as any social statement.

Emily is initially restless as a ghost, wanting to return, but the dead mostly want to forget life as soon as possible, as it is too painful to remember, knowing it has gone. It matters not that their lives may be viewed as trivial, because to them, as they lived them, they were not. As Emily relives her 12th birthday she becomes horrified noticing the details she and her parents missed at the time and is overcome with a sense of loss. As the Stage Manager suggests, it is only saints and poets who come close to appreciating life's wonder while still living. But at the play's end, while night falls, life goes on.

The Stage Manager is the most central role in the play, and it is he we get to know best. Affable, charming, and very knowledgeable, he continually directs the audience's vision of Grover's Corners. He sets each scene and describes any missing props, offering a visual picture of what the missing scenery might have supplied. He provides the necessary background of the town and its people, with the assistance of a local professor and the editor of the town's newspaper. As a narrator, he is able to bridge any gaps in time, for he speaks to the audience and the actors directly, telling the latter which scenes to play, or when to leave in order to move things along, and even acts some of the minor roles himself (such as Mr. Morgan, the owner of the town drugstore; an old lady, Mrs. Forrest; and the minister at the wedding), thus participating in the action. He also provides a philosophical commentary on the events we witness. In many ways he is related to the omniscient narrator Wilder used in his novels: someone who knows everything about the characters' past, present, and future, even how and when they will die.

THEMES

Mrs. Gibbs's advice to the dead Emily, who is deciding which moment of her past to revisit, to "Choose the least important day in your life. It will be important enough" reveals much of Wilder's theme. Wilder recognizes the brevity of human life on a cosmic scale and the commonplace fact of sadness and suffering in those lives, so much so, that sadness and suffering are in some sense a part of those lives and what gives them shape. From the start we know from the Stage Manager that many of these people will die. Emily and George have nine brief years of marriage before he is left to mourn her loss with his four-year-old son, but the fact is, they had nine years of happy marriage. Such moments of happiness are reflected in the lives of most of the town's inhabitants. What Wilder asks is that along with Emily we rediscover the simple joy of living—beyond pain, frustration, and failure—and relish the little details, because that is what life is about, and their ordinariness is what makes them so special. As Wilder states in his preface to *Three Plays*,

Our Town "is an attempt to find a value above all price for the smallest events in our daily life" (xi)—a timely message for the Depression age and the relevance of which has not lessened over the years.

Wilder's vision is so broad he offers a picture of life in its entirety, even to death. His vision is one of the essential timelessness and universality of the human condition. He viewed those living in the twentieth century as existing very much the same as those living in any previous century in the broadest sense: all are born, live, love, and die, with only variations on this theme. Always interested in ancient cultures, Wilder has the Stage Manager point out the similarity between the daily routine of families in the ancient Babylonian empire and in Grover's Corners, and has him place a copy of the play in a time capsule to enable people a thousand years from now to know what life was like in a New England village at the turn of the century. The point is, nothing ever really changes, and if we take a step back in the timescale, individual lives should hardly matter at all in the grander scheme of life, they appear so briefly in its design. And yet, each tiny detail of life matters greatly to the person living it, or at least, Wilder suggests, it should.

It is the common human failure to appreciate the smallest events in daily life that *Our Town* laments. Upon arrival in the cemetery, Emily remarks that she never knew "how in the dark live persons are." As a ghost, Emily restlessly longs to rejoin the living, but after reliving her 12th birthday, she comes to see that the past is forever changed by the knowledge of what is to come, and one cannot happily go back. She also gains a new appreciation of the wonder of life itself, and this is the central lesson Wilder is trying to convey. Emily asks the Stage Manager, "Do any human beings ever realize life while they live it?—every, every minute?"; "No," he answers, "The saints and poets, maybe—they do some," but the suggestion is that most of us are too busy living life to pause and recognize its wonderful detail as it passes. The question is one of time, and the relative brevity of human life in the bigger scheme of creation. Earlier in the play, the Stage Manager requests only a short lecture from Professor Willard, because, as he adds, "unfortunately our time is limited." The line should take on a deeper significance beyond the obvious.

Despite many erroneous evaluations of the play as presenting a happy and naïve view of life, Wilder actually fills his play with death and a fair amount of suffering. For example, when the Gibbses are first introduced we are told the manner of their deaths before we know much else about them. He portrays many of the darker aspects of human nature alongside the good. Rather than create a New England idyll, Wilder is offering a balanced view about life as he saw it, as one of his dead suggests in act 3 when she declares, "My, wasn't life awful—and wonderful." But while he allows Simon Stimson to rail against life, Wilder does not allow him the final say, having Mrs. Gibbs tell him off and offer a wider vision: "Simon Stimson, that ain't the whole truth and you know it." It may be this refusal to become despairing or overly cynical that makes the play finally, despite its harsh undertones, appear so affirmative. As the Stage Manager insists, "There's something way down deep that's eternal about every human being," and in this lies hope for every human being.

HISTORICAL CONTEXT

Inspired by the poem "Lucinda Matlock" in Edgar Lee Masters's *Spoon River Anthology*, *Our Town* takes place at the beginning of the twentieth century. The play depicts the easy community of small-town America, as represented by Grover's Corners, New Hampshire—the kind of town where everyone knows everyone, and the daily rituals of milk and paper deliveries evoke a simpler but full existence.

The timing of *Our Town* could not have been better for a nation caught between two World Wars and trying to cast off the pall of the Depression. Despite its darker elements, on the surface at least, it appeared to offer its audiences a glimpse of their better selves and better times. Wilder's optimism was partly based on his view that the Great Depression was not such a bad period when viewed through the larger lens of time. Thus he rarely dwelled on this specific period, even while he was writing for people who had mostly suffered through it. For Wilder, the Depression was no better or worse than any other period, and life simply goes on.

In his preface to *Three Plays,* Wilder explains: "*Our Town* is not offered as a picture of life in a New Hampshire village.... It is an attempt to find a value above all price for the smallest events in our daily life" (xi). In other words, Wilder was striving to present a picture of life that could be generally applied to all people of all cultures. Thus, Emily's farewell speech is not to an explicitly American culture and lifestyle at the turn of the century, but to the details of daily life that are, for the most part, universal: "Mama and Papa ... clocks ticking ... food and coffee. And new-ironed dresses and hot baths ... and sleeping and waking up." The fact that so many countries around the world have successfully mounted productions of the play is testament to the fact that this leap of the imagination may have worked.

However, although Wilder tries to stress the universal to present a picture of humanity in its broadest sense, it is, yet, undeniable that *Our Town* is saturated by what can be seen as profoundly American values and history. The stage manager frequently reminds us of that history as he points out the seventeenth-century flagstones in the cemetery and the iron flags on the graves of the Civil War veterans. Throughout the play we hear references to particularly American events, from the coming of the Mayflower and the decimation of American Indians, through the Revolutionary War, the Louisiana Purchase, the Monroe Doctrine, the rise of Ford automobiles, World War I, and other references to American culture and lifestyle. These details could have made this an especially American story, only that they finally serve to make the play's vision more concrete, grounding it further in daily life by giving that life a sense of history and the past, which, of course, is evident in any culture.

LITERARY STYLE AND DEVICES

The apparent simplicity and incredible popularity of the play make us forget its fundamentally radical style and theme at the time it was produced. In a period when realism dominated the stage, like Bertold Brecht in Germany and Luigi Pirandello in Italy, Wilder sought a different means of presentation, stripping away props and scenery to encourage audiences to pay closer attention to the cast and what is said. But where Brecht and Pirandello sought to alienate their audiences, Wilder seeks to engage them both emotionally and intellectually. With its bare stage, *Our Town* transcends a particular time and place, presenting a universal vision of what Wilder saw as the meaning of life, lived from day to day, wonderful in the very details of its ordinariness. As Wilder explains in his preface to *Three Plays*, he began writing plays to try and "capture not verisimilitude but reality" (xi).

In another "preface" for the play that Wilder wrote for the *New York Times*, he explains his decision to approach from an archeologist's point of view, given his training in that field. He sought to discover the larger issues of life from close observation of the smallest details, just as archeologists piece together how someone lived long ago from the tiny pieces of everyday evidence they unearth. *Our Town* is constructed in much the same way as a jigsaw puzzle. Being disinterested in conflict—usually at the core of most theatrical plots—Wilder prefers instead to present an episodic structure that, once all the pieces come together, will depict the life of a town. What is more, these episodes have no firm continuity, as the narrative flow is interrupted by set pieces such as Professor Willard's geography lecture or the Stage Manager interrupting the wedding ceremony to go back in time to the start of the couple's romance.

Though made up of a series of what might seem like set pieces, the disparate acts are tied together with various common threads, including the singing of the same hymn, "Blessed Be the Tie That Binds," in each act. Each act, however, has an explicit function. Act 1 depicts the daily life of Grover's Corners. The emphasis is on social rather than individual relationships—we are learning here about the nature of a community, a town, rather than single people. In act 2, we gain closer focus on Emily and George as representatives of their typical families and, in a sense, representatives of humankind's "urge to merge." As Mrs. Gibbs declares, "People are meant to go through life two by two. 'Tain't natural to be lonesome." These are the two whose actions (marriage and children) will ensure the continuity of the town. We get a little closer to George and Emily through Wilder's affecting descriptions of their courtship, but they are really never more than representatives, and our emotional involvement is more for the abstract concept than the particular ideal. George and Emily symbolize youth and all its promise.

The third act transports us to an even more universal plane as we go through death to contemplate eternity and are awarded with the knowledge that it is the tiniest detail of the here and now that makes life worth living, whatever its precariousness. Although the focus seems to be on Emily, there is a whole community of the dead backing her up and sharing her insight, so that it remains more representative than specific. Despite a stage populated by the dead, what we are made to realize is that life in the collective persists, whatever its individual brevity or sadness, and that, Wilder insists, is cause for celebration.

Arthur Miller was to recognize Wilder's use of expressionism in his 1956 essay "The Family in Modern Drama." Miller felt that as a general rule, while realism lends itself to the presentation of family relationships, wider social ones are more effectively depicted using expressionism. Its greater emphasis on symbolism and theatricality help expressionism to delineate the nature of social forces with a clarity sometimes too blurred by the fine details of realism. Wilder wished to break the boundaries of time and place, to present a play that would transcend such restrictions; expressionism allows him to do that, just as it allows a play that on the surface may appear so dated, to be ultimately timeless.

SITUATION OF WORK

Wilder's work offers an interesting alternative to the more downcast views advanced through the plays of dominant contemporaries, including the squalid family sagas and politicized agitprop of Clifford Odets, or the dark, naturalistic dramas of Sidney Kingsley. Wilder was, by contrast, more upbeat, and sadly, as a consequence, not taken as seriously by many critics for a long time. However, by the 1990s, critics were beginning to better appreciate what Wilder had contributed to American theater.

Wilder—much as Arthur Miller, who would soon follow—loved the theater and felt it was the most social of all the arts, allowing for an immediate, community experience—a place where human beings can share a sense of their own humanity. His plays have been shared possibly the most of any American playwright. *Our Town* is the number-one seller from the Samuel French catalog, which indicates the continued frequency with which this play is performed. Between the spring of 1939, when the amateur and stock rights to perform the play became available, and the end of 1940, 795 productions were mounted. The play has remained popular with professional acting troupes too; for example, between 1970 and 1999 it was performed 91 times in professional theaters. The play is generally believed to be performed at least once each night somewhere in America.

The play's attraction is due to many aspects, including its cheapness to produce, given the lack of scenery and simple props and costumes; its large cast with good parts for old and young; and the swiftness of its emotional appeal and impact. Audiences are drawn to what they see as the play's optimism and affirmation of traditional American morality and values in what seems on the surface a fairly simple, folksy drama. Such views clearly put him at odds to the far more dyspeptic O'Neill. Yet *Our Town* has its darker side too, filled with discontent, waste, pettiness, and hypocrisy, as well as unfulfilled hope and promise, as Grover's Corners is ultimately shown to us "warts and all."

The play continues to have great popular success, but it has also won its share of critical acclaim. Playwright Donald Margulies, in his foreword to the 2003 reprint of the play, suggests that it could be "*the* great American play" (xi), as he describes his transition from viewing it as a corny piece of nostalgia to realizing its true subversive power. Drama critics both then and now have tended to lionize Wilder for his philosophical themes, alongside his innovations and experimentation. Many credit him with revitalizing American theater in the 1930s. Theater critic Travis Bogard views Wilder as a man who, along with O'Neill, freed the American theater from its traditional forms through his experimental productions. Though many of the play's conventions, such as its direct address, telescoping of time, lack of scenery, and use of mime and a narrator, may not seem unusual now, next to the comedies mostly playing on Broadway in 1938, they were truly radical.

Wilder's importance to American theater is partly due to his rejection of the widely popular dramatic realism of his day in favor of technical experimentation, coupled with an interest in the older theatrical forms and conventions of the Greek and Renaissance playwrights. Both Luigi Pirandello in Europe and Eugene O'Neill in America were experimenting with theatrical convention, but Wilder was the first to break so many of the usual conventions of character and plot in a single work. The fact that he adapted many of these ideas from other sources—including the telescoping of time from Japanese Noh theater; the breaking of the fourth wall (which usually determines that an actor pretends the audience is not there) from Europeans like Pirandello; the use of mime; no scenery and a chorus figure (a narrator who both comments on and takes part in the action) from ancient Greek theater; and the use of soliloquies, asides, and greater reliance on the actor from Renaissance theater—make him no less innovative, as he was the first to place all of these techniques side by side on the modern stage.

Wilder's influence can most evidently be seen in the empathetic work of Tennessee Williams, Arthur Miller, and August Wilson, with the latter two, especially, displaying a similar humanistic concern with society and people's place within that scheme. Like Wilder, Williams, Miller, and Wilson do not allow their evident sympathy for their characters to spill out into sentimentality. Other writers, including Edward Albee and John Guare, have been influenced by Wilder's ability to innovate and mix old and new theatrical styles to create something fresh and original. As theater scholar Robert Corrigan wrote in 1964 about Wilder's innovative techniques, "[They] have made it possible for his plays to communicate to audiences all over the world—and for this reason in most European countries, his work is considered the most representative and significant product of the modern American theater" (1075).

CRITICAL RECEPTION

Already a successful novelist, Wilder also wanted to conquer the realm of drama, and *Our Town* allowed him to do just that, but the way was not entirely smooth. Despite a mutual admiration, working with Jed Harris as director proved to have its pitfalls, as he and Wilder disagreed over sections of the text and the way some of the characters should be portrayed. Although audiences generally liked the play, many critics were initially uncertain.

The play's initial tryout took place in Princeton, New Jersey, on January 22, 1938. It received a highly negative review from *Variety*, suggesting that it was the season's most extravagant waste of talent. However, audience response was favorable, so it moved to Boston for a proposed two-week run. It was still the Depression and theater attendance was not at its best anywhere, but attendance in Boston was poor, and the decision was made to close after only a week. Reviews were better, but still cautious, as many critics seemed confused by the play's avant-garde techniques and were uncertain regarding the play's apparently mundane subject matter. Audiences, however, continued to enjoy the play, so Harris decided to move it to New York early, opening on February 4, 1938. Despite a standing ovation on opening night, reviews even here remained mixed, although most recognized the play's originality. But the public kept coming, they were able to move to a bigger theater, and the play was eventually credited a success. So far, it has been revived in New York five times.

Gaining the Pulitzer Prize helped boost ticket sales of this initial production, as did Wilder's taking over as Stage Manager for a two-week stint. It closed after a respectable 336 performances and then went out on a lengthy national tour of 12 major cities. The tour's proposed run was never completed, as Harris argued with Frank Craven, the actor playing the Stage Manager, and canceled the tour partway through. However, the play continued to be produced throughout the United States at an alarming rate, soon making it one of the most seen plays in America. Biographer Gilbert Harrison reported how novelist Willa Cather wrote to Wilder about Americans living abroad weeping with homesickness when they read the play (187–88). Its screen adaptation in 1940 widened that audience, as did several major radio broadcasts. To broaden its appeal, Wilder even allowed the initial 1940 movie production to change the ending and allow Emily to live, only to have dreamed she had been dead. It also became a popular play to produce abroad, suggestive of its truly universal appeal.

On the negative side, critics such as the *New Yorker's* Robert Benchley saw the play as "so much ersatz" and wondered if it was "dramatic" enough to be a real play (26), while Marxist critic Michael Gold continued to abhor what he saw as Wilder's refusal to portray middle-class family life as anything but comfortable (qtd. In Tappan Wilder 115). Eleanor Roosevelt declared that it had "moved her and depressed her beyond words.... I am glad I saw it but I did not have a pleasant evening" (qtd. in Simon 144). George Jean Nathan saw it as a "stunt," feeling the third act was too mystical and speculative to work (65). But critics from *Herald-Tribune*, *World Telegram*, *Brooklyn Daily Eagle*, and *Sunday Mirror* all praised the play's staging, acting, direction, and themes (Tappan Wilder 115). Brooks Atkinson, of the *New York Times*, was enamored of *Our Town* from the start and gave it some of its most positive reviews, suggesting that through this work Wilder had "escaped from the formal barrier of the modern theatre into the quintessence of acting, thought and speculation" and "transmuted the simple events of human life into universal reverie" (18). Atkinson also called the

play "hauntingly beautiful" and "less the portrait of a town than the subli-
mation of the commonplace" (18).

While earlier critics tended to celebrate its softer, more nostalgic side, later
critics grew more aware of its harsher underpinning. As playwright Lanford
Wilson suggests, "*Our Town* is a deadly cynical and acidly accurate play" (36).
In 1997, the U.S. Postal Service honored Wilder by placing him on a stamp,
and in the background was depicted a New England landscape to remind
people of the play for which he is best known.

SUGGESTED READINGS

Atkinson, Brooks. Rev. of *Our Town*, by Thornton Wilder. *New York Times*, February 5,
     1938: 18.
Benchley, Robert. Rev. of *Our Town*, by Thornton Wilder. *New Yorker*, February 12,
     1938: 26.
Blank, Martin, ed. *Critical Essays on Thornton Wilder*. New York: G.K. Hall, 1996.
Blank, Martin, Dalma Hunyadi Brunauer, and David Garrett Izzo, eds. *Thornton Wilder:
     New Essays*. West Cornwall, CT: Locust Hill, 1999.
Bogard, Travis. *Contour in Time*. New York: Oxford University Press, 1972.
Bryer, Jackson R., ed. *Conversations with Thornton Wilder*. Jackson: University Press
     of Mississippi, 1992.
Burbank, Rex. *Thornton Wilder*. Boston: Twayne, 1978.
Castronovo, David. *Thornton Wilder*. New York: Ungar, 1986.
Corrigan, Robert. *The Modern Theatre*. New York: Macmillan, 1964.
Cowley, Malcolm. "The Man Who Abolished Time." *Saturday Review of Literature* 39
     (October 6, 1956): 13–14, 50–52.
Dean, Alexander. "*Our Town* on the Stage." *The Yale Review* 27.4 (June 1938):
     836–38.
de Koster, Katie, ed. *Readings on Thornton Wilder*. San Diego, CA: Greenhaven,
     1998.
Gold, Michael. "Wilder: Prophet of the Genteel Christ." *New Republic*, October 22,
     1930: 266–67.
Goldstone, Richard H. *Thornton Wilder: An Intimate Portrait*. New York: Dutton, 1975.
Goldstone, Richard H., and Gary Anderson. *Thornton Wilder: An Annotated
     Bibliography of Works by and about Thornton Wilder*. New York: AMS, 1982.
Haberman, Donald. *Our Town: An American Play*. Boston: Twayne, 1989.
Harrison, Gilbert A. *The Enthusiast: A Life of Thornton Wilder*. New Haven, CT:
     Ticknor & Fields, 1983.
Herron, Ima Honaker. *The Small Town in American Drama*. Dallas, TX: Southern
     Methodist University Press, 1969.
Kuner, Mildred Christophe. *Thornton Wilder: The Bright and the Dark*. New York:
     Crowell, 1972.

Lifton, Paul. *Vast Encyclopedia: The Theatre of Thornton Wilder*. Westport, CT: Greenwood, 1995.

Margulies, Donald. Foreword. *Our Town*. By Thornton Wilder. New York: HarperCollins, 2003: xi–xx.

McCasland, Elizabeth Barron. *The Philosophy of Thornton Wilder*. New York: Carlton, 1976.

Miller, Arthur. "The Family in Modern Drama." *Atlantic Monthly*, 197 (April 1956): 35–41.

Nathan, George Jean. Rev. of *Our Town*, by Thornton Wilder. *Scribner's Magazine*, May 1938: 65.

Siebold, Thomas, ed. *Readings on* Our Town. San Diego, CA: Greenhaven, 2000.

Simon, Linda. *Thornton Wilder, His World*. Garden City, NJ: Doubleday, 1979.

Stephens, George D. "*Our Town*: Great American Tragedy?" *Modern Drama* 1.4 (February 1959): 258–64.

Walsh, Claudette. *Thornton Wilder: A Reference Guide, 1926–1990*. New York: G.K. Hall, 1993.

Wilder, Amos Niven. *Thornton Wilder and His Public*. Philadelphia: Fortress, 1980.

Wilder, Tappan. Afterword. *Our Town*. By Thornton Wilder. New York: Harper Collins, 2003: 113–72.

Wilder, Thornton. *"American Characteristics" and Other Essays*. Ed. Donald Gallup. New York: Harper & Row, 1979.

———. *The Collected Short Plays of Thornton Wilder*. 2 vols. New York: TCG, 1997 and 1998.

———. *The Journals of Thornton Wilder: 1939–1961*. Ed. Donald Gallup. New Haven, CT: Yale University Press, 1985.

———. "A Preface for *Our Town*." *New York Times*, February 13, 1938, sec. 2: 1.

———. *Three Plays by Thornton Wilder*: Our Town, The Skin of Our Teeth, The Matchmaker. New York: Harper, 1957.

Wilson, Lanford. "*Our Town* and Our Towns." *New York Times*, December 20, 1987, sec. 2: 36.

2

Tennessee Williams
A Streetcar Named Desire
1947

BIOGRAPHICAL CONTEXT

Born Thomas Lanier Williams on March 26, 1911, in Columbus, Mississippi, he was the second child of Edwina Dakin Williams (daughter of an Episcopal clergyman) and Cornelius Coffin Williams, a lively traveling salesman. While his father was on the road, Williams lived mostly at his grandparents' rectory, with his mother and older sister, Rose. In 1918 his father was promoted to manager within the International Shoe Company, and the family relocated to the industrial center of St. Louis and soon after added a third child, Walter Dakin. They bought a gloomy house, in which his parents constantly argued, and Rose, who was possibly schizophrenic, withdrew into her collection of glass animals.

Frail and overly protected by his mother, especially after a near-fatal bout of diphtheria when five, Williams was a target for school bullies. His weakness and lack of physical prowess disappointed his father, who called him "Miss Nancy." But Williams was intellectual, and partly as escapism from a life he hated, wrote short stories, reviews, essays, and travel articles. An early story, "Isolated," was printed in his junior high school newspaper, and he won money from advertising and magazine contests. His first professionally published story was "The Vengeance of Nitocris" (1928) in *Weird Tales*, based on an episode from Herodotus, for which he was paid $35.

In 1929 Williams attended the University of Missouri to study journalism. Here he drank to cover his shyness, and discovered the drama of Anton Chekhov, August Strindberg, and Henrik Ibsen, whose work inspired him to become a playwright. In 1930, he wrote his first play, *Beauty Is the Word*, which took sixth place in a play contest. Unfortunately, after failing ROTC in his third year, his father refused to pay his tuition and sent him to work in his company's warehouse, where Williams was appalled by the monotony of the work. He continued to write at night, but by 1935 the oppression of the job led to a nervous breakdown and Williams's belief that he had had a heart attack (he was a hypochondriac). He went to recover with his grandparents in Memphis. Here his first play was produced by the Memphis Garden Players: a one-act farce about two sailors on shore leave called *Cairo, Shanghai, Bombay!*, cowritten by Doris Shapiro.

He returned to St. Louis to enroll at Washington University. Entering its playwriting competition with *Me, Vashya*, he was disappointed with only an honorable mention. During this time he became involved with the Mummers, a local amateur theater group that produced his first longer works, *Candles to the Sun* (1936), a Marxist melodrama set in the Alabama coalfields, and the socialist exposé *Fugitive Kind* (1937), set in a St. Louis flophouse during the Depression. The mental state of his sister, Rose, had worsened (she would later be institutionalized and given a prefrontal lobotomy), and Williams, fond of his sister, could not face her deterioration. With aid from his grandmother, he attended a playwriting course at the University of Iowa, where he wrote but was unable to produce *Spring Storm*, about couples in a Mississippi Delta town troubled by social taboos, and *Not about Nightingales*, an exposé of conditions in a Pennsylvania prison.

After graduating in 1938, he traveled around America gathering ideas and material, taking menial jobs, and writing poetry and short fiction as well as plays. It was with the story "The Field of Blue Children," published in 1939, that he first called himself Tennessee Williams. Impressed by some one-act plays (later published in 1948 as *American Blues*), the Group Theatre awarded Williams a special $100 prize. The plays were a mix of scenarios about family responsibility, unfulfilled dreamers, risk takers, and a dreamlike fantasy he would later expand into *Camino Real* (1953). Although prefiguring common themes in Williams's work, none of these plays were deemed ready for production, but their promise found Williams a literary agent, Audrey Wood, who worked with him for the next 30 years.

Wood secured grant money for Williams to write full time, and he completed *Battle of Angels* for the Theatre Guild, opening in Boston in 1940, with plans to transfer to New York. It proved a disaster, severely panned by reviewers, and with its mix of religious and sexual content, it was strongly criticized by the Boston City Council. Even with revisions, the play closed after two weeks. After further revisions, Williams eventually had moderate success with this play about repressed passion and sexual sterility under the title *Orpheus Descending* (1957). But in the meantime, severely dejected, Williams returned to menial labor, first in New Orleans and then in New York.

Exempt from military service because of cataracts and close to penniless, Williams received from Wood a scriptwriting contract with MGM at $250 a week, from May to November in 1943. He adapted an earlier short story, "Portrait of a Girl in Glass," into the screenplay *The Gentleman Caller*, in which he expanded the role of the mother to accommodate the studio's request for a Lana Turner vehicle. Rejected by the studio, the screenplay was rewritten and became *The Glass Menagerie* (1944), which Wood got produced in Chicago. Despite an initial poor attendance, positive critical reviews stirred audiences to come, and it became the hit for which Williams had been waiting. Opening in New York in 1945, it won numerous awards and ran for nearly two years.

Glass Menagerie was heavily autobiographical. Narrated by a son, "Tom," who ran away to escape a mindless job in a shoe factory, the play depicts Tom's vision of the life and plight of the domineering mother and painfully shy sister he lived with but then abandoned. In his production notes for the play, Williams spoke of his desire to create a revitalized lyrical theater of feelings, which he termed "plastic theater." He effectively used lighting and music motifs to complement characters and action, and had envisioned a screen device to convey images and captions to the audience, although this element was dropped by the play's director as too distracting and is rarely included in productions. However, the play, as produced, did much to enthuse other playwrights, such as Arthur Miller and William Inge, who were stunned by its poetic artistry. Though with less emphasis on the sexual and violent motifs in much of Williams's work, the play introduced themes that would become apparent in later plays: illusion vs. reality; fear of isolation; need for understanding of the dispossessed; as well as clashes between sensitive and worldly people, Southern and Northern lifestyles, and the practical against the ideal.

While *Glass Menagerie* brought Williams to public attention, it was not until *A Streetcar Named Desire* (1949) that his reputation would be securely cemented. In the interim, Williams disappointed critics with a collaboration he had written with Donald Windham: a comic adaptation of a D. H. Lawrence story, *You Touched Me!* (1945). The following year he published *"27 Wagons Full of Cotton" and Other One-Act Plays*, full of experimental pieces and risky themes. It contained a number of interesting plays, including *The Last of My Solid Gold Watches*, a sympathetic study of an aging salesman who would prefigure Arthur Miller's Willy Loman, as well as *The Lady of Larkspur* and

Portrait of a Madonna, which both depict precursors of *A Streetcar Named Desire*'s Blanche DuBois. The first is in the form of an aging prostitute who lives under a pretense of gentility, and the second with a middle-aged spinster unaware of her impending commitment to a state asylum; like Blanche, both are sensitive and sympathetic portraits. Williams again went traveling in search of a less complicated life, initially to Mexico, where he began *The Poker Night.* On returning to America, he joined fellow writer Carson McCullers on Nantucket Island and rewrote *Poker Night* into *Streetcar.*

Streetcar opened in December 1947 and ran for two years. Its intriguing plot, fascinating characterizations, and excellent production made it a tremendous success, winning Williams his first Pulitzer, as well as Donaldson and New York Drama Critics' Circle awards. It made Marlon Brando, who played Stanley Kowalski, a household name, especially after the successful movie version, which followed in 1951. Although European critics were more skeptical, performances were well attended and the public declared it a hit, to establish Williams's reputation as a playwright on an international scale. Despite some minor letdowns, such as his next play, *Summer and Smoke* (1948), about the repressed love of a Southern spinster, which had been written before *Streetcar* and was considered less well crafted, Williams wrote a series of popular plays during the 1950s. He also published several short-story collections, including *"One Arm" and Other Stories* (1948) and *Hard Candy* (1954), many of whose stories were used as springboards for plays, as well as a lurid novel, *The Roman Spring of Mrs. Stone* (1950), and a mediocre book of poetry, *Winter of Cities* (1956).

In his 1975 *Memoirs,* Williams chronicles an adolescent and unconsummated sexual attraction for a female, but also his realization by the 1940s that he was homosexual. He admits to having adopted a promiscuous lifestyle after this discovery, with a series of pickups and short-term relationships. But in 1948, he was reunited with an earlier acquaintance, Frank Merlo, with whom he then stayed (although not exclusively) until Merlo's death in 1963. It was for Merlo, of Sicilian descent, that he wrote *The Rose Tattoo* (1951), a celebration of sexual love set amid a Sicilian community, which was another hit. Not every 1950s work was popular; critics and audiences were bemused by the obscure, nonrealistic *Camino Real* (1953), but the more realistic *Cat on a Hot Tin Roof* (1955), with its Southern setting, focus on a single family in crisis, and strong characterizations, was more satisfying and won him his second Pulitzer.

In 1956, Williams wrote the screenplay for *Baby Doll,* about an infantile wife and her sexual awakening amid violent circumstances. Although its sensationalized advertising drew large crowds, it was lambasted by critics who found its subject matter amoral and unhealthy. The following play, *Orpheus Descending* (1957), was also lurid and violent. Concerned about his mental state, friends persuaded him to enter psychoanalysis. He was a psychological mess: stressed out from work, suffering from alcoholism and constant hypochondria, in addition to growing bouts with claustrophobia and fear of suffocation. The deaths of his grandfather in 1955 and his father in 1957 only deepened his depression. This immersion in the psychoanalytical prompted his next play, *Suddenly Last Summer* (1958), considered by many to be his most shocking, in which a young woman relates having witnessed her homosexual cousin being cannibalized, for which antagonistic relatives are trying to have her lobotomized. It was a surprising success, followed by *Sweet Bird of Youth* (1959), about two aging dreamers vainly searching for happiness. But critics grew tired of the psychological babble between the troubled couples in *Period of Adjustment* (1960) and wished for something new.

Williams's last major hit was *The Night of the Iguana* (1961), about a disparate group of travelers working through problems in a run-down tourist spot in Mexico. His output continued, but plays like *The Milk Train Doesn't Stop Here Anymore* (1962), in which a young man helps an old woman to die peacefully, and *In the Bar of a Tokyo Hotel* (1969), about the pain and isolation of an artist, were seen as rehashing old ideas, and people grew weary of Williams's psychoses played out onstage. The death of Merlo in 1963 had sent Williams back to an even stronger dependency on drugs and alcohol, and although he would recover from this after an extended hospital stay at the close of the decade, he would have little future artistic success. A number of his earlier works were revived, and *Small Craft Warnings* (1972), in which a seamy group of derelicts in a bar explain their lives, ran Off-Off-Broadway to moderate reviews. But most of his work of the 1970s up until his death in 1983 (having choked to death on the cap from a pill bottle) was short lived and unpopular, although certain plays since, such as *Vieux Carré* (1977), with its boardinghouse collection of the spiritually and physically dying, have begun to be rediscovered, as have some of his earlier "failures."

PLOT DEVELOPMENT

Set in Elysian Fields, a poor section of New Orleans, *A Streetcar Named Desire* opens with blues music filling the air, to express "the spirit of life which goes on here." Stanley Kowalski arrives home, with a package of meat for his wife, Stella, before going out bowling. Stella follows on to watch. Meanwhile, her older sister, Blanche DuBois, arrives, dressed in an unsuitable white party outfit and horrified by her surroundings. Having taken two streetcars named Desire and Cemeteries to get here, she is looking for refuge. The Kowalskis' neighbor, Eunice, assures Blanche she has the right place and, learning who she is, discusses the family estate in Mississippi, Belle Reve, and Blanche's job as a schoolteacher. Eunice lets Blanche into the apartment while she fetches Stella.

Spotting some whiskey, Blanche drinks but clears up the evidence; she is nervous. Stella runs in and they embrace. Blanche asks her to turn off the glaring over-light, not wishing to be seen closely in the light. She asks for a drink, then criticizes Stella's home. Stella is anxious, wondering why her sister has come. Blanche tells her she has been given a leave of absence from school for her health, then criticizes Stella's appearance as she demands compliments about her own. Stella accepts this patiently. Stella has married for love, but Blanche disapproves and acts shocked at Stella's evident passion for Stanley. Blanche confesses she has lost the family estate and talks about the string of family deaths to which she tended.

While Stella washes her face to recover from this news, Stanley returns. He and his friends arrange to meet for poker the following night. Blanche greets him as he removes his shirt, notices how much liquor has been drunk, and welcomes her coldly. When he asks about her former husband, a faint polka plays. Blanche declares the boy is dead and that she feels sick.

The following evening, Blanche bathes in preparation for a night out with Stella. Stella tells Stanley that Belle Reve was lost and asks him to be nice to Blanche. Stanley is concerned over what happened to the estate, pointing out that he has a right to anything his wife owns. He pulls out Blanche's clothes and jewelry, implying that she bought them with estate money, but Stella insists these are inexpensive items, and losing her temper, storms outside. He confronts Blanche as she dresses. She is flirtatious, fishing for compliments; he is gruff and terse. She sends Stella to fetch a coke and offers to tell Stanley anything he wants to know, getting out her papers. To her horror, he snatches some letters from her husband, whom she confesses she hurt. She gives him the estate papers, and he tells her Stella is pregnant, something Stella had asked him not to mention. Blanche congratulates Stella as they head out for the evening.

The third scene shows Stanley playing poker with Mitch, Steve (Eunice's husband), and Pablo. Stanley is winning, and he teases Mitch, who still lives with his mother. Mitch goes to the bathroom, and Blanche and Stella return. Stella introduces Blanche, Stanley is rude, and Blanche decides to have another bath. She meets Mitch coming out of the bathroom and is struck by his politeness, asking her sister about him. Stella goes to the bathroom, and Blanche puts on the radio as she begins to undress. Stanley objects and barges in to switch it off. Mitch bows out of the game, going to the bathroom again, and talks to Blanche while he waits. She asks him for a cigarette and notices an inscription on the case. It was from a girl Mitch once knew who died young. They hit it off as Blanche presents herself as a refined lady, saying she rarely drinks and is Stella's younger sister.

Blanche switches the radio back on, and Stanley, who has been getting aggravated with their chatting, storms in and tosses the radio out the window. Stella angrily objects, calling Stanley a drunk animal and asking them all to leave. Stanley chases Stella into their room and hits her. The others pull him away, calm him down, throw him into the shower to sober up, and run off home, while Blanche takes Stella to Eunice's for safety. Distraught, Stanley calls Eunice on the telephone and, getting a rebuff, goes outside and screams for Stella. Stella comes down, rejoins her husband, and they passionately embrace before heading off to the bedroom. Blanche is horrified, but Mitch sits and talks, and calms her down.

The next morning, Blanche tries to understand how Stella could have returned to Stanley. Stella explains how on their wedding night he smashed the lightbulbs, and it excited her. Still thinking Stella might leave Stanley, Blanche talks about having met the wealthy-but-married Shep Huntleigh and suggests sending him a telegram to ask for money. Blanche realizes she cannot stay much longer, but Stella insists she is quite happy with Stanley. While Blanche denigrates Stanley as a primitive, brutish animal to try and change her sister's mind, Stanley returns and listens in. Pretending he has just arrived, he grins at Blanche as Stella embraces him.

Some days later, while Blanche composes a letter to Huntleigh, Eunice and Steve fight, and Eunice storms off, with Steve running after. Blanche tries to be jovial, but Stanley's antagonism is clear. He is asking around about her and finding out unpleasant details that she denies, but she is visibly shaken. Steve and Eunice return, having made up, and Stanley heads to the bar. Blanche worriedly asks Stella if she has heard anything about her, confessing she was not "so good the last two years or so." Stella gets Blanche a drink, and Blanche explains her hope that Mitch will propose—they have been dating—and offer her a refuge. Stella thinks this is possible and goes to join Stanley and the others.

While Blanche is waiting for Mitch, a young newsboy arrives. Blanche flirts with him and kisses him before sending him away, declaring she has to be good. He leaves as Mitch arrives for their date. They return at two in the morning. Mitch admits he likes her and comes in for a drink. They clumsily flirt, and Mitch admits he has discussed Blanche with his mother; she is dying and wants him settled. They talk about loneliness, and Blanche recounts her marriage to Allan Grey, whom she discovered embracing another man, and who killed himself when she told him, while they were dancing the "Varsouviana," that he now disgusted her. Mitch responds compassionately and they embrace in mutual need.

By September, to Stanley's annoyance, Blanche is still there. While she sings "It's Only a Paper Moon" in the bath, preparing for her birthday party, Stanley tells Stella he has information about Blanche's recent life. She was asked to leave her school after getting mixed up with a student, and she has a reputation of a virtual town whore. Stella admits Blanche is flighty, but insists this is an exaggeration. However, Stanley has already told Mitch, who has lost interest in marriage. Stanley plans to give Blanche a bus ticket home and force her to leave.

A few hours later at the birthday party, Mitch has not shown, and Blanche is putting on a brave face. Upset at Stanley, Stella criticizes him and he throws his crockery to the floor, telling her never to talk to him that way. She cries, and Blanche, beginning to panic, telephones Mitch to find out what has happened, but he is not home. Stanley tries to comfort his wife, reminding her how it was before Blanche came. He then gives Blanche the ticket, which makes her run to the bathroom to throw up, as the "Varsouviana" plays. Stella demands that Stanley explain why he is being so cruel, but as he does, she goes into labor and they rush to the hospital.

Later that evening, Blanche has been drinking when Mitch arrives. Excited to see him, she tries to straighten up, but his gruffness gets her nervous. He demands to see her in the light and that she tell him the truth. She replies that the reality does not matter, for she tells "what *ought* to be truth." But he pulls off her light shade and switches on the light; in its harsh glare she confesses all Stanley discovered was true. A vendor comes to the door crying "Flores para los muertos" (flowers for the dead), and sending her away, Blanche begins to fall apart, recalling how she first began to sleep around with soldiers from the local camp. Mitch embraces her but tells her he cannot marry her. She sends him away.

Blanche continues to drink and is packing as Stanley arrives home. Stella is in labor and he has been sent to sleep. Blanche tells him an old admirer has invited her on a cruise. He takes his shirt off and has a drink. The more Blanche talks, the more obvious it is that her cruise is a lie. She also invents a scene in which Mitch begged for her forgiveness, and she refused to accept. Stanley calls her on these lies, mocking her appearance and her refined veneer. Surrounded by menacing shadows, Blanche tries to telephone Huntleigh but does not know the number. Stanley has put on the silk pajamas he wore on his wedding night to celebrate his impending fatherhood and taunts Blanche. In fear, she backs into the bedroom and he follows. She breaks a bottle and threatens him with it. Disarming her, he declares they have "had this date with each other from the beginning!" and carries her to the bed. The blues music suggests what happens next.

Some weeks later, Stella packs Blanche's things while the men play poker. Blanche has told her what happened, but rather than believe it and lose Stanley, Stella is sending Blanche to a state institution. Confused, Blanche thinks she's going with Huntleigh and prepares for a trip. Both she and Mitch are visibly upset when they hear one another through the doors. Blanche begins to panic, fearing a trap. Stella and Eunice calm her and, when the doctor arrives, take her out to meet him. She realizes this is not Huntleigh and runs back in. The doctor and the matron come after her, and Stella cannot watch, guiltily hiding outside with Eunice as comfort. Mitch swings at Stanley, holding him responsible, but ends up sobbing on the table. As Blanche resists, the matron gets rough, but the doctor charms her into going along peacefully. Stella calls after, but Blanche ignores her, and Eunice hands Stella her baby boy. Stanley calls to his wife and she wails, then he comforts her as the blues music swells. Steve calls for "seven-card stud," and life returns to normal.

CHARACTER DEVELOPMENT

Some critics have suggested that Williams's homosexuality allowed him greater insight into female characters than many of his heterosexual contemporaries, and women are certainly at the center of many of his plays. In *Streetcar* it is Blanche DuBois, a grown woman, struggling to survive in a world she barely understands. After a youthful marriage to a man whom she later discovers to be gay, and drives to suicide by her disgust, Blanche begins using sex as an escape from a guilty and stultifying life. Haunted by her passing youth, she preys on young boys, until virtually chased from town after a scandal with a student from the school at which she taught. Blanche's perverse and tortured sexuality is balanced against the healthy sexuality of her sister, Stella. Stanley may be attracted to both, but it is Stella who wins as she delivers him a healthy child, and Blanche is taken off to a mental hospital.

Blanche is fatally divided, caught between the desire to be a lady—young, beautiful, and concerned with old-fashioned Southern ways—and a bohemian—erring and excessive in her appetites. In New Orleans, Blanche hides her real age and shady past as she tries to attract a decent man to clean up her life. She nearly fools Mitch into believing her to be the lady she insists she is. But her attraction to young men will continue to cause trouble; it led her into an unsuitable marriage, lost her job, and she cannot resist flirting with the newspaper boy. It is quite likely that marriage to Mitch would not have solved her difficulties, for she is a fatally divided person. Blanche seeks love, but her very nature works against her ever finding this. Her guilt over all she has done will never allow her to enjoy a real relationship, as deep inside she does not see herself as worthy.

In opposition to the deathly whiteness of Blanche is her younger sister, Stella, who is healthy, pregnant, and full of life. Stella loves Blanche, but unlike her sister, has rejected her refined Southern heritage in favor of a more brutal, low-class existence with Stanley, who offers her a life of the senses. Stanley provides her with all she needs, including an exciting, guilt-free sexual relationship. In comparison to Blanche, Stella seems open and sincere, but she is not naïve and will only allow Blanche so much leeway; although she humors her sister to keep things smooth, she knows what Blanche has become and is largely unimpressed with her airs. At the close of the play she allows Blanche to be taken to the asylum, because to acknowledge that her husband has raped her sister would ruin a marital relationship on which she depends, and, in this matter, she chooses ignorance over truth.

Stanley sees Blanche as a disruptive force in his household, as Stella picks up Blanche's snooty habits and grows critical of him. His response is to become increasingly belligerent. He truly loves Stella and at times shows her great tenderness, which makes him only fight all the harder to keep her. He has no time for illusions and insists on facing reality, which clearly puts him at odds with Blanche. Williams continually depicts him in animal terms—bringing home the meat, eating like a beast, pacing, howling—and points out Stanley's "animal joy in his being." Being at heart an animal, Stanley likes to display his strength and control, and protects his territory with increasing violence, beginning with throwing the radio out the window. He attacks Blanche for losing Belle Reve and spoils Blanche's relationship with Mitch by telling him what he has found out about her recent life. His final act of aggression is his virtual rape of Blanche.

Mitch is possibly the most sympathetic character in the play with no darker side to his nature. Stella, after all, for all of her open-mindedness, abandons her sister to a state institution. Still carrying around a cigarette case given him by a dying girl he once liked, Mitch is sensitive, but also naïve by the way he so readily accepts Blanche's performance. It is little wonder Blanche sees in him a possibility of salvation. Still living with his mother, Mitch has had little experience of life, and is only now being allowed to contemplate marriage because his mother is dying. He does, however, abandon Blanche when she needs him most. She may have given him the runaround, but if he truly loved her, her past should not matter. Instead, he sees her as someone too dirty to live in the same house as his mother. Yet his attack on Stanley at the close, and subsequent sobbing, indicates Mitch's awareness that he may have made a mistake and condemned himself to a life of loneliness by his intolerance.

THEMES

Streetcar illustrates many of Williams's central concerns, including the consequences of nonconformity and the seemingly inevitable destruction of sensitive or romantic souls by those who are insensitive or materialistic. With the play taking place in the Elysian Fields district of New Orleans—a run-down tenement section of town in the French Quarter with which Williams had become familiar on several extended visits—the name becomes an ironic allusion to paradise. Instead, this play is full of sex and deadly violence, which the steamy atmosphere of its New Orleans location, snatches of blues music, and streetcars named Desire and Cemeteries evoke. Both Stella and her neighbor, Eunice, have tempestuous marriages, in which sex is the glue that holds them together. Yet the men find Blanche's sexual excesses unforgivable; even Mitch, who is painfully alone, cannot bring himself to marry her.

The name of the family mansion Blanche has lost, Belle Reve, means "beautiful dream" and indicates the dream life Blanche creates, trying to avoid the truth—the most awful being having forced her gay husband into suicide by her disgust. It is this past that forever threatens to overwhelm her, indicated by the continual intrusion of the "Varsouviana," which was playing at the ball during which her husband killed himself. Blanche lives in a fake world of sentimental illusion because reality would destroy her, and she constantly bathes herself, as if she can wash away the taint of her guilt. Her white dress and her name, meaning "white woods," do not indicate innocence, but a paucity of spirit. Her star sign of Virgo (the virgin) is an ironic joke because of her growingly evident promiscuity, but even that is just a part of her act and is not the real Blanche. It is a form of escape just like the alcohol. She had begun to see soldiers from the camp to escape a dreary home life tending to dying relatives, and it had just escalated to where she could only win young boys eager for their first experience or married men, like Shep Huntleigh, not looking for serious relationships. On the surface she seems vivacious and flirtatious, but this is a sham, for when her guard drops, we see how frightened and drained of life she really is.

A major part of the dramatic conflict in the play is between a dying aristocracy, represented by Blanche, and the cruder, but more vital, working class who live in this region, represented by Stanley. Blanche arrives and instantly looks out of place in her white clothes, looking as if she were going to a garden party. Her younger sister, Stella, having recognized that the family fortune is lost, has given up all pretensions to noble birth, glad to be pulled down from the pillars of the old family home, and preferring instead the more vibrant life offered by her adoring but volatile Polish husband, Stanley.

Blanche's arrival on the scene and subsequent demands disrupt Stanley and Stella's happy home, and as her presence threatens to destroy the contentment they have found, Stanley becomes increasingly antagonistic toward his sister-in-law. The sides of conflict are drawn between gentility and commonness, illusion and reality, death and passion, and each side uses sex to forward its claims. Blanche cannot understand the coarseness of her sister's new lifestyle, where violence and sexuality openly mingle, but her own sexual history threatens to undermine the credibility of the civilized refinement she proposes. Meanwhile, Stanley has no patience with Blanche's airs and graces, and reacts, as with everything else, passionately. Feeling threatened by a woman who has invaded his home, constantly criticizes his manners, and has the potential to sour his relationship with his wife, he is delighted to be able to expose her as a fraud.

Stanley's declaration that they have "had this date with each other from the beginning!" before he takes Blanche into the bedroom is ambiguous. Blanche has flirted with him, as she admits to Stella, and as she does with every man, but that she holds a secret passion for her sister's husband is unlikely. She finds his coarseness more revolting than titillating, and her acceptance of his attentions is more a spiritual surrender than anything. Stanley may have taken her flirting at face value and, being a realist, now acts on it, but it is also a spiritual victory for him, rather than an attempt at sexual fulfillment. Given his evident vitality, it was clear that Stanley would triumph all along, yet it is a mark of Williams's power that he gets us to sympathize with the misguided, misinformed, and ultimately mistreated Blanche. Although Stanley and Blanche are at irreconcilable odds, both have a complexity that allows each to be both villain and victim.

Elysian Fields may be a kind of paradise for men like Stanley who embrace lives of the senses and are completely comfortable in their sexuality. He is self-assured and does what he wants, taking off his shirt in company and refusing to fake politeness for his sister-in-law. Always himself, he plays no games, having a lack of pretension and perception that Williams wants us to respect; Stanley sees through Blanche from the start. He has a permanency and strength about him that contrasts to Blanche's impermanence, fragility, and sexual uncertainty—Blanche wants to be a "lady" but feels continually tripped up by her sexual desire, which she feels society demands she suppress. Blanche and Stanley both strive to win Stella to their side, but Stanley is the eventual victor. The world he offers Stella is full of color and genuine passion, a world from which Blanche is utterly alienated and can only fear. Stanley has no refinement, but he truly loves life, and women. Stella is attracted to him as a female to a strong male. They fight and make up, just like their neighbors, Eunice and Steve, and these bouts of violence seem just a spillover from the sheer passion of their existence and nothing about which to be truly alarmed.

The play's final image evokes the Holy Family, with Stella and Stanley standing in tableau and Stella holding her son; it suggests that here is the future of the world—working-class Stanley and his violent spirit having beaten back the forces of imagination and art—and it will be a world in Stanley's image. However, Stella is sobbing, and it is clear that her life has changed (as may have Mitch's, who also sobs). For her to continue her previous existence, she will have to live in an illusion, just like her sister (by denying her husband is a rapist). In the 1951 movie version, under pressure from the studio to present a more morally acceptable ending in which a rapist cannot escape without punishment, it is made to look as if Stella is prepared to take the child and leave her husband at the close, but there is no sense of this in Williams's original script.

HISTORICAL CONTEXT

Part of the play's historical background is its subtle commentary on the deterioration of the old agrarian South since the Civil War. *Streetcar* heralds a new way of life and the vital possibilities, despite Williams's reservations, of the expanding postwar urban-industrialized society. To many, Blanche represents the fallen myth of the antebellum old South—a South of supposed refinement, generosity, and gentility in which accomplished women married handsome beaus and lived happily ever after on their wonderful plantations. The Civil War exposed the lie in this, as such grandeur had largely been built on the back of a slave population now freed and, by the twentieth century, becoming increasingly independent. Although she would like to be, Blanche is no Southern belle; she is a virtual prostitute who has lost the family mansion and seduces young boys. Stanley, on the other hand, is the brute, naturalistic force of the future of the city—the animalistic man who will sweep away the past myths without conscience, while fathering the new generation with Stella.

At the time the play was first produced, shortly after World War II, Broadway was largely dominated by musical comedies and revivals of classics, with few new plays being produced. But in this postnuclear, post-Freudian age of anxiety, full of political and social upheaval, audiences were growing increasingly unsatisfied with the pat endings of the drama being performed. Something edgier would better suit the times, and Williams provided just that with the loose structure and moral ambivalence of *Streetcar*. The boldness of the play's sexuality both excited and spoke to fantasies held by a nation too long repressed. References to the recent war (Blanche meeting off-duty soldiers and the past army duty of Stanley and his friends) gave the play a realistic immediacy and suggested that the way forward in a period of such uncertainty was to be like Stanley: to reject the past and work on building a new and better world for oneself.

Elia Kazan, the play's first director, had envisaged Blanche as the play's protagonist, yet even in his production it was Stanley who seemed to gain the greater sympathy. Midcentury audiences cheered him on to attack Blanche and saw little wrong in his actions. In more enlightened feminist times, toward the end of the century, the patriarchal aspects of Stanley's behavior are less accepted and Blanche has become a more sympathetic heroine. Williams, however, intended a balance between these two as each has a soft side and a harsh side, and both act in context to the stakes that are set to gain or keep what they want. Both share the "desire" of the title, and the play is fraught with sexual politics. Indeed, theater scholar Philip Kolin suggests that "*Streetcar* defined desire in 1947, and refines it with each succeeding decade of performance" (*Williams's* A Streetcar 2).

LITERARY STYLE AND DEVICES

Williams's characterizations can be related to those he admired in the work of Anton Chekhov; both portray people whose inability to communicate honestly will cause their lives to spin out of control. Many critics have recognized similarities between *The Cherry Orchard* (1904) and *Streetcar*, in their dual concern about the passing of an older order and more genteel way of life as brash interlopers take over; Stella is particularly Chekhovian in her passive acceptance of events. Furthermore, like Chekhov, Williams's attention to detail is tremendous, as images signify and echo throughout the play. Williams was also a keen admirer of D. H. Lawrence, even publishing a tribute to him in 1951, *I Rise in Flame, Cried the Phoenix*. Much of Williams's work is suffused with Lawrencian notions and symbols, and like Lawrence, he was also unafraid to explore both the darker side of sexual obsession as well as the pleasures of sexual union.

Blanche is a living death wish, and Williams surrounds her with symbolism to underline this. She constantly bathes to wash away the taint of her past and seeks solace in drink and dreams; it is as if she wishes to obliterate her true self. On one hand, we see her as overly sensitive—she never really gets over Allen's death, as depicted by the constant refrain of the "Varsouviana"—yet on the other we can also see her as being punished by Williams for her insensitive cruelty toward a homosexual. She hides behind the shade of her paper lantern, but this will be ripped away to reveal all by both Mitch and Stanley. Blanche is exposed as a mess of contradictions that can never be resolved. It is this, perhaps, that allows her tragic status, coupled with her final determination to salvage her dignity in the face of disaster.

Blanche ran to her last refuge with Stanley and Stella, but they offer no safety, as they are too involved in themselves. They eventually tire of this annoying third person and get rid of her the only way they know, violently. In the final scene Blanche's light shade has been replaced, and she returns to her dreamworld, where it seems safer. It is debatable as to whether she ends up truly mad or just creates an alternate reality to survive. The sound of the locomotive rushing in suggests the forces working on Blanche from both within and without—she is cornered. The train will crush her as she has nowhere left to which she can escape, except, perhaps, within her own psyche.

Despite the expressionistic elements woven throughout *Streetcar*, which express Blanche's mental torment and deterioration, the action is mostly realistic. The play's complex levels of reality are partly what make it unique for its time. Its objective reality offers the audience psychologically realistic characters, while a more subjective reality complements these within a symbolic framework presented through language and staging. Such realism and theatricality are usually at odds, but Williams blends them so that neither overwhelms the other. This allows him to simultaneously reflect both an inside and outside reality—what a character believes or hopes is happening to him or her, against what society is actually doing to him or her. The episodic structure only serves to heighten this distinction, as it is largely guided by the ups and downs of Blanche's perception of her relationship to the world around her.

The play is divided into 11 scenes with no act division. In the initial production it was decided to have the usual two intervals, after scenes 4 and 6. In terms of time this made sense, as it divides the play into the three significant seasonal periods over which it takes place, the spring of Blanche's arrival, the summer of her hope of a second chance, and the fall of her exposure, defeat, and removal to the state institution. It also divides the play into three distinct moods, with the beginning section being distinctly more comic, the middle in a more romantic vein, and the final section approaching tragic dimensions.

SITUATION OF WORK

Scholar Matthew Roudané credits Williams with virtually single-handedly animating American drama in the middle years of the century and providing the link between older playwrights—Eugene O'Neill, Susan Glaspell, Clifford Odets, Thornton Wilder—and those who came after—Arthur Miller, Lorraine Hansberry, Edward Albee, Sam Shepard, David Mamet. "Williams succeeded in expanding the boundaries of theatricality itself," Roudané explains, by "combining a lyricism and experimentalism that revolutionized American drama after World War Two" (1). No doubt inspired by the psychological insight of plays by Susan Glaspell and Elmer Rice, the social dimensions of Clifford Odets and Thornton Wilder, and the vast experimentation and often salubrious subject matter of Eugene O'Neill, Williams built on what they had started and contributed much that was his own.

Only Arthur Miller, among Williams's contemporaries, attained the same major status. Even though their styles and subject matter are very different, Miller credits Williams as having inspired him to continue writing, especially with *Streetcar*. In his autobiography, *Timebends*, Miller explains how he was amazed by the play's sheer vitality, with its liberated and liberating use of words, and felt that it paved the way for the acceptance of a new form of drama that America could proudly call its own. Miller saw Williams's use of language as a kind of poeticized realism that produced an everyday speech for his characters with a lyrical quality, allowing playwrights to escape from the language-bound realism of nineteenth-century drama that had dominated even the work of O'Neill up to this point.

Although Williams's frequent choice to explore his basic themes through seemingly degenerate characters and sordid situations has created controversy, he has mostly done so with such compassion and understanding that his audience finds themselves on the side of the disenfranchised, disadvantaged, and disillusioned, whom they formerly despised. The play was certainly considered shocking, much in the way plays of O'Neill had been, in its recognition of the centrality of sexuality in people's lives, but it was also recognized as being searingly truthful.

Because of his Southern roots and the Southern settings or characters in many of his plays, Williams, in some ways, shares more with twentieth-century Southern fiction writers than other dramatists of his period. His concern with

the past glory but current decay of the South, the violence caused by intolerance and isolation, the difficulty of honest communication, and the lonely
search for value in a chaotic world links him to writers like William Faulkner
and Carson McCullers, the latter of whom was a close personal friend and
whose work he greatly admired.

Critics generally agree that Williams has one of the most distinctive poetic
voices and depths of compassion ever witnessed on the American stage.
Harold Bloom describes him as "the most literary of our major dramatists" (2).
Streetcar's impact in 1947 was "especially strong," as Harold Clurman recognized, because at that time it was "virtually unique as a stage piece that is
both personal and social" (52); Williams had found a way to combine the
two. A Williams play, during his peak, was both moving and highly dramatic, and *Streetcar* is considered by many to be his best, if not the pinnacle
of all American drama. It was voted the most important American play of
the twentieth century by the American Theatre Critics Association. At a
1990 forum organized by Philip Kolin, in which various playwrights offered
their views on *Streetcar* (and they were overwhelmingly in awe), Robert E.
Lee declared: "There are very few nearly perfect plays. *Streetcar* is one of
them. It is indigenous to the speaking theatre" (qtd. in Kolin "A Playwright's
Forum," 188). Williams, like Wilder, had a U.S. Postal Service stamp com-
memorating his work, and its inclusion of a streetcar behind the author's portrait indicates a clear sense of the centrality of this play in both Williams's own
work and the national consciousness.

CRITICAL RECEPTION

More exciting and more adult than the popular but softer *The Glass
Menagerie*, *Streetcar* seemed to contain many of the previous play's good
qualities and combined them with a more sensual and exciting plot, as well
as a richer and subtler use of imagery and theme. *Streetcar* can be read as a
kind of compendium of Williams's entire canon, with its marginalized or
psychically wounded character types, pitted against those who run counter to
such types; his thematic preoccupations with time, sexuality, and the harshness and vulgarity of much of existence; and the psychological realism of the
characters, set against the departures from realism in the play's staging.

Williams once suggested that any play script is merely a blueprint for a
performance, and the fortunate confluence of talent on the initial production
of *Streetcar* certainly aided its success. Directed by Elia Kazan, with stage and
lighting designed by Jo Mielziner, Marlon Brando as Stanley, and Jessica Tandy
as Blanche, backed by a stellar cast, this production strongly had the odds in its

favor. Kazan and Mielziner, especially, helped create a play that did more than simply mimic reality and offered something that remained believable, even while it became more fluid and indeterminately real. Excellent acting made the characters, too, appear more credible. Audiences were allowed to recognize that they were in a theater, but that need not negate the authenticity of what they would witness. After highly successful tryouts in Boston, New Haven, and Philadelphia, when *Streetcar* opened in New York on December 3, 1947, at the Barrymore Theatre, at the final curtain the audience cheered for 30 minutes. It ran for 855 performances and became the first play ever to win all three of the Pulitzer, Donaldson, and New York Drama Critics' Circle awards.

While some critics were shocked by the play's subject matter, some also felt it was too loosely structured, and others too pessimistic. But there were other critics who saw all of these aspects merely as additional strengths, alongside its depth of characterization, innovative stylistic devices and visual imagery, and lyrical force. Louis Kronenberger described it as "the most creative new play ... the one that reveals the most talent, the one that attempts the most truth" (250), and Howard Barnes declared Williams to be a successor to Eugene O'Neill (qtd. in Kolin *Williams's: A Streetcar* 1). Even 20 years later Martin Gottfried could still state it was "perhaps the most romantic, poetic and sensitive play ever written for the American theater" (250).

The play has remained very popular, with several New York revivals and further movie treatments. Like few other plays, *Streetcar* truly entered the consciousness of the American people, witnessed by continual references to its characters, dialogue, and situations throughout both low and high culture. As Thomas Adler suggests, the play has become "an ingredient in our popular mythology," having "entered into and become the property of the public imagination" (7), and Blanche DuBois and Stanley Kowalski have, as Kolin suggests, "taken up residence in world theatre and culture. They are Williams's most colorful, memorable yet indeterminate creations" (*Williams's A Streetcar* 3).

SUGGESTED READINGS

Adler, Thomas P. A Streetcar Named Desire: *The Moth and the Lantern*. Boston: Twayne, 1990.

Berkman, Leonard. "The Tragic Downfall of Blanche DuBois." *Modern Drama* 10 (December 1967): 249–57.

Bloom, Harold, ed. *Modern Critical Interpretations: Tennessee Williams's* A Streetcar Named Desire. New York: Chelsea House, 1988.

Boxhill, Roger. *Tennessee Williams*. New York: Macmillan, 1987.

Chesler, S. Alan. "*A Streetcar Named Desire:* Twenty-Five Years of Criticism." *Notes on Mississippi Writers* 7.2 (fall 1974): 44–53.

Clurman, Harold. "*Streetcar.*" *Tomorrow,* February 1948: 52.

Crandell, George C., ed. *The Critical Response to Tennessee Williams.* Westport, CT: Greenwood, 1996.

————. *Tennessee Williams: A Descriptive Bibliography.* Pittsburgh: University of Pittsburgh Press, 1995.

Devlin, Albert J., ed., *Conversations with Tennessee Williams.* Jackson: University Press of Mississippi, 1986.

Gottfried, Martin. *A Theatre Divided: The Postwar American Stage.* Boston: Brown, Little, 1967.

Griffin, Alice. *Understanding Tennessee Williams.* Columbia: University of South Carolina Press, 1995.

Gunn, Drewey Wayne. *Tennessee Williams: A Bibliography.* Metuchen, NJ: Scarecrow, 1980.

Hayman, Ronald. *Tennessee Williams: Everyone Else Is an Audience.* New Haven, CT: Yale University Press, 1993.

Jackson, Esther Merle. *The Broken World of Tennessee Williams.* Madison: University of Wisconsin Press, 1965.

Kolin, Philip C., ed. *Confronting Tennessee Williams's* A Streetcar Named Desire: *Essays in Cultural Pluralism.* Westport, CT: Greenwood, 1993.

————. "*A Streetcar Named Desire:* A Playwrights' Forum." *Michigan Quarterly Review* 29 (spring 1990): 173–203.

————. *Tennessee Williams: A Guide to Research and Performance.* Westport, CT: Greenwood, 1998.

————. *Williams's* A Streetcar Named Desire. New York: Cambridge University Press, 2000.

Leverich, Lyle. *Tom: The Unknown Tennessee Williams.* New York: Crown, 1995.

Martin, Robert A., ed. *Critical Essays on Tennessee Williams.* New York: G.K. Hall, 1997.

McCann, John S. *The Critical Reputation of Tennessee Williams: A Reference Guide.* Boston: G.K. Hall, 1983.

Miller, Jordan Y., ed., *Twentieth-Century Interpretations of* A Streetcar Named Desire. Englewood Cliffs, NJ: Prentice-Hall, 1971.

Murphy, Brenda. *Tennessee Williams and Elia Kazan: A Collaboration in the Theatre.* New York: Cambridge University Press, 1992.

Roudané, Matthew C., ed., *The Cambridge Companion to Tennessee Williams.* New York: Cambridge University Press, 1997.

Savran, David. *Communists, Cowboys, and Queers: The Politics of Masculinity in the Work of Arthur Miller and Tennessee Williams.* Minneapolis: University of Minnesota Press, 1992.

Spoto, Donald. *The Kindness of Strangers: The Life of Tennessee Williams.* Boston: Little, Brown, 1985.

Voss, Ralph F., ed. *Magical Muse: Millennial Essays on Tennessee Williams*. Tuscaloosa: University of Alabama Press, 2002.

Weales, Gerald. *Tennessee Williams*. Minneapolis: University of Minnesota Press, 1965.

Williams, Dakin, and Shepherd Mead. *Tennessee Williams: An Intimate Biography*. New York: Arbor House, 1983.

Williams, Tennessee. *The Collected Poems of Tennessee Williams*. Ed. David Roessel and Nicholas Moschovakis. New York: New Directions, 2002.

———. *Collected Stories*. New York: New Directions, 1985.

———. *Memoirs*. Garden City, NY: Doubleday, 1975.

———. *Plays*. 2 vols. New York: Penguin, 2000.

———. *27 Wagons Full of Cotton: And Other One Act Plays*. Norfolk, CT: New Directions, 1946.

Windham, Donald, ed. *Tennessee Williams's Letters to Donald Windham, 1940–1965*. New York: Holt, Rinehart and Winston, 1976.

3

Arthur Miller
Death of a Salesman
1949

BIOGRAPHICAL CONTEXT

Arthur Asher Miller was born October 17, 1915, in New York City, the second child of Gittel "Augusta" and Isidore Miller. Augusta was a first-generation American whose father had emigrated from Poland, while Isidore himself had emigrated from Poland at the age of six. An older brother, Kermit, and a younger sister, Joan, made up the Miller family, although there was also the extended family of aunts, uncles, and cousins from whom Miller developed many of his characters when he became a playwright.

Miller's upbringing was solidly Jewish, providing him with a strong moral and ethical center that is evident in his works and life. He began life in an attractive apartment overlooking Central Park, but at 14, just before the Wall Street Crash, the family relocated to a small house in Brooklyn as Isidore was finding his finances stretched. Before being financially ruined by the Crash, his father owned and ran a women's clothing business. Miller simultaneously hated and admired his father. He was annoyed at his father's incapacity to fully recuperate, both economically and emotionally, from the Depression, yet he was able to recognize the man's worth. This ambivalence toward his father lies at the core of many of the ambiguously presented father figures, including Willy Loman, a seemingly strong man who loves his children, yet leads them to suffer because of certain weaknesses. In hindsight, Miller realizes that it was the system that failed, rather than his father, but at the time it was difficult to lay the blame elsewhere.

Having a better reputation for sports than academics, he was something of a Biff Loman at high school. He graduated in 1932, and trying to continue his education, unsuccessfully pursued a night school degree at New York City College. He began a series of short-term jobs—from singing on a local radio station to truck driving—to save the $500 he would need to attend the University of Michigan as a full-time student.

It was partly Miller's growing interest in politics that attracted him to the University of Michigan, with its notoriety as a radical enclave. Although his high school grades had been poor, Miller persuaded the dean to accept him on probation, and by 1934 he had sufficient funds to attend. Enrolling as a student in journalism, he wrote for the student newspaper during his first year. Then, during his 1935 spring vacation, Miller spent six days writing his first play, No Villain, to enter the Avery Hopwood Writing Awards. The Hopwood Awards are competitive financial awards given by the University of Michigan, and Miller needed the prize money to stay enrolled. He chose to write a play because he felt it was closer to real life, and he won a prize for drama the following year. In 1937, his rewrite of this play No Villain, retitled They Too Arise, won a scholarship award from the Bureau of New Plays and was produced in Ann Arbor and Detroit. Miller switched his major to English and enrolled in a playwriting seminar given by Professor Kenneth Rowe. Miller credits Rowe with teaching him about the dynamics of constructing a play. Miller won another Hopwood Award in 1937 for Honors at Dawn.

On graduating from Michigan in 1938, he returned to New York to join the Federal Theater Project. This project was a government-run national agency that had been formed to provide salaries for artists during the lean Depression years. Unfortunately, soon after signing on, the project was shut down on suspicion that it had been infiltrated by communists. For the next few years, Miller wrote radio plays for shows like Columbia Workshop (CBS) and Cavalcade of America (NBC). Not all of his plays were aired, but it gave him a lucrative opportunity to develop and refine his writing skills. However, Miller was discontent writing for commercial radio, feeling restricted and confined by the demands of the networks and their advertisers. He continued to write stage plays for himself and search for a producer.

In 1940, he married his college sweetheart, Mary Slattery, and by 1944 the couple had a daughter, Jane, and Miller had his first Broadway play produced, The Man Who Had All the Luck. The play was about a prosperous business-man, David Beeves, who cannot accept his good life and considers suicide. It explored key Miller concerns: family relationships and the impact of success, failure, and materialism on people's lives. A poor production may have been at fault, but it closed after only six performances. Discouraged by the way the play was received, Miller considered quitting playwriting for good. Turning his hand to fiction, he wrote Focus (1945), a controversial novel exploring issues of American anti-Semitism, which was a moderate success. However, the playwright could not be silenced, and he began work on a new play about success, guilt, and responsibility, revolving around another controversial issue: war profiteering.

In 1947 he and Mary had their second child, Robert, and Miller found a producer for his new play, *All My Sons,* about a father who gets away with selling faulty aircraft parts to the air force, but ultimately pays the price as his sons turn against him. Championed by *New York Times* theater critic Brooks Atkinson, who welcomed such a serious work in a theater he saw growing too socially trivial, *All My Sons* won solid reviews, some major awards, and professional recognition for Miller as a playwright. It also provided him with funds to purchase an estate in Roxbury, Connecticut, to use as a vacation home for the family.

For his next play, Miller felt the Red Hook shipping area of Brooklyn might offer something interesting on which to write. His research gave him the material for a film about waterfront corruption, *The Hook,* which was never produced, and a later play, *A View from the Bridge* (1955). But on meeting his uncle Manny Newman at a matinee performance of *All My Sons* and asking how he was doing, he got a new idea. Instead of replying, Manny had gone straight into saying how well his sons were doing, as if he felt he had to build them up in competition against their successful playwright cousin. The fact that Manny did not even pause before taking their conversation in an unexpected direction gave Miller the idea to write a play without transitions, where the dialogue would flow from one scene to the next without any apparent breaks. Instead of using a chronological order, in which single events followed one another, he wanted to create a form that displayed the past and the present as if they were both occurring at the same time. In this way he would be able to transmit to the audience exactly what was going on inside the mind of his protagonist; indeed, an early title for the play was *The Inside of His Head.* This would become the play that would make his permanent mark: *Death of a Salesman.*

In the spring of 1948, Miller spent six weeks writing *Death of a Salesman* in a small writing studio he built for himself in Roxbury. Miller had been interested in carpentry since he was a teenager, when he bought a stack of lumber to build a porch onto the family house. He gave Willy Loman the same love of craftsmanship and working with wood. Miller's uncle Manny became a prototype for Willy Loman: someone who worked with his hands, and a salesman with a wild imagination and tendency to brag. Manny would manipulate the truth to his own advantage and saw everything as some kind of competition that he and his family had to win. He was also prone to black moods and bouts of despair, and probably committed suicide. Manny's eldest child, Buddy, like Willy's son Biff, was athletic and popular, and the younger son, Abby, like Willy's younger son Hap, was a ladies' man.

Salesman premiered on February 10, 1949, at the Morosco Theater in New York City. Enthusiastic reviews swiftly made it the must-see play of the season, and Miller garnered nearly every award available. At times comic, yet also poetic, tragic, and with a realistic veneer that made it easy to involve any audience, *Salesman* was a new type of serious play that merged the forms of realism and expressionism to suggest new directions and possibilities for all of American drama. It has become, perhaps, the best-known American play worldwide.

After *Salesman*, Miller returned to his film script for *The Hook*, which he wanted Elia Kazan to direct, having built up a strong relationship with him during Kazan's expert direction of both *All My Sons* and *Salesman*. Knowing from the start that it would be difficult to get backing for such a controversial movie, especially given the growing paranoia of the times, Miller still felt he had a social duty to expose the corruption he had witnessed. Unfortunately, he was entering an era when social responsibility was being conflated with Communism, and studios felt it too dangerous to back such projects. Miller would not be working with Kazan again until the 1960s.

To avoid repetition, Miller's biography from this point will be continued at the start of the next chapter, on *The Crucible*.

PLOT DEVELOPMENT

The play begins as an elderly traveling salesman, Willy Loman, arrives home, late and exhausted. Upset he has sold nothing, Willy is comforted by his wife, Linda, who tries to calm and cheer him. Their oldest son, Biff, is visiting after a long absence, and their younger son, Hap, is staying with them too. Relations are strained between Biff and his father, partly because of Biff's evident lack of ambition in life—especially considering the promise his father still believes him to have. Willy starts to reminisce, trying to recall better days to cheer himself up, as his sons wake up and overhear him.

Willy goes to the kitchen to get a snack, and the scene switches to the boys' room, where they discuss their father's condition. Biff is as unhappy as Willy regarding his own lack of advancement, but cannot admit this to a father against whom he holds an unspoken grudge. Hap just wants to avoid anything unpleasant, preferring for his brother to deal with Willy rather than get involved himself. Although he confesses he is discontent with his life as a deceitful womanizer, Hap seems unlikely to change. The brothers talk about going into business together, but it is an idle dream from which they are soon distracted by their father, who has begun to talk loudly.

Willy is remembering his sons as young boys and recalls the fatherly advice he gave about how being well liked is all a man needs to get on in the world—advice that we see has badly influenced his sons, making them too self-assured, lazy, and lacking in a moral underpinning. Willy boasts of his exploits, lying to make himself look better, and his sons are of an age where they still believe and idolize their father. Bernard, the son of Willy's friendly neighbor, Charley, comes to warn Biff that he is failing his math class. Although the Lomans show contempt for the studious Bernard, his more serious attitude will be the one that achieves the only success among this group, and we soon learn how poorly the Lomans are actually doing. Willy is not a good salesman, and they are struggling to pay their bills.

We are brought to understand that Willy has been unfaithful. His guilt over this is exacerbated by Linda being so loving and supportive. Willy's memories, which started contentedly, turn unpleasant as he recalls a darker past: his guilt over his adultery, as well as Biff's laziness, thievery, and impending failure to graduate. Willy is plunged back into the present and finds Hap in the kitchen trying to calm him down.

Willy has made enough noise to wake the neighbors, and Charley comes over in evident concern for his friend. He stays to play cards and asks Willy to work for him, but Willy rudely refuses. Willy recalls his older brother, Ben, and conjures up a rare visit Ben made in the past. Charley becomes confused because he can hear only Willy's side of the conversation; the two argue and Charley leaves. The dream takes over and we learn of the influence Ben has had on Willy over the years. Ben has not seen Willy for years. He abandoned him at the age of three, but Willy admires Ben because Ben became rich. Ben is a hard man, without compassion, which has helped him become a successful businessman, pursuing lucrative land deals in Alaska and running diamond mines in Africa. The dream again turns sour, as Willy recalls Biff being caught stealing lumber at the time of this visit. He returns to the present and goes for a walk.

Biff joins his mother to find out what is wrong with Willy. Linda instinctively tries to calm Biff's fears, but then decides to let him know that his estrangement from his father is the root of the problem. She tries to get answers from Biff as to why he is antagonistic to Willy, but Biff is evasive. Although he has not told her, Linda knows that Willy has been taken off salary, is unable to make any sales to earn commissions, and is borrowing money off Charley to hide the fact. Linda criticizes both her sons for their wasteful and selfish lives, and for not caring about their father. Biff, reluctantly, promises to stay around to help, but Linda demands more, telling him that Willy has been trying to kill himself.

Willy returns from his walk and he and Biff begin to argue. Considering what he has just learned, Biff backs down and tries to cheer up his father. Biff suggests that he might go and see an old employer, Bill Oliver, with whom he was once supposedly a favorite, to get a loan to start up his own business. Hap encourages this idea by suggesting that he and Biff are planning a sporting goods partnership, and they get Willy enthused by this dream. For a moment the whole family is excited, until Willy and Biff fall back into arguing, after Biff defends his mother when Willy treats her dismissively. Linda tells Biff to make up, which he does in order to keep the peace. Willy finally goes to bed, to dream of Biff's greatest moment, when he won the high school football championship. Biff goes to remove the rubber tube Linda discovered, which Willy has hidden to assist in his suicide.

The second act begins the following morning. The boys have left, but Linda and Willy breakfast together and speak hopefully of the future. The boys plan to meet their father later in the day for a celebratory dinner. Willy decides to demand he be given a desk job at the company, but it is clear on his arrival there that his boss, Howard Wagner, has little time for him. Fascinated by his latest acquisition, a wire recorder, Howard hardly listens to what Willy says. Willy makes his request, and Howard unsympathetically refuses. Willy tells him about Dave Singleman, an old-time salesman who had inspired Willy as a younger man to go into sales. Howard is not interested, and as soon as he can, fires Willy. The shock sends Willy back into his past to seek advice from his brother, Ben.

Willy recalls a job opportunity Ben had once offered him to go to Alaska, and how Linda had encouraged him to turn it down. He again recalls Biff's championship game, then returns to the present outside Charley's office, where he has come to borrow more money. The adult Bernard, now a successful lawyer, is waiting to see his father and talks to Willy. He asks after Willy's family. Envious of Bernard's success, Willy lies about Biff's prospects but cannot resist asking Bernard how he managed to do so well while Biff turned out so poorly. Bernard asks him why Biff ruined his chances by refusing to retake the math class. Avoiding an answer, Willy gets argumentative and Charley comes to break it up.

Charley again tries to get his friend to accept a job, but Willy responds angrily. Charley gives him the money he needs, and Willy goes to meet his sons for dinner. Hap is already at the restaurant picking up a girl. Biff arrives and has come to his senses, realizing that the dream the family had constructed of him borrowing money from Bill Oliver and becoming a successful businessman was entirely unrealistic. Oliver did not remember who he was, and in revenge Biff stole his fountain pen. When Willy arrives, Biff insists his father face the truth and tries to tell him, but Willy refuses to listen and forces Biff to create a happier version of his meeting. As Biff gets frustrated, Willy returns once more to the past, and we see Biff arriving in Boston to ask his father for advice after flunking his math class, only to find him with another woman. Willy is distracted by his memories, and his strange behavior gets Biff so worried that he falls back on the lie to calm his father down, telling him that Oliver will loan the money. It nearly works, but Biff cannot keep up the pretense. Willy wanders off to the washroom in a reverie, and Biff vainly appeals to Hap for help. Distraught, Biff leaves, and Hap follows with two women, callously leaving his father alone in the washroom, where Willy relives the whole experience of Biff losing faith in his father and every-thing else thereafter. Finding himself abandoned by his sons, Willy goes off to buy some seeds.

The boys arrive home late to find their mother fuming at the way they treated their father, and she is determined to throw them both out for good. Hap tries to smooth things over, but Biff, to Linda's horror, wants to confront his father again. Willy is outside planting seeds, and Biff and Linda go to him. Willy is chatting with Ben, discussing a plan to kill himself so that Biff will get the insurance money to start his own business. As Ben casts doubt on whether the insurance company will pay out, Biff interrupts, telling his father that he has decided to leave for good. As Willy curses Biff, his son tries one final time to get his father to face the truth, confronting him with the rubber tube and declaring the whole family to be fakes.

Biff speaks the truth as he sees it: Hap has a lowly job without prospects and is wasting his life, he himself is a thief and a bum who has never held down any kind of job, and he declares that his father is a "dime a dozen" like the rest of them. His father refuses to accept any of this, accusing Biff of spite, but when Biff breaks down into tears, he understands that his son still loves him. Ignoring everything else Biff has said, Willy concentrates on this one uplifting truth and decides to go through with his suicide plans so that Biff will have enough money to make a success of his life. The family goes to bed, and Willy drives off to crash his car for one last time.

At the close of the play there is a short scene titled "Requiem," which takes place with Willy's family and Charley standing before his grave as they discuss what his death means. Hap seems determined to follow in his father's footsteps, forever the dreamer, while Biff refuses to fall back into that world of deceit. Charley is sympathetic, suggesting that dreams are all that some men have, while Linda is shown to be utterly lost without her husband.

CHARACTER DEVELOPMENT

Willy Loman's whole life seems to have been a sellout; his sons have turned out badly, and his relationship with Biff has soured. But although a braggart and adulterer, Willy Loman is not a bad man, and he is loved by all who are close to him. It is their love that allows us to see his better side and sympathize with his plight. Willy also loves his family and tries to give them what he feels they are worth, even sacrificing his own life. Unlike his father and brother, Willy stayed with his family and tried to be responsible. Willy's problem is that he wants to be successful, but he has not been given the personality, the ability, or the luck to achieve this goal. Overweight, over-talkative, and now overage, he has become redundant in a business world that only ever tolerated him in the first place. But Willy refuses to give up without a fight. He is a human being and demands the respect and dignity most human beings deserve, and this determination makes him heroic.

Willy is the salesman of the title, but the first salesman whose death we hear of is Dave Singleman. Willy idealizes Singleman's death, but realistically, the man passed away on a train still trying to make that big deal; despite the many who attended his funeral, he died alone. Salesmen must always be on the move, and such a life inevitably wears people down. Singleman was a salesman of the past who could still manage to get by on being liked; Willy attempts to emulate Singleman's life in a less sentimental age. Working against greater odds, Willy runs out of steam, and it is his death with which the play ends. His funeral is not nearly so well attended, indicating a society in which people hold less importance, which seems to finally invalidate Willy's insistence on personality being the key to success.

Willy recalls his idealized past as both an escape and an attempt to discover what went wrong. Convinced his current unhappiness is due to his failure to make his mark in the business world, he searches for the answer to the question he has asked all his life: how do you become successful? Willy has convinced himself that the answer is to be well liked, and he passed this belief on to his sons. However, Miller makes it clear that being well liked has little to do with success. Miller uses various characters in the play to exemplify how people get ahead through hard work (Charley and Bernard), inheritance (Howard), or sheer luck (Ben). Neither Howard nor Ben wastes any time trying to be liked, and both are depicted as selfish, impolite, and rich.

Related by his recording device (an early version of a tape recorder) to cold technology, Howard foreshadows the hard-hearted businessmen who decimate their workforces as cheaper automation takes over. Howard has not worked for his success; he inherited it from his father. He has no time for his father's old salesman and does not listen to what Willy tries to tell him. Howard represents a new development in the business world: the uncaring and exploitative way of doing business, in which being well liked holds no relevance, and all that matters is the profit line.

Ben, as a self-made man, tells his tale of finding a fortune in the African jungle as if it were a solution, but it is merely a boast. Ben was a selfish man, and he survives the jungle by plundering it. His father had left a wife and two young sons to seek success in Alaska and was never heard from again. Ben similarly ignores family responsibility as he follows the father's footsteps. Ben's hardness helped him survive, and he has made a fortune by luck. Charley, on the other hand, is successful, content, and a nice guy. Charley is satisfied with moderate success without feeling compelled to be the best, and he does not take shortcuts but relies on steady, hard work. Ever in the background, not forcing himself but trying to help his unfortunate neighbor through a difficult time, Charley loves and respects Willy in a way that few others do. Charley passes on his values to his offspring, as Willy does, but his are clearly the better values by which to live, for his son, Bernard, is a caring, compassionate adult, as well as a highly successful lawyer.

As a youth, Biff was led to believe that since he was "well liked" he could get away with anything. He begins to steal: a football from school, lumber for the house, a crate of balls from Bill Oliver. Willy is desperate that Biff should succeed in life, so instead of punishing him, he condones the thefts and makes excuses, neglecting to instill in his son the moral values a parent should teach a child. Biff appears successful in high school as a football player, but reaps no benefit from this as he never goes to college. Initially he had planned to retake the math course he needed, but he catches his father with a mistress. Biff's self-confidence dissipates as he loses respect for his father. As a result of this, his belief in the fantasies his father has fed him cannot be maintained. Out in the real world, away from the destructive influence of his father, Biff begins to recognize his own true nature, and he replaces his father's dream with one of his own. Whether Biff can achieve his dream of working with the land is not as important as the fact that it is more suited to his nature than trying to be a hotshot businessman.

Hap does not reach the same level of awareness as his brother. Since his childhood Hap has admired his father and older brother, forever fighting for their attention and approval. Biff left home, but Willy remained as a role model, and Hap has become a pale imitation of his father. Bereft of even the few decencies Willy retains, such as a conscience and a sense of responsibility, Hap presents an entirely disreputable figure. Despite his supposed love and respect for his father, Hap has no compunction about abandoning Willy in a bar when he is clearly distressed, even denying that Willy is his father to escape embarrassment. He would rather chase women, even though he has as little respect for them as he shows to Willy, and sleeps with the wives and girlfriends of his bosses in petty revenge.

Linda's central importance seems to be as a voice of protest and outrage against what is happening to her husband. She insists that "attention must be paid" to Willy and his suffering. As Linda recognizes, Willy is a human being and it *is* a terrible thing that happens to him. Dreams, illusions, and self-deceptions feed the action of this play; Linda, in contrast, seems very much planted in reality with her concerns over house payments, mending work, insurance premiums, and her husband's care. She knows exactly what her sons are and does not hold back in telling them, especially when they hurt her husband. Yet despite Linda's clear sight, she allows her family's dreams to flourish; she even encourages them. It is only when they are dreaming of a brighter future that the family can operate together, and for Linda, the truth is a small sacrifice to pay for the happiness of her family.

THEMES

Miller's strong sense of moral and social commitment runs throughout the play. The aims of *Salesman* are twofold. Firstly, Miller wanted to write a social drama confronting the problems of an ordinary man in a conscience-less, capitalistic social system. Secondly, he wanted that same play to be a modern tragedy that adapted older tragic theories to allow for a common man as tragic protagonist. Willy's apparent ordinariness should not blind us to his tragic stature; Miller insists that a common family man's situation can be as tragic as the dilemmas of royalty, because he ties his definition of heroism to a notion of personal dignity that transcends social stature. Willy is heroic because he strives to be free and to make his mark in society despite the odds against him. Though he is destroyed in the process, he is motivated by love, and his destruction allows for learning to take place. Through Willy's sacrifice, Biff is able to accept his father's love while recognizing the empti-ness of the dream Willy espoused. Willy Loman had accepted at face value overpublicized ideas of material success and therein lies his tragedy. His downfall and final defeat illustrate not only the failure of a man but also the failure of a way of life.

A central thematic issue in this play is Miller's consideration of the problematic and elusive "American Dream" of success, and how success is interpreted by society. Miller sees many people's lives being poisoned by their desire to be successful. People like the Lomans are doomed to try for success but fail, with all the resulting guilt that such failure brings. Others, like Ben and Howard, display an ability to make money, which deems them successful, but at the cost of their own moral integrity. Charley and Bernard, on the other hand, are successful, but do not allow their desire for wealth to run their lives. This enables them to maintain their moral integrity and offer us a potential solution to this social problem that, Miller believes, lies at the heart of American democracy.

The Loman family survives intact for many years largely through their capacity to dream. Such dreams are highly ambivalent, especially when they turn out to be so patently false; they may provide a momentary respite from a harsh reality, but are they not more destructive in the long run? When Biff is led to dream that he and Hap can start a business on a loan from Bill Oliver, we see the family revitalized and Willy gain the strength to go and ask for a better job. But to feed the dream Biff has to reinvent not only his own abilities, but also his relationship with Mr. Oliver. Such dreams can never be fulfilled, as they are based on lies. While the dream is maintained it may grant strength, but as soon as reality intrudes, the dream is shattered and lays the dreamer open to harsh disillusionment.

But the question remains in the play, is it possible to live in dreams? Charley tells us, "A salesman is got to dream," and seems to suggest that Willy had no other option. But where do Willy's dreams originate? It is evident that Willy's family experience has been influential in his development. Both Willy's father and older brother, Ben, are portrayed as archetypal pioneers—men who have successfully tamed the West—whom Willy is tempted to emulate, despite their evident self-absorption and lack of compassion. However, their sense of freedom and adventure clashes with Willy's more humane sense of responsibility and his caution; for Willy is not only the product of his family upbringing, but a product of a far wider array of cultural myths and values. It is little wonder that Willy is unable to find happiness, for he is being continuously influenced by conflicting ideologies, which can never allow him to feel any satisfaction.

The play also explores the changing role of capitalism in society and its impact on people's lives. Willy Loman is living in a time when the nature of business itself is undergoing intrinsic changes, partly due to the capitalist pressure to make more money and become more efficient. *Death of a Salesman* depicts a definite clash between capitalistic business and morality. It is clear that Miller would prefer us to follow the example of Charley rather than Howard or Ben. Ben abandons his family, Howard ruthlessly fires an old man, and Hap admits to taking bribes; none of them feel any remorse, and a capitalist system encourages such behavior. The best way to survive in such a system is to become a better and more ruthless capitalist than your fellow workers. However, a character such as Charley seems to have found a way to survive in business with his morality intact; he is able to do this largely by limiting his expectations and refusing to ignore the plight of others.

The desire to be successful, and the fact that a capitalistic society encourages such a desire, leads to a third major theme in the play: Miller's consideration of the force of materialism in people's lives. In the search for the "good life," people like the Lomans surround themselves with many things above and beyond the necessities of life. However, these goods are only available at a price, and not everyone in society can afford all that the advertisers convince them they must have to be considered happy. The Lomans try to keep up, with a refrigerator, a vacuum, and a new car, but they find themselves in a constant state of worry that they may not be able to meet all their payments. However, they do not dare be satisfied with less.

The issue of family and the relationship that exists between members of a family are also of great interest to Miller. Father figures abound in Miller's work, and like Willy Loman, they are often portrayed as highly ambivalent characters. In the 1940s the father was still viewed as the provider of life, both biologically and economically. Fathers were also responsible for teaching their children proper morals and values, through instruction and by setting themselves up as good examples. Children should be able to view their father with the proper mix of awe, devotion, and love. A major problem occurs with fathers like Willy Loman, because they prove themselves to be so fallible. They fail to exhibit the right morals and values in their own lives, thus making it hard for children to respect and follow their lead. The kinds of relationships Willy and Charley have with their sons are very different. They teach their offspring different sets of values, and we can see by their sons' resulting success or failure as to who was in the right. While Willy teaches Biff and Hap that all they need to be successful is to be well liked, Charley makes sure Bernard understands that he has a better chance to get ahead through hard work.

HISTORICAL CONTEXT

Although Willy Loman's situation is often described as timeless, *Salesman* can be read as an illustration of the historical economic interests and forces operating on American society from the turn of the century to when the play was written. This was a period of major changes in the economic structure of America. Willy witnessed the pioneers' sense of hope and possibility at the beginning of the new millennium, a time when his father and brother both left home to embrace such possibilities to the full. He lived through the wild prosperity of the 1920s, a period when he felt he could become successful in the big city, through to the 1929 Wall Street Crash, which marked the start of the Great Depression. The Depression lasted throughout the 1930s, and Willy evidently found his products increasingly hard to sell in a period when nobody had money to buy anything but necessities.

With the economy being jump-started for the 1940s by the increased market demands and industrial advances of World War II, Willy saw a renewed sense of vigor in the American economy, which probably created much of the hope he places in the prospects of his sons. The play was written and set in 1948, at the time when forces of capitalism and materialism came to the fore, and technology made its greatest inroads into the lives of everyday people. *Salesman* depicts the impact of these forces on the lives of an ordinary family—the Lomans. It is little wonder that so many of those watching the original production felt that they were witnessing their own story or that of a family member.

The Lomans are depicted as social failures in their inability to make money and live happily and comfortably, but the deeper question asked by the play is whether this failure is because of their own inadequacies or caused by society's unrealistic standards of success? In Miller's opinion, the blame of failure should not be attached to insignificant cogs in the social machine, like the Lomans, but attributed to the larger social forces that operate in people's lives. Economics plays an important part in the creation of such forces. By the time the play was written, Miller saw business matters at odds with conventional morality, with humanity threatened by the onset of technology and the growing pressures of ownership; all these issues are reflected in the dilemmas of the Loman family and the other characters to whom they are economically linked.

LITERARY STYLE AND DEVICES

Written in a style that has become known as "subjective realism," *Salesman* carefully blends a realistic picture of a salesman's home and life in the post-Depression years with the subjective thoughts that are going through its central protagonist's head. The play's clever use of time, which allows the audience to view both past and present occurring at the same moment on the same stage set, fully captured the concept of simultaneity after which Miller had been striving. The Lomans act and sound like natural, everyday people, facing everyday social and domestic concerns. However, Willy's flashback dream sequences, the increasingly evident symbolism of various stage effects (lighting and sound), and the play's subtle protest against accepted social expectations also satisfy the requirements of an expressionistic work.

Miller's lengthy setting and character descriptions offer valuable clues for interpretation. Willy is presented as living in a claustrophobic urban setting indicative of the harsh life he has chosen. His home is surrounded by apartment houses that emanate a threatening orange glow. When memory takes over, this glow gives way to a more dreamlike background with shadowy leaves and music, evoking a happier pastoral era. At the close of the play, however, we see the looming "hard towers" of the apartment building dominating the setting once more. When Willy initially goes from the real world into his first reverie, the apartment houses in the background are faded out, and the lighting suggests that the stage is covered with leaves, as the opening pastoral music reasserts itself. With this change in atmosphere, Willy's dreamworld of the past is re-created for the audience as it occurs in Willy's memory.

The opening setting provides the background for Willy Loman's life and some of the rationale behind his death. The faint pastoral melody, played on a flute, recalls both Willy's father, who played such an instrument, and the pastoral dream that may have suited Willy's nature better than the harsh world of business he chose. Miller's emphasis on the refrigerator in the kitchen and a silver athletic trophy above Willy's bed represents the only achievements in Willy's life—a few basic luxuries for the house and a fleeting winning moment from his family's past. The refrigerator, we later learn, is on the verge of breaking down, and the trophy was won by Willy's oldest son, Biff, just before he dropped out of high school and became a vagrant. Willy's activities, aside from his job as a salesman, are part of a symbolic network. He plants seeds just as he plants false hopes: both will die and never come to fruition, largely because the house has become enclosed by the city. The front porch, constructed out of stolen lumber, is indicative of how their lives, as well as their house, have been built on something false. Willy does not fit into the modern world of machinery; likewise, the values he espouses, where deals are made with a smile and a handshake, are those of a bygone age. To illustrate this point, Miller frequently depicts Willy's uneasy relationship with machinery such as his car, his refrigerator, and Howard's recording machine.

The names of characters also provide insights. Willy is a childish version of the more adult William, indicating an intrinsic immaturity in his nature. The Loman men all need to grow up and find true direction in their lives, especially Willy with his unrealistic dream of wanting everyone to like him. Loman has been read as indicating Willy to be a "low-man," common and insignificant, as opposed, perhaps, to Dave Singleman, the salesman who is "singled" out. Miller, however, declares this was unintentional, for he picked the name of Loman subconsciously from a movie he had once seen: *The Testament of Dr. Mabuse*. For Miller, the name Lohmann as used in the movie evokes the voice of a "terror-stricken man calling into the void for help that will never come" (*Timebends* 178), and this certainly applies to Willy Loman.

In contrast, the names of Willy's sons seem highly ironic. Biff seems to indicate an abrasive nature and someone who will have to fight to get what he wants, but Biff's life so far has been marked by his inability to stick with anything and to quit anytime things get to be too hard. Born Harold, but called Happy by his friends, Biff's brother, Hap, invokes a happy-go-lucky personality. However, we soon learn that this is a deluded happiness; Hap isn't happy at all and pushes his inner discontent to one side.

SITUATION OF WORK

Miller's influence on American drama can be seen as both general and specific. Alongside Eugene O'Neill and Tennessee Williams, he is a major pioneer in the development of both a serious and distinctly American theater, and *Salesman* is his single most important work in this regard. The play suggested new theatrical possibilities with its unique blend of realism and expressionism, as well as offering a challenge to previous definitions of tragedy.

Soon after the play opened, Miller wrote an article for the *New York Times* entitled "Tragedy and the Common Man," in which he insisted that "the common man is as apt a subject for tragedy in its highest sense as kings were" (*Theater Essays* 3). This started a heated debate regarding the nature of tragedy, which has continued ever since. Traditional views of tragedy assume a hero who is either upper class or very intelligent, and who challenges, because of some personal flaw in his nature, the moral values of his society. For daring such a challenge, the hero suffers, to prove to audiences that their society and its values are inviolable.

Willy Loman is clearly not the usual tragic hero; he is lower middle class and none too clever. The world he inhabits is that of amoral, capitalistic big business, rather than one with any clear moral values. However, Miller insists that Willy Loman is a tragic hero, and *Salesman* a tragedy. He argues that tragic heroes are defined by their willingness to sacrifice everything in order to maintain their personal dignity—whatever their station in life. Loman has a faulty vision of what makes a person successful, which makes him flawed, but regardless of the opposition and the ultimate cost to himself, he refuses to give up that vision, which makes him, in Miller's eyes, a tragic hero. This new definition of tragedy has been explored by numerous playwrights since.

The dramas of social criticism from the 1920s and 1930s had slight influence on the society they critiqued, and myths of success continued to flourish in America, unabated. But *Salesman*'s exposure of the darker aspects of the American Dream was widely accepted, partly because the attack was so sympathetic. Miller exploded those American myths, both old and new, which seemed to ensure success, and brought into common view the empty materialistic values infecting much of American society. After *Salesman*, playwrights could rely on a large proportion of their audiences having a different perception of the faults within American society.

Miller's commitment to serious drama and openness toward experimentation, as shown in *Salesman*, has influenced many younger American playwrights, including Edward Albee, August Wilson, and David Mamet. They write plays that display similar social concerns, with the same degree of craft, design, and attention to language. There are also plays that display a specific influence, for example, Lorraine Hansberry's *A Raisin in the Sun* (1959), which portrays the Youngers, a family who, despite their ethnicity, is very similar to the Lomans. Both families struggle to survive and progress in a society that seems antagonistic to their dreams. Mamet's *Glengarry Glen Ross* (1984) can also be viewed as an update of *Salesman*, with one of its central protagonists, Shelley Levene, being a modern-day version of Willy Loman. Both elderly, they are tired men, worn out by a world that has been antagonistic and hostile to their dreams.

CRITICAL RECEPTION

Response to *Salesman* was tremendous, both in its Philadelphia tryouts and its Broadway opening; audiences and critics had been riveted. Miller won a string of major awards, including the Pulitzer Prize, the New York Drama Critics' Circle Award, the Theater Club Award, and the Tony Award. The play was soon performed throughout America and Europe. The published script became a best seller and the only play ever to be a Book-of-the-Month Club selection.

The director, Elia Kazan, who had successfully produced Miller's earlier play, *All My Sons*, persuaded Miller to accept Lee J. Cobb as Willy Loman, even though Miller had written the part for a small man. Cobb made the part his own, although Dustin Hoffman also made a mark on the role in 1984, playing it more closely to Miller's original vision. Jo Mielziner designed a set and lighting that helped convey Loman's mental state, and Alex North provided music. Robert Coleman of the *Daily Mirror* called the play "emotional dynamite" and reported that "sobs were heard throughout the auditorium, and handkerchiefs were kept busy wiping away tears" (360). Brooks Atkinson declared it "superb," commenting on its poetry and calling it a "wraith-like tragedy" (27). Richard Watts asserted that "under Elia Kazan's vigorous and perceptive direction, '*Death of a Salesman*' emerges as easily the best and most important new American play of the year" (359).

The play's portrait of Willy Loman managed to strike an emotional chord that continues to reverberate. A man of his time and yet also, somehow, timeless, Loman has attracted international audiences and continues to interest them even to the present day. Theater scholar Brenda Murphy talks about "the ease with which audiences all over the world have understood and sympathized with the plight of Willy Loman, and have grasped the issues of the play" (126). The 1983 production of *Salesman* in Beijing, The People's Republic of China, at the People's Art Theater, which Miller himself directed, was a landmark in foreign diplomacy. Aside from the Chinese production and numerous American and European productions, the play has been successfully produced in countries as diverse as South Africa, Korea, Japan, Mexico, the Soviet Union, and Australia. There have also been at least seven movie and television versions.

SUGGESTED READINGS

Abbotson, Susan C. W. *Student Companion to Arthur Miller*. Westport, CT: Greenwood Press, 2000.

Ardolino, Frank. "Like Father, Like Sons: Miller's Negative Use of Sports Imagery in *Death of a Salesman*." *Journal of Evolutionary Psychology* 25.1–2 (March 2004): 32–39.

Atkinson, Brooks. "At the Theatre." *New York Times*, February 11, 1949: 27.

Bhatia, Santosh K. *Arthur Miller: Social Drama as Tragedy*. New York: Humanities, 1985.

Bigsby, C.W.E. *Arthur Miller*. Cambridge: Cambridge University Press, 2004.

———, ed. *Arthur Miller and Company*. London: Methuen, 1990.

———. *The Cambridge Companion to Arthur Miller*. Cambridge: Cambridge University Press, 1997.

Bloom, Harold, ed. *Arthur Miller*. New York: Chelsea House, 1987.

———. *Arthur Miller's* Death of a Salesman. New York: Chelsea House, 1988.

———. *Modern Critical Views: Arthur Miller*. New York: Chelsea House, 1987.

———. *Willy Loman*. New York: Chelsea House, 1991.

Carson, Neil. *Arthur Miller*. London: Macmillan, 1982.

Centola, Steven, ed. *The Achievement of Arthur Miller: New Essays*. Dallas, TX: Contemporary Research, 1995.

———. *Arthur Miller in Conversation*. Dallas, TX: Northouse & Northouse, 1993.

Coleman, Robert. "*Death of a Salesman* Is Emotional Dynamite." *Daily Mirror,* February 11, 1949. *New York Theatre Critics' Reviews* 10 (1949): 360.

Corrigan, Robert W., ed. *Arthur Miller: A Collection of Critical Essays.* Englewood Cliffs, NJ: Prentice-Hall, 1969.

Evans, Richard I. *Psychology and Arthur Miller.* New York: Dutton, 1969.

Gottfried, Martin. *Arthur Miller: His Life and Work.* New York: Da Capo, 2003.

Griffith, Alice. *Understanding Arthur Miller.* Columbia: University of South Carolina Press, 1996.

Harshburger, Karl. *The Burning Jungle: An Analysis of Arthur Miller's* Death of a Salesman. Washington, DC: University Press of America, 1979.

Hayman, Ronald. *Arthur Miller.* New York: Ungar, 1972.

Huftel, Sheila. *Arthur Miller: The Burning Glass.* New York: Citadel, 1965.

Koon, Helen Wickam, ed. *Twentieth Century Interpretations of* Death of a Salesman: *A Collection of Critical Essays.* Englewood Cliffs, NJ: Prentice-Hall, 1983.

Marino, Stephen A. *A Language Study of Arthur Miller's Plays: The Poetic in the Colloquial.* New York: Mellen, 2002.

———, ed. *"The Salesman Has a Birthday": Essays Celebrating the Fiftieth Anniversary of Arthur Miller's* Death of a Salesman. Lanham, MD: University Press of America, 2000.

Martin, Robert A., ed. *Arthur Miller: New Perspectives.* Englewood Cliffs, NJ: Prentice-Hall, 1982.

Martine, James J. *Critical Essays on Arthur Miller.* Boston: Hall, 1979.

Miller, Arthur. *Arthur Miller's Collected Plays.* New York: Viking, 1957.

———. *Echoes down the Corridor: Collected Essays—1944–2000.* Ed. Steve R. Centola. New York: Viking, 2000.

———. "In Memoriam." *New Yorker,* December 25, 1995 and January 1, 1996: 80–81.

———. *The Man Who Had All the Luck.* New York: Penguin, 2004.

———. *Mr. Peter's Connections.* New York: Penguin, 1999.

———. *The Portable Arthur Miller.* Ed. Christopher Bigsby. New York: Penguin, 1995.

———. *The Price.* New York: Viking, 1968.

———. *The Ride down Mt. Morgan.* New York: Penguin, 1992.

———. *The Theater Essays of Arthur Miller.* Ed. Robert A. Martin and Steven R. Centola. Rev. ed. New York: Viking, 1996.

———. *Timebends: A Life.* New York: Grove, 1987.

Moss, Leonard. *Arthur Miller.* 2nd ed. New York: Twayne, 1980.

Murphy, Brenda. *Miller: Death of a Salesman.* Cambridge: Cambridge University Press, 1995.

Murphy, Brenda, and Susan C. W. Abbotson. *Understanding* Death of a Salesman. Westport, CT: Greenwood Press, 1999.

Nelson, Benjamin. *Arthur Miller: Portrait of a Playwright.* New York: McKay, 1970.

Otten, Terry. *The Temptation of Innocence in the Dramas of Arthur Miller.* Columbia: University of Missouri Press, 2002.

Ribkoff, Fred. "Shame, Guilt, Empathy, and the Search for Identity in Arthur Miller's *Death of a Salesman*." *Modern Drama* 43.1 (spring 2000): 48–55.

Roudané, Matthew C., ed. *Approaches to Teaching Miller's Death of a Salesman*. New York: MLA, 1995.

———. *Conversations with Arthur Miller*. Jackson: University Press of Mississippi, 1987.

Scanlan, Tom. *Family, Drama, and American Dreams*. Westport, CT: Greenwood, 1978.

Schlueter, June, and James K. Flanagan. *Arthur Miller*. New York: Ungar, 1987.

Shockley, John S. "*Death of a Salesman* and American Leadership: Life Imitates Art." *Journal of American Culture* 17 (summer 1994): 49–56.

Trowbridge, Clinton W. "Arthur Miller: Between Pathos and Tragedy." *Modern Drama* 10 (1967): 221–32.

Watts, Richard. "*Death of a Salesman* A Powerful Drama." *New York Post*, February 11, 1949. *New York Theatre Critics' Reviews* 10 (1949): 359.

Welland, Dennis. *Miller: The Playwright*. 2nd ed. New York: Methuen, 1983.

Yim, Harksoon. "Arthur Miller's Theory of Tragedy and Its Practice in *All My Sons, Death of a Salesman*, and *The Crucible*." *Publications of the Mississippi Philological Association* (1996): 57–63.

Yoon, So-young. "Willy Loman's Portrait: Trauma of the Absence of the Father." *Journal of Modern British and American Drama* 16.3 (December 2003): 181–209.

4

Arthur Miller
The Crucible
1953

BIOGRAPHICAL CONTEXT

Continuing on from the biography of Miller in the previous chapter, Miller enters the 1950s. This period was a difficult decade in artistic circles, as Senator Joseph McCarthy and the House Committee on Un-American Activities (HUAC) were trying to purge the entertainment industry of what they saw as Communist subversives out to undermine America. Many were accused of Communist sympathies and found themselves out of work. In 1950, Miller adapted Henrik Ibsen's *An Enemy of the People* for Fredric March and his wife, Florence Eldridge, who had been blacklisted from movie roles. They all saw the parallel in its tale of a man accused by a kind of "mob-hysteria" of threatening the well-being of the larger society. Given the climate of the times, the production was not a great success, and Miller was accused by the press of creating anti-American propaganda.

A number of people, such as Miller's close colleague Elia Kazan and fellow playwright Clifford Odets, admitted having had socialist sympathies to HUAC, and named others. Such betrayals lie at the heart of later plays *A View from the Bridge* (1956) and *After the Fall* (1964). Kazan's friendship with Miller fell apart for a number of years following his testimony. When Miller was subpoenaed in 1956, he refused to cooperate. He was cited for contempt, but had the conviction overturned on appeal. Miller wrote *The Crucible* in 1953, and it draws a clear parallel between the American anti-Communist paranoia of the period and the 1692 witch trials of Salem, exposing both to be maliciously motivated with ritualistic public denunciations of largely innocent people. He had spent much of the previous year researching witch trials at the Historical Society in Salem, Massachusetts, to ensure that the play would have an accurate historical basis. It premiered in 1953 in New York City in a production by Jed Harris that Miller saw as too cold and stylized, and was greeted by a mixture of praise, suspicion, and contempt for its evident parallels to HUAC's "witch hunts." It was not until two years later, when a better production appeared, that critics proclaimed it a "great" play. Since then, with its clear message of resistance against tyranny, *Crucible* has grown to be Miller's most widely produced work.

Earlier, in 1950, Miller first met Marilyn Monroe; initially resisting her charms, he later capitulated. His mounting celebrity and the pressures of a writing career had put tremendous strain on his marriage, and meeting Marilyn was the final straw. Miller was attracted to both Marilyn's intense sexuality and her vulnerability, and she seemed to hope that Miller would be able to protect her from the hostile world she saw around her. In 1956, he divorced Mary and married Marilyn, accompanying his new wife to England, where she was making a film. While there, Miller revised *A View from the Bridge* into two acts for Peter Brook to produce in London; the play had appeared a year earlier in New York in a one-act format, on a double bill with Miller's nostalgic drama about life in an auto-parts warehouse, *A Memory of Two Mondays*.

The late 1950s into the 1960s were difficult times for Miller. Apart from the troubles with HUAC, which had made producers wary, his second marriage did not go well, and there would be a series of deaths of those closest to him. Distracted by personal problems, Miller faced a creative slump. The only main work that emerged from this period was the result of an attempt to help his wife, who was growing frustrated by her insipid roles. Miller adapted an earlier short story he had written, "The Misfits," into a screenplay. However, Marilyn's insecurities made filming a nightmare, and the finished movie opened in 1961 to mediocre reviews. Miller would write about this experience 43 years later in *Finishing the Picture* (2004). Before the film opened, he and Marilyn divorced. He saw she was in trouble but felt powerless to help, and he could no longer watch her destroy herself. That same year his mother died. The following year, 1962, six months before Marilyn died, Miller married his third wife, Ingeborg Morath, a professional photographer whose stable nature he found preferable to the roller-coaster relationship he had had with Marilyn.

In Inge, Miller seemed to find his ideal wife, as they lived contentedly for the next 40 years until Inge's death in 2002 from cancer. They had two children, Daniel and Rebecca, and collaborated on a number of books of reportage, including *In Russia* (1969) and *Chinese Encounters* (1979), for which Inge took the photographs and Miller wrote the text.

In 1964 he wrote *After the Fall*, which conveys the psychological drama taking place in the head of Quentin as he tries to place his life, loves, and fears into perspective; many critics chose to read Quentin as a surrogate for Miller himself, especially given the presentation of Quentin's three wives, who seemed remarkably close to those of Miller. The play drew fierce disapproval from many critics for what they felt was a vindictive portrayal of Marilyn (who had died while Miller was completing the play). Depicting the interrogation of suspected Jews by Nazi officials in Vichy France, *Incident at Vichy* (1964) was produced that same year.

In 1965 Miller was elected president of PEN, an international organization of playwrights, poets, essayists, and novelists formed after World War II to combat censorship and nationalistic pressures on writers. In 1969 he visited Czechoslovakia to show support for writers there, and met Václav Havel, then a famous dissident writer, but who later became the democratic president of Czechoslovakia. Havel became the inspiration for Sigmund in Miller's 1977 play *The Archbishop's Ceiling*, which depicts a group of writers trying to survive against threats of suppression. After his presidency of PEN expired, Miller continued to work with the organization to assist writers in trouble across the globe.

In 1968, *The Price* premiered in New York City and saw a return to more familiar Miller territory: the division and connection between family members. *The Price* had the longest run of a Miller play for some time, but Miller continued to experiment with new forms. In 1974 he wrote a musical called *Up from Paradise*, which was a revised version of his 1972 rewrite of the Cain and Abel story, *The Creation of the World and Other Business*. Neither met much success, nor did *The American Clock* (1980), with its moving collage of American life in the 1930s. A television screenplay based on Fania Fenelon's Holocaust experiences, *Playing For Time* (1980), had moderate success, but Miller continued to explore theatrical limits, switching to one-acts, producing *Elegy for a Lady* and *Some Kind of Love Story* in 1982, and *Clara* and *I Can't Remember Anything* in 1987. All four center on two main characters who, through conflicts over their differing views of reality, either grow, or fail to grow, toward a deeper appreciation of their own shortcomings, strengths, and responsibilities. The plays use minimalist or highly representational sets and make great use of lighting, sound, and image to get their points across.

Despite a lack of critical acclaim for his newer works, Miller did not slacken into the 1990s. In 1991 a one-act version of *The Last Yankee*, depicting the pressures facing married couples in a postmodern age of chaos and insecurity, was produced, with an expanded two-act version coming two years later. Also, 1991 saw *The Ride down Mt. Morgan*, about one man's ego and the troubles he causes in his desire for complete autonomy, which premiered in London, England. The choice of England was a reflection of Miller's growing despair over getting fair press in America. The year 1994 saw a return to Miller's interest in both the Holocaust and the 1930s with *Broken Glass*, which had successful runs on both Broadway and London stages. Many saw this realistically rendered tale of a woman's paralysis and her husband's inability to face his complicity in this as a return to the earlier style of Miller, albeit somewhat stripped. However, 1998 produced the ethereal *Mr. Peter's Connections*, a firmly experimental play with multiple timelines and blurring of reality. His plays of the new century showed a decided comic turn, with the 2002 satire on politics and the media, *Resurrection Blues*, and his thinly disguised version of what happened on the set of *The Misfits*, *Finishing the Picture* (2004). Inge died in 2002 and Miller's companion of later years was the painter Agnes Barley. He died on February 10, 2005, at his home in Connecticut.

PLOT DEVELOPMENT

Set in Salem, Massachusetts, in 1692, *The Crucible* begins in the bedroom of Reverend Samuel Parris's daughter, Betty. Parris kneels in prayer, weeping at the bedside of his comatose 10-year-old daughter. He sends away the family slave, Tituba, but allows entry to his teenage niece, Abigail Williams, and young Susanna Walcott, who tells him the doctor suspects witchcraft. Although Parris insists that "unnatural causes" cannot be at fault, he has already sent for the Reverend Hale to look into such possibilities.

Prior to Betty's coma, Parris caught her and Abigail dancing "like heathens" in the forest. The shock of discovery caused Betty to faint, and she has not regained consciousness. Parris is more worried about how his enemies may use this against him than about his daughter's health. He presses Abigail for details, and she insists they were only dancing. Abigail was dismissed from the Proctors' service seven months prior, and although she insists it was maliciousness on Elizabeth Proctor's part, her uncle is suspicious. Locals Ann and Thomas Putnam, clearly determined to believe the worst, arrive with stories of Betty flying like a witch. Their daughter, Ruth, is also behaving strangely. Ann lost seven babies prior to Ruth, an occurrence not uncommon in the seventeenth century, but is determined to blame someone. She had sent Ruth to Tituba, whom she believes to have supernatural powers, to discover who "murdered" her babies.

The Putnams press Parris to publicly declare witchcraft abroad, and he agrees to lead the gathering villagers in prayer. These three leave and Abigail remains to talk with the Putnams' servant, Mercy Lewis. They are joined by

Mary Warren, who replaced Abigail as the Proctors' servant. The girls discuss what really occurred in the forest: Mercy had been naked, and Abigail had drunk blood to conjure against Elizabeth Proctor. Mary Warren had only watched, but she is the most fearful of what will happen once the truth comes out. Abigail shakes Betty to wake her, and Betty revives. She tries to fly out the window but is held back by Abigail, who threatens them all to stay quiet. Betty reverts to her coma as John Proctor enters to fetch Mary.

Proctor sends Mary home, and Mercy follows, leaving he and Abigail together. Abigail tells Proctor no witchcraft was involved, but she is angered by his refusal to have anything more to do with her. They have had relations in the past, and Abigail refuses to believe that Proctor does not prefer her to his wife, even though he insists otherwise.

A psalm about Jesus drifts in from outside, and Betty screams. Parris, the Putnams, and Mercy Lewis rush in to see what is happening, joined by two respected elders of the village, Rebecca Nurse and Giles Corey. Rebecca calms Betty down with her presence, and suggests that the children's odd behavior is just childish mischief. Proctor is angered by the superstitions of Parris and the Putnams, accusing Parris of being a poor preacher. They squabble, Rebecca tries to calm them down, and Putnam joins in the accusations, just as Reverend Hale arrives.

Proctor leaves as Hale examines Betty. Hale insists the others accept his authority, and they relate their suspicions. Rebecca disapproves of their malicious tone and leaves, while Giles questions Hale about his wife's tendency to read books. Parris and Hale question Abigail about the children's exploits in the forest, and she accuses Tituba of calling the devil and making her drink blood. Tituba is brought in to defend herself, but Abigail seems the more credible. Tituba is fearfully led into confessing complicity with the devil to save her own life, and to name others as witches. Abigail adds more names and Betty joins her, as the adults scurry to arrest the accused.

Act 2 begins eight days later in the Proctors' house. There is tension between Elizabeth and Proctor; both speak and behave overcautiously. Proctor wishes Elizabeth to be warmer toward him, while she is suspicious he still sees Abigail. Their servant, Mary, is an official of the court, which has been set up in town to try the accused. Matters have escalated, and there are now 14 people in jail faced with hanging unless they confess to witchcraft. The town supports the trials, as Abigail leads the girls to accuse more people. Elizabeth asks Proctor to stop this dangerous nonsense, but he is uncertain if anyone will believe him if he denounces Abigail. Elizabeth suspects Proctor is reluctant because of feelings for Abigail, but he angrily denounces her jealousy as unfounded. Arriving home, Mary deflates their argument.

Mary gives Elizabeth a small rag doll, called a poppet, which she made in court. The girls have accused 25 more people, and the court has declared Goody Osburn must hang. If the accused confess their allegiance with the devil, they go to jail, but if they refuse to confess, they are hanged as unrepentant witches; a declaration of innocence carries little weight. Even Elizabeth has come under suspicion (from accusations by Abigail), but the court apparently dismissed the idea when Mary defended her.

After Mary goes to bed the Proctors worry. Realizing that she is in danger, Elizabeth asks Proctor to talk to Abigail. Proctor agrees to go, just as Hale arrives. Although convinced that witchcraft is about, Hale is unsure of the girls' accusations and is investigating further. He questions the Proctors about their religious adherence, asking Proctor to name the Ten Commandments. Proctor significantly forgets "adultery," until delicately reminded by his wife. Elizabeth presses Proctor to tell Hale about Abigail's admission there was no witchcraft involved. Hale is shocked, but Proctor is reluctant to testify to this in court and put his word against Abigail's.

They are interrupted by Giles and Francis Nurse arriving to announce their wives have been arrested on charges of witchcraft. This news shakes Hale, but he insists they accept the justice of the court and allow no one to be above suspicion. The marshal arrives to arrest Elizabeth, asking for a poppet that he has been told is Elizabeth's and proves her witchery. Abigail has stuck herself with a needle and declared that Elizabeth sent a spirit to do this; they find a needle sticking in the poppet. Mary explains the poppet and needle are hers, and Proctor rips the warrant, but they insist on taking Elizabeth. Rather than cause trouble, Elizabeth agrees to go. Proctor promises to free her shortly. Giles and Proctor urge Hale to see the girls' accusations as fraudulent, but Hale stands firm that such confusion would not have fallen on the town if all were innocent. In the guilt of his recent adultery, Proctor falls quiet. As everyone leaves, Proctor remains with Mary, whom he insists must speak to clear Elizabeth. In fear of Abigail, Mary refuses, but Proctor says he is prepared to confess his own adultery to destroy the court's faith in Abigail.

There is an additional scene at this point, not always included, which Miller added during the initial production. Five weeks after Elizabeth has been arrested, the day before her trial, Proctor secretly meets Abigail to warn her to tell the truth or be exposed, but Abigail does not believe him. She seems close to madness, displaying a continued passion for Proctor and paranoia about the township. Her body is covered in scars she believes were caused by spirits, despite the implication they are self-inflicted.

In act 3 we move to an anteroom outside the courtroom. Next door Judge Hathorne questions Martha Corey. When her husband, Giles, speaks in her defense, he is brought into the anteroom for questioning. Governor Danforth, leading the panel of judges, demands Giles be less disruptive and offer his evidence in a proper affidavit. Meanwhile, Francis Nurse, whose wife, Rebecca, has been condemned, insists to the shocked judges that the girls are lying. They threaten him with contempt, but he stands firm. Proctor enters with Mary, who has agreed to tell the truth about the girls' deceit.

Although Hathorne and Parris are against even considering the girls as false, Danforth listens. He questions Proctor regarding his motivation for presenting Mary, fearing Proctor is trying to undermine the court rather than just save his wife. We learn that Elizabeth has declared herself pregnant, although the judges are uncertain if this is true. Proctor insists his wife would never lie. To test him, they offer to let Elizabeth live to give birth if Proctor will drop his protest, but he refuses, as too many other innocents are condemned. Danforth angrily agrees to hear the deposition.

Proctor shows a list of people that Francis has compiled who believe Elizabeth, Rebecca, and Martha are innocent. To Francis's dismay, the judges decide to arrest all these people for examination. Proctor offers Giles's deposition accusing Thomas Putnam of prompting his daughter to cry witchery on people to get their property. Danforth insists that Giles name his witness, but knowing that to name the man would send him to jail, Giles refuses and is arrested for contempt. Next, the judges read Mary's deposition. Danforth harshly questions Mary, but she stands firm. The girls are brought in to face their accuser, and Danforth asks them to respond. Abigail insists Mary lies, and diverts the men to argue over Elizabeth's poppet, but Proctor redirects their attention to Abigail, insisting she is trying to murder his wife. His accusations of Abigail laughing during services and leading the girls to dance naked affect Danforth. Hathorne asks Mary to show how she pretends to faint in court, but Mary cannot do this without the proper atmosphere. This restores the judges' belief that she is lying.

Danforth questions Abigail, but her insistence of innocence weakens his resolve. Abigail pretends Mary has sent a spirit against her, and the other girls join in, accusing Mary. Mary becomes hysterical, losing control, so Proctor calls Abigail a whore and confesses his adultery. Abigail denies the charge, so Danforth calls for Elizabeth (whom Proctor has told us never lies) to support Proctor's accusation. Not knowing that her husband has confessed, Elizabeth cannot publicly betray him, so she lies and declares no adultery took place, making her husband look the liar. The girls again pretend Mary's spirit attacks them, and fearfully, Mary cries out against Proctor to save herself. All the judges, except Hale (who now denounces the proceedings), are convinced by this performance and have Proctor arrested.

Act 4 takes place three months later inside the jail, where Sarah Good and Tituba, who confessed themselves witches, now languish. Danforth and Hathorne are concerned that Parris and Hale praying with the condemned might indicate a weakening of their support. Hale is trying to persuade the condemned to confess, in order to save their lives. Parris enters to declare that Abigail and Mercy have stolen his savings and absconded. A nearby town, Andover, is rebelling against the witch courts, and the girls fled in case Salem follows suit. There is fear of riot, and Parris's life has been threatened; he suggests they postpone the hangings, but Danforth refuses. To pardon others would cast doubt on the guilt of those 12 already hanged.

If one of the accused would confess, it would make the others look guilty, so Danforth suggests using Elizabeth to lead Proctor to confess. Hale pleads with Elizabeth to get Proctor to lie to save his life. She is suspicious, thinking this a trick, but offers to speak with him. Proctor is brought in, and they are happy to see each other. Left alone, Elizabeth tells how Giles died under torture. Proctor suggests he may as well confess and live, as he feels too dishonest to hang with such morally pure people as Rebecca and Martha. Elizabeth assures him she does not see him as dishonest, and confesses her own feelings of blame in his adultery, because she has been cold. As Hathorne reenters, Proctor declares he will confess, and the judges are elated.

As they lead Proctor to admit he has bound himself to the devil, Rebecca is brought in to witness in the hope she will follow suit. She adamantly refuses and is shocked at Proctor. The judges ask Proctor to damn the others, saying he saw them with the devil, but he refuses to name anyone but himself. He signs his confession but cannot hand it over, not wanting it publicly displayed, knowing it will badly reflect on the other condemned. Overwrought, he admits his confession is a lie. Proctor realizes he is not so morally bad and rips the confession apart, choosing to die beside the others rather than become a hypocrite. Danforth orders the hanging to proceed, and Proctor and Rebecca are taken outside. Parris and Hale beg Elizabeth to get Proctor to change his mind, but she honors his decision and refuses. The curtain falls to the sound of the drums heralding the executions.

In an afterword, Miller relates subsequent events, in which Parris is forced from office, Abigail becomes a Boston prostitute, and Elizabeth eventually remarries. Twenty years on from these proceedings, the government awarded compensation to the victims still living and to the families of the dead.

CHARACTER DEVELOPMENT

Although the original John Proctor was not a major figure in the Salem trials, Miller's Proctor is the central protagonist of *Crucible*. Proctor represents the voice of common sense in the play, being rightly skeptical of the whole court. A freer thinker than many of his neighbors, he insists that the whole idea of witchery is a sham. However, this is a period of time when common sense has vanished, and his skepticism just makes him appear more suspicious to the biased judges. Proctor's honestly motivated dislike of Reverend Parris, as an ungodly materialist, and subsequent refusal to attend church or have his third son baptized also work against him. Proctor is very human and not without fault; not only is he impatient and quick to anger, but also an adulterer. However, he is fully repentant, and Miller expects us to forgive him his lapse, even if he cannot do so himself. He loves his wife, Elizabeth; he is keen to please her and does all he can to save her after her arrest, even to the point of endangering himself.

Proctor faces the dilemma of the innocent person who must falsely confess to a crime in order to save his own life. He considers telling this lie because he feels guilty over an adultery for which he has not been punished. He realizes, too, that were it not for his former relationship with Abigail, his wife would not be in danger. Proctor's ultimate refusal to go along with the confession indicates his awareness that he has a responsibility to himself and his community, and he would rather hang than participate in the false judgment of either. Through Proctor and the others who die with him, Miller wishes to show the heroism of these victims, in order to lead us to recognize and celebrate the existence in the world of such personal integrity.

Elizabeth Proctor, like her husband, is a sensible person, which is why she too finds it hard to believe in witchcraft. She begins the play angry and suspicious of her husband, having recently discovered his adultery. But her pregnancy is evidence that she and Proctor have continued relations since Abigail left. Bravely, she allows herself to be taken to jail, sure of her innocence. Elizabeth's love for her husband is emphasized by her lying for him about the adultery (her first ever lie) in an effort to save him embarrassment; it is ironic that it is this lie that condemns him in the eyes of the judges. Her suffering in jail causes her to reflect on her former treatment of Proctor, and in their final meeting she confesses she has been cold to him in the past. She takes partial responsibility for driving him into the arms of Abigail.

Reverend Parris was previously in business in Barbados and now runs his ministry like a business. He has estranged honest men like John Proctor because of his evident materialism and concentration on negative aspects of their religion. Any dissension from his views he translates into personal persecution. As a minister of God, he strikes an ungodly figure, being petulant, selfish, conceited, unmerciful, and awkward in his relationships with others, especially children. Parris's first thought on his daughter's bewitching is how it affects him and his standing in the community. It is he who brings in the witch finders, and he is a staunch advocate of condemning anyone the girls name without allowing any proper defense.

The Reverend John Hale begins the play a conceited figure, seeing himself as a superior intellect to these villagers and happily determined to uncover their evil spirits. Events conspire to make him reassess his beliefs, and we watch as his convictions are eroded by doubt. His questioning comes too late, but it helps expose the closed logical system of the judges when one of their number turns so strongly against them. In contrast to the other judges, by honestly considering the evidence before him, Hale shows himself to be more rational and conscientious. Recognizing the deception of the girls, he denounces the proceedings and tries to save the victims, but he has become too cynical. Urging people he knows are innocent to confess in order to save their lives casts aside any possibility of them having honor or nobility. He becomes a lost figure, not knowing in what to believe and unable to understand the Proctors' noble behavior.

Judge Hathorne is described as a "bitter, remorseless" man, and he is certainly more concerned with his own power than he is with uncovering the truth. His refusal to even listen to others makes him contemptible, but Danforth is worse. Deputy Governor Danforth is a grave figure, equally determined, but more sophisticated than his fellow judges, which makes him more dangerous. Although he listens to counterarguments, it is not with an open mind, and when he hangs the condemned with full knowledge of their innocence, saying it is for a higher good, we should recognize in him an evil force.

Thomas Putnam is a sour man filled with grievances against others, which have been created mostly by his own imagination and sense of self-importance. Greedy and argumentative, Putnam is not above manipulating truth and law to his own vindictive ends, and it is entirely credible he persuaded his daughter, Ruth, to cry out against men whose lands he desires. His wife, Ann Putnam, is no less self-absorbed and vindictive, and for a religious woman, ascribes far too much value to silly superstition. The Putnams are the worst face of Puritanism, but Giles and Martha Corey, along with Rebecca and Francis Nurse, offer a kinder picture. Even though Giles may be argumentative, it is without malice, and he has a courage that reminds us of the strength of the pioneer stock from which he sprang. At heart he is a good man, and he dies for his beliefs no less bravely than John Proctor. Martha Corey and Rebecca Nurse are ideal Puritans

who live their faith, showing kindness and compassion to others, and displaying a gentleness in their lives, which is rightly respected. Francis Nurse is the
opposite of Thomas Putnam, being a man who puts others before himself,
living a genuinely moral life.

Tituba and Sarah Good confess to witchery rather than hang, and they are
readily believed, as neither has a good reputation in the town. The first group
hanged were of a similar low standing, which is why Salem went along with
the judges' decisions. Sarah Good is a vagrant, and as a black foreigner, Tituba
has already been judged by this racist township as having an allegiance to dark
forces. They survive, but there is no triumph in their survival as they lose everything by confessing to something they have not done.

Abigail Williams is the most complex of the girls who cry out against their
elders. She has been awakened to her sexuality a few months previously after
a brief affair with her former employer, John Proctor, and is no longer content
to play the role of meek serving girl. An orphan who has been dependent on
her churlish uncle Parris, Abigail sees in Proctor someone who treated her as
a woman rather than a childish nuisance. Her desire for him seems to transcend the physical, and she has magnified the importance he holds in her life
beyond reasonable expectation. Abigail cleverly uses the town's superstitious
leanings to her own advantage, to claim greater respect in the community
and revenge herself upon Elizabeth, whom she sees as having "blackened" her
name with her dismissal, and who kept her from Proctor. The way she sacrifices former friends like Tituba to the court, without care, suggests an amo-
rality in her nature. She eventually turns on her beloved Proctor in an act of
self-preservation, and when the possibility of rebellion arises, she quickly flees,
stealing Parris's savings on the way, just to prove her truly disreputable nature.

Mercy Lewis, Susanna Walcott, Betty Parris, Ruth Putnam, and Mary
Warren are among the young girls who follow Abigail's lead. All have led
limited lives up until this point, bullied by employers and forced to be quiet
and subservient. Abigail offers them a chance to be at the center of attention
and treated as special. They are attracted to the power they see themselves
holding over the townspeople as they deceitfully offer the judges any names
they like.

THEMES

Salem, Massachusetts, in the spring of 1692, is described as a newly founded,
religiously devout township. A communal society has formed, backed by an
autocratic theocracy to help it attain the discipline necessary for survival; they
are naturally suspicious of individuality, seeing it as a threat to their imposed

sense of order. Salemites have worked hard to survive, constantly threatened by the surrounding wilderness. Concentrating on survival has left them little opportunity to misbehave, but ironically, although their recent ancestors came to this land to avoid persecution, they have become intolerant and are constantly judging each other's behavior. Their way of life is strict and somber, and the witch trials offer them a release of pent-up frustration and emotion. Under the guise of morality they are given the opportunity to express envy and hostility toward their neighbors, and take vengeance.

Miller insists that while McCarthyism may have been the historical occasion of *Crucible*, it is not its theme. We never go inside the courtroom, because Miller is not interested in the proceedings as much as the motivations behind them and the fears of those involved. One issue concerning Miller is the tension people experience between conscience and their predilection toward selfishness, and the inevitable moral consequences of allowing the latter an upper hand. *Crucible* exposes the extent to which many people use troubled times, such as the trials, to pursue selfish ends. In contrast to these types, Miller elevates and celebrates people of individual conscience, such as the Nurses and the Proctors, who refuse to do this.

Crucible depicts how unscrupulous people, from the Putnams to the trial judges, declare the presence of evil to cripple whomever disagrees with them, not just religiously but politically and socially. Such people assume a moral high ground, so anyone who disagrees is deemed immoral and damned. Tituba and the children were trying to commune with dark forces, but if left alone, their exploits would have bothered no one—their actions are an indication of how people react against repression rather than anything truly bad. But Miller sees evil as being at large in the world, and he believes that everyone, even the apparently virtuous, has the potential to be evil given the right circumstances, even though most people would deny this. Miller offers Proctor as proof—a good man, but one who carries with him the guilt of adultery. However, men like Danforth also fit this category, because they do evil deeds under the pretense of being right.

In *Crucible*, Miller wanted to go beyond the discovery of guilt, which has motivated his plots in earlier plays, to a study of the results of such guilt. He centers this study on John Proctor, a man with an initially split personality, caught between the way in which others see him and the way he sees himself. His private sense of guilt leads him into an ironically false confession of having committed a crime, although he later recants. What allows him to recant is the release of guilt given to him by his wife's confession of her coldness and refusal to blame him for his adultery. Elizabeth insists that he is a good man, and this finally convinces him that he is.

Miller sees *Crucible* as a companion piece to *Death of a Salesman* in the way both explore the realm of conscience. Through Willy Loman and John Proctor, Miller examines the conflict between a person's deeds and that person's conception of himself. While Loman never resolves this conflict and consequently never discovers who he is, Proctor finally comes to some understanding, evidenced in the way he claims his identity in the form of his "name." In *Crucible*, Miller explores what happens when people allow others to be the judge of their conscience; in *Salesman* the central character does not get this far, as Loman refuses to allow his guilt any reality. What both plays do is explore the social forces that operate on people, to show the falsity of our belief in individual human autonomy. Both Proctor's and Loman's actions are largely dictated by forces outside of themselves, which seem to demand of them reactions and sacrifices they have little choice but to give. Total freedom, Miller suggests, is largely a myth in any working society.

Some critics like to view *Crucible* as a debate on the theme of marriage, and what a marriage requires to make it work. Issues of trust, love, and what one partner owes the other are all discussed in the play. It is partly Giles Corey's idle tongue and lack of trust in his wife that get her hanged. But it is the marriage of John and Elizabeth Proctor that lies at the play's center, along with the love triangle Miller creates between Abigail and the Proctors. When we consider that at the time of writing this play, Miller himself was pursuing an adulterous affair with Marilyn Monroe while still married to Mary Slattery, it is unsurprising to find such issues explored.

John and Elizabeth love each other, but seven months before where the play begins, John had an affair with their serving girl, Abigail. We do not know how long this may have continued had not Elizabeth discovered her husband's adultery, but Proctor insists it was nothing more than animal passion. Abigail is sent away, but the trust between the married couple has shattered, and all ease between them gone. Insecure of her own attractiveness, Elizabeth looks for signs that her husband continues to stray. Tortured by guilt at what he sees as a moment of weakness, Proctor vacillates between apologetic attempts to make his wife happy and anger at her continued distrust. It is not until both suffer at the hands of the court that they come to an understanding of each other and their mutual love. Each is willing to sacrifice everything for the sake of the other. Proctor tries to free Elizabeth by blackening his own name with a public confession of adultery, while she lies for the first and only time in her life to save him from ignominy. Their final scene together is highly touching, as we see Elizabeth declare her love, and willingness to sacrifice that love, by allowing Proctor to die rather than relinquish his integrity.

HISTORICAL CONTEXT

Miller's interest in the Salem witch trials was partly prompted by reading Marion Starkey's *The Devil in Massachusetts*. While researching witch trials at the Historical Society in Salem, Massachusetts, Miller found the core of his plot in Charles W. Upton's nineteenth-century book, *Salem Witchcraft*. Here he found references to most of the main characters who appear in his play. In terms of the play's historical accuracy in portraying the Salem witch trials of 1692, in a note at the start of the play script Miller declares his play is predominantly accurate in regard to facts, but he has made some changes for "dramatic purposes." The major changes are the fusing of various original characters into a single representative, reducing the number of girls "crying out" and judges, and increasing Abigail's age. While he based characters on what he learned through letters, records, and reports, he asks them to be properly considered as "creations of my own, drawn to the best of my ability in conformity with their known behavior" (Weales 2).

The printed play contains extensive notes detailing the historical background of Salem society in the 1690s, along with detailed facts regarding the actual lives of the main characters involved. Miller wanted his critics to know that he had not made up these events, but that people really allowed such things to occur. These notes illustrate the extensive research that Miller undertook to write *Crucible*. And yet there have been criticisms of the play's historical inaccuracies, despite Miller's opening disclaimer.

However, there are many details in the play that are firmly supported by trial transcripts and other records of the time, such as Tituba's confession, Sarah Good's condemnation on being unable to cite the Ten Commandments, Rebecca's steadfastly claimed innocence, Giles Corey's complaints against his wife preventing him from saying his prayers, and Mary Warren's poppet being given to Elizabeth. The notable details that appear to have arisen more from Miller's imagination are the presentation of Abigail and her lust for Proctor; the development of both the Proctors, with John, especially, depicted as a liberated thinker for those times; and Proctor's subsequent confession and recantation. Miller also makes Governor Danforth a lot more accommodating than the original, who would never have listened to any counterarguments. It was the moral absolutism of many Puritans of that era, which allowed no dissent, that Miller wished to capture and expose. The original prosecution was truly as blind to the facts and relentless as they appear in the play, and there were many, like the Putnams, who took full, mercenary advantage of the situation.

HUAC had been set up in 1938 and had been behind the closing of the Federal Theater Project, which Miller had briefly joined. However, there was not the right political and cultural climate in America to allow HUAC to become really powerful until the 1950s. Spurred on by Senator Joseph McCarthy, the committee sought to expose and restrict anyone in government positions, the military, or the arts whom the committee suspected of harboring Communist sympathies or beliefs, which it saw threatening the American way of life. Artists, actors, and writers were subpoenaed to prove that they were not or had not been active in the Communist Party. If they confessed to any Communist activity, then they were expected to name names of anyone else involved, or they would be sent to jail for contempt.

In order to further restrict potential subversives among the artistic and intellectual community, a blacklisting system, by which anyone even rumored to have "Red" sympathies would be refused work or prevented from displaying his or her art, came into creation. Many artists went along with whatever the committee asked, rather than face jail or loss of livelihood. By the time that fears of Communist expansion were assuaged, and the committee's bullying tactics and McCarthy's own self-aggrandizing agenda were finally exposed, many people had lost careers, reputations, and even their lives.

Miller initially resisted the idea of depicting the HUAC hearings in the form of an old-fashioned witch trial as too obvious. However, as the HUAC hearings grew more ritualistic and cruelly pointless, he could no longer resist, despite the obvious risks, for the parallels were far too apt to ignore. He saw how both sets of hearings had a definite structure behind them, designed to make people publicly confess. In both cases, the "judges" knew in advance all of the information for which they asked. The main difference was that Salem's hearings had a greater legality, as it was against the law in America to be a witch in the 1690s, but not a Communist in the 1950s. Miller does not attempt a one-to-one analogy between his characters and those involved in HUAC, because this would have made the play too temporal. The reason the play has remained so popular is that it offers more than a simple history lesson of either the original witch trials or of HUAC—what Miller explores are the prevailing conditions that precipitate such events. The play, however, as critic James Martine suggests, "struck its own effective blow at McCarthyism" (10).

LITERARY STYLE AND DEVICES

Miller created his own poetic language for this play, based on the archaic language he had read in Salem documents. Wanting to make his audience feel as though they were witnessing events from an earlier time, yet not wanting to make his dialogue incomprehensible, he devised a form of speech for his characters that blended into everyday speech, using an earlier vocabulary and syntax. Incorporating more-familiar archaic words like "yea," "nay," or "goodly," Miller creates the impression of a past era without overly perplexing his audience.

While Miller's mastery of language seems most evident in the way he manages to create an apparently period, everyday speech, it rises to the level of poetry with its sophisticated metaphors. The "crucible" of the title is a place where something is subjected to great heat to purify its nature—as are the central characters of Proctor, Elizabeth, and Hale. All endure intense suffering to emerge as better, more self-aware individuals. Complex imagery is built up through the concerns and the language of the play—ideas of heat and light against cold and dark are played off against our common concepts of heaven and hell, good and evil. Numerous images of cold and winter, along with the hardness of stone, are used to indicate the harshness of the Puritan life. These people are trapped in a cycle of toil, unrelieved by leisure (singing, dancing, or any frivolous behavior is not allowed). Their lives are limited by both the hard landscape they strive to tame and their own restrictive religion. Abigail tells John that he is "no wintry man," which is true in that he refuses to abide by many of the strictures of his community and is determined to have a mind of his own.

For the people of Salem, Satan is alive and nearby in the dark forest. The forest acts as a representation of hell to be avoided at the cost of sin, and godly folk stay home at night. The main sin is sex, which has been notoriously equated with the devil by way of original sin. The girls dance illicitly in the dark woods, around a fire (another hellish symbol), some naked, while Abigail drinks blood to cast a spell on Elizabeth, in order to try and break up a marriage. Abigail's devilment is continually reinforced by the symbols that surround all she says and does: she has been initiated into the joys of sex by her former employer through her "sense for heat," and still feels Proctor "burning" for her. He is described in his adulterous lust as a "stallion"—in other words, less than human.

By fixating so much on sin, the religious right, represented by men like Parris and Danforth, become sinful and turned from God. Early in the play Proctor accuses Parris of preaching too much "hellfire and bloody damnation" and saying too little about God; this becomes a kind of prophecy as Parris and the judges become more devilish in their treatment of others. It is significant that where they send the supposedly "saved" Sarah Good and Tituba, who have falsely confessed, becomes for the women a hell from which they pray to be saved by the devil. The fires of hell seem to consume the supposedly righteous rather than the "guilty" witches.

SITUATION OF WORK

The Crucible is Miller's most resilient play in that its sheer craft makes it nearly impossible to produce a bad production, and that its subject and theme continually fascinate audiences throughout the world. As critic and scholar Gerald Weales suggests, "Anyone with a touch of conscience, a hint of political interest, a whisper of moral concern will be drawn to *The Crucible*" (xvii). It has become the most performed of Miller's plays and, after *Our Town*, possibly the most performed of any American drama.

Not as innovative or experimental as *Salesman*, its influence is in a social and historical context more than a literary one. For Miller, art has only ever been of use when it tries to change society for the better, and *Crucible* is the play he wrote that is most informed by that purpose. In one sense, the play's ability to span from 1692 Salem to its contemporary times implies a study of the nature of America itself, with some striking lessons. But these lessons are in the responsible role of authority and the rights of the individual, which speak to people who have never even heard of Salem or Senator McCarthy. It is this timeless aspect that gives the play its universal appeal.

Dan Sullivan, a reviewer for the *Los Angeles Times*, describes Miller as a "father figure" for American theater artists, who is most notable for his "integrity" and pursuit of truth (qtd. in Bigsby 192). Writers have a profound respect for Miller and feel inspired to assist in his lofty goal of trying to make the world a better place in which to live. Christopher Bigsby's book, *Arthur Miller and Company*, is a telling summary of what many contemporary writers feel about Miller: what they owe him, why they admire him, and what they have learned from him. Throughout the book, writers, along with directors and actors who have been involved with his work, offer their opinions and assessments of Miller. Men like Ralph Ellison, Joseph Heller, and William Styron speak of Miller's importance and contribution to American art; playwrights David Rabe and Edward Albee praise his writing and social commitment. Kurt Vonnegut sums up their admiration when he describes how Miller's plays "speak movingly about America to almost all Americans, while telling the truth about America" (qtd. in Bigsby 10).

Although its first production was not as successful as hoped, *Crucible* nevertheless secured Miller's reputation as one of America's most important playwrights. It also helped remind people of an American theatrical tradition, advanced by the agitprop plays of the 1930s, of drama that went beyond diversion or entertainment to seriously address key social and political issues.

CRITICAL RECEPTION

Despite its later success, the play's initial reception was poor, though this may have been partly a fear of the repercussions of liking a play that was critical of current politics. It may have won Tony and Donaldson awards for best play, but many critics had been quick to condemn both play and playwright. After *Salesman,* some critics had felt let down and saw *Crucible,* in comparison, as less innovative, and therefore a step backward. Walter Kerr felt it was too mechanical and overtly polemic. Reviewer Eric Bentley notably attacked the play, claiming that Miller's naïve liberalism and depiction of innocence reduced it to melodrama. Even Miller's staunch ally, Brooks Atkinson, had reservations.

Crucible first appeared on Broadway at the Martin Beck Theater in New York in January 1953, but it was not until the 1960s that it became widely popular, perhaps needing some separation of time from the Communist hunts of HUAC, against which it so bravely spoke. On reflection, many critics who had originally found fault with the play came around, such as John Gassner, who by 1960 had come to see *Crucible* as a powerful drama that surpassed most others of its era.

There had also been difficulties with the initial production. Unwilling to ask his usual director, Elia Kazan, due to Kazan's testimony to HUAC, Miller had to find someone else to direct. Despite a reputation of being difficult, Jed Harris was chosen. His working relationship with Miller was strained from the start. Harris disliked Miller's choice of Arthur Kennedy to play Proctor and demanded a series of rewrites from Miller in an unsuccessful attempt to undermine the playwright's confidence in order to gain full control of the production. His direction of the play was very static, as he had characters make speeches to the audience rather than each other, and often kept them frozen in tableaux while speaking their lines. This approach made critics view it as cold, unemotional, and lacking in heart. After initial mixed reviews, Harris withdrew and left Miller to try and salvage the production. Improvements were made, but not enough to save this production.

Crucible has been successfully performed countless times since, and has also been filmed more than once. Miller enjoyed the 1950s movie, retitled *The Witches of Salem,* for which French playwright and philosopher Jean-Paul Sartre wrote the screenplay, but felt that the Marxist references Sartre had included were a little too heavy-handed. The version of *Crucible* with which Miller has been most closely involved, and for which he rewrote some scenes, is the 1996 version starring Daniel Day-Lewis (who soon after married Miller's daughter Rebecca), which was filmed on Hog Island, Massachusetts, and produced by Miller's son, Robert.

SUGGESTED READINGS

To avoid repetition I have omitted general biographies and criticisms of Miller's work that appear in the previous chapter, and only recorded writings more specific to this individual play.

Alter, Iska. "Betrayal and Blessedness: Explorations of Feminine Power in *The Crucible*, *A View from the Bridge*, and *After the Fall*." *Feminist Rereadings of Modern American Drama*. Ed. June Schlueter. Rutherford, NJ: Farleigh Dickinson University Press, 1989: 116–45.

Ardolino, Frank. "Babylonian Confusion and Biblical Inversion in Miller's *The Crucible*." *Journal of Evolutionary Psychology* 24.1–2 (March 2003): 64–72.

Atkinson, Brooks. "*The Crucible*." *New York Times*, February 1, 1953, sec. 2: 1.

Bentley, Eric. "Miller's Innocence." *New Republic*, February 16, 1953: 22–23.

Bigsby, C.W.E, ed. *Arthur Miller and Company*. London: Methuen, 1990.

Bloom, Harold, ed. The Crucible: *Modern Critical Interpretations*. New York: Chelsea House, 1999.

Booth, David. "Dubious American Ideal: Gender and Historical Knowledge in *The Crucible*." *Soundings: An Interdisciplinary Journal* 84.1–2 (spring-summer 2001): 31–49.

Bredella, Lothar. "Understanding a Foreign Culture through Assimilation and Arthur Miller's *The Crucible* and Its Dual Historical Context." *Text, Culture, Reception: Cross-Cultural Aspects of English Studies*. Eds. Rüdiger Ahrens and Heinz Antor. Heidelberg, Germany: Winter, 1992. 475–521.

Caruso, Cristina C. "'One Finds What One Seeks': Arthur Miller's *The Crucible* as a Regeneration of the American Myth of Violence." *Journal of American Drama and Theatre* 7.3 (fall 1995): 30–42.

Dukore, Bernard F. Death of a Salesman *and* The Crucible: *Text and Performance*. Atlantic Highlands, NJ: Humanities, 1989.

Ferres, John H. *Twentieth Century Interpretations of* The Crucible. Englewood Cliffs, NJ: Prentice-Hall, 1972.

Gassner, John. *Theatre at the Crossroads*. New York: Holt, Rinehart and Winston, 1960.

Hendrickson, Gary P. "The Last Analogy: Arthur Miller's Witches and America's Domestic Communists." *Midwest Quarterly* 33.4 (1992): 447–56.

Kerr, Walter F. "*The Crucible* Retells Salem's Violent Story." *New York Herald Tribune*, February 1, 1953, sec. 4: 1.

Lowe, Valerie. "'Unsafe Convictions': 'Unhappy' Confessions in *The Crucible*." *Language and Literature* 3.3 (1994): 175–95.

Marino, Stephen. "Arthur Miller's 'Weight of Truth.'" *Modern Drama* 38.4 (winter 1995): 488–95.

Marlow, Stuart. "Interrogating *The Crucible*: Revisiting the Biographical, Historical and Political Sources of Arthur Miller's Play." *Staging a Cultural Paradigm: The Political and the Personal in American Drama*. Ed. Barbara Ozieblo and Miriam López-Rodríguez. New York: Lang. 79–100.

Martin, Robert A. "Arthur Miller's *The Crucible*: Background and Sources." *Modern Drama* 20 (1977): 279–92.

Martine, James J. The Crucible: *Politics, Property, and Pretense*. New York: Twayne, 1993.

Miller, Arthur. "Again They Drink from the Cup of Suspicion." *New York Times*, November 26, 1989, sec. 2: 5, 36.

———. "Why I Wrote '*The Crucible*.'" *New Yorker*, October 21–28, 1996: 158–60.

Otten, Terry. "Historical Drama and the Dimensions of Tragedy: A Man for All Seasons and *The Crucible*." *American Drama* 6.1 (fall 1996): 42–60.

Pearson, Michelle. "John Proctor and the Crucible of Individuation in Arthur Miller's *The Crucible*." *Studies in American Drama* 6.1 (1991): 15–27.

Plakkoottam, J. L., and Prashant K. Sinha, eds. *Literature and Politics in Twentieth Century America*. Hyderabad, India: American Studies Research Centre, 1993.

Schissel, Wendy. "Re(dis)covering the Witches in Arthur Miller's *The Crucible*: A Feminist Reading." *Modern Drama* 37.3 (1994): 461–73.

Starkey, Marion L. *The Devil in Massachusetts*. New York: Knopf, 1949.

Valente, Joseph. "Rehearsing the Witch Trials: Gender Injustice in *The Crucible*." *New Formations* 32 (autumn-winter 1997): 120–34.

Weales, Gerald, ed. The Crucible: *Text and Criticism*. New York: Viking, 1971.

5

Eugene O'Neill
Long Day's Journey into Night
1956

BIOGRAPHICAL CONTEXT

Eugene Gladstone O'Neill was born in 1888, to James and Ella Quinlan O'Neill. His father's acting career meant the family was constantly on the move, except when they summered in the family cottage in Connecticut. O'Neill was actually born in Barrett House, a New York hotel. From the age of seven, O'Neill was sent to a variety of authoritarian boarding schools. In his first year of attendance at Princeton University, he dropped out after being suspended for breaking a window, and went to live in New York, where he began to frequent Greenwich Village and attend plays.

O'Neill's whole life was largely tormented and unhappy; rarely seeing his family, he learned of their disorders from a distance, and was closest to his older brother, Jamie. Much like the characters in *A Long Day's Journey into Night*, his mother was addicted to morphine and had once considered becoming a nun; his father a skinflint and disappointed in an acting career that had trapped him in a single role; and Jamie, a derelict drunk. A younger brother, Edmund, died in infancy from measles. A heavy drinker like the rest of the men in his family, he tried to commit suicide in 1911, and once roomed with a youth who successfully took his own life. Both his parents and older brother would die between 1920 and 1923, leaving him alone.

Poor marriage choices did little to help. In 1909 his girlfriend, Kathleen Jenkins, became pregnant, and they married. They spent little time together as two weeks later he went to Honduras on a six-month mining expedition, from which he contracted malaria, and was touring as a stage manager when his son, Eugene, was born in 1910—a son who would become an alcoholic and die by suicide in 1950, despite a successful college career. Later that year, O'Neill signed up for a sea voyage as a working passenger and was gone for another two months. He and Kathleen divorced in 1912, and he moved into a run-down Lower Manhattan flophouse, Jimmy-the-Priest's, which he would feature in later plays, living a dissolute life, in between further sea trips.

O'Neill was diagnosed with mild tuberculosis in 1912, and it was during his convalescence, in which he read voraciously, that he decided to become a playwright. Having lived all his young life backstage watching his father perform, O'Neill understood how plays were constructed, so drama seemed a natural choice. He was also determined to write something better than the sentimental, melodramatic fare in which his father acted. There may be melodramatic moments in his plays, but they are created by far more complex characters and situations, unlike the plot-driven, oversentimental dramas commonly produced.

O'Neill's earliest plays, begun in 1913, were mostly short experimental pieces reflecting his experience with life on the sea, some of which were published in "Thirst" and Other Plays (1914), underwritten by his father. Based on these, O'Neill was invited to attend English 47, a playwriting course at Harvard, run by George Pierce Baker. Baker would also tutor such playwrights as Edward Sheldon, Philip Barry, and Sidney Howard. Unable to afford more than a year, he returned to New York and tried, unsuccessfully, to interest small theaters in his work. However, he also made friends with George Cram Cook, Susan Glaspell, and others, who, dissatisfied with commercial theater, would form the Provincetown Players in 1915 in Cape Cod, Massachusetts. They would produce his first plays the following year: Bound East for Cardiff and Thirst. The first was a play about life on board a ship (part of a series of plays about the crew of the SS Glencairn), and the second a grotesque study of three characters trying to survive on a life raft. When the group moved to New York later that year, O'Neill returned with them and produced several more one-acts over the following seasons.

During this period he met Agnes Boulton, a writer, whom he married in 1918 and who bore him two children: a son, Shane, who would become a drug addict and die young, and a daughter, Oona, whom he renounced in 1943 when she married film actor Charlie Chaplin, 36 years her senior, against his wishes. In the mid-1920s he fell in love with the actress Carlotta Monterey, divorcing Agnes in 1929 to marry Carlotta. It was a tempestuous marriage, and his new wife was, at times, overprotective to the point of alienating friends.

A personal life full of failure was balanced against an incredibly successful professional life. In 1920 O'Neill conquered Broadway with his Pulitzer-winning *Beyond the Horizon*, a naturalistic work relating the tragic fate of the disparate Mayo brothers. One is practical, the other a dreamer, and both fall for the same girl and are led to pursue lives and careers antithetical to their natures, which end in misery. Audiences had enjoyed his one-acts and were ready for a full-length piece. The play ran for an entire season and established him as the most promising playwright of his generation.

The Emperor Jones was produced that same year, solidified his reputation, and introduced expressionism to American theatergoers. Its tale of Brutus Jones, who had fled America to become ruler of a West Indian isle through fear, superstition, and unscrupulous means, offers a parody of race relations at the time. Jones's subjects revolt and are joined by the ghosts of his past in tracking him down to kill him. The play's gripping use of monologue, unusually compelling black characters (for the time period), and expressionistic format with its innovative use of setting, light, and sound to draw the audience into Jones's psyche made it both an original and stunning contribution to American drama.

O'Neill dominated American drama from the 1920s. Between 1920 and 1934, 21 new O'Neill plays premiered in New York—from the expressionistic supernaturalism (O'Neill's term for a blend of realism and symbolism) of *The Hairy Ape* (1922), his most chilling presentation of the alienated modern man, through historical costume dramas *The Fountain* (1925), based on Ponce de Leon's search for the fountain of youth, and *Marco Millions* (1928), which tracks the material seduction of Marco Polo, to his epic 13-act trilogy, *Mourning Becomes Electra* (1932), an updated version of Aeschylus's *Oresteia*, about the fateful fall of a once-great family, set during the American Civil War. He continually experimented beyond expressionism, with the evocative staging of *Desire under the Elms* (1924), masks in *The Great God Brown* (1926), a different use of masks coupled with chorus in *Lazarus Laughed* (1928), and even comedy in *Ah, Wilderness!* (1933). O'Neill also covered nearly every emotionally powerful and controversial issue of his time—materialism, adultery, prostitution, incest, modern alienation—so that several of his plays were banned in various cities. He even explored miscegenation in *All God's Chillun Got Wings* (1924), which drew instant censorship.

O'Neill's plays were not all critical and commercial successes, but he rarely repeated himself, and he won two more Pulitzers during his lifetime, for the tale of a prostitute's attempt at reformation, *Anna Christie* (1921), and the psychological thriller and exploration of desire, *Strange Interlude* (1928), in which he had characters speak their thoughts aloud, and grace the stage for nearly six hours. On winning the Nobel Prize in 1936, he was only the second American to be so acknowledged, even though by this time he was beginning to decline both physically and emotionally. Depressed by the onset of World War II and, as his disease progressed, unable to hold even a pen, he was reluctant to allow much of his later material to be produced, especially after the comparative failure of *The Iceman Cometh* (1946) and *A Moon for the Misbegotten* (1947). When he died, as he had been born, in a hotel, in 1953, he felt sadly distant from the theater, to which he had contributed so much.

From 1934 until the 1940s O'Neill had been extensively working on what he hoped to be his best contribution to the theater: a lengthy cycle of plays depicting the effects of acquisitiveness on the Harford family, entitled *A Tale of Possessors Self-Dispossessed*. An ambitious project, it was never finished, and most of the material he destroyed shortly before his death; only *A Touch of the Poet* (1957) and the unfinished *More Stately Mansions* (1962) survived. But in 1939, O'Neill had briefly set aside this project to work on other material, and he produced the predominantly realistic, though complex *Iceman*, *Long Day's Journey into Night* (1956), *Hughie* (1958), and *Moon for the Misbegotten*.

Long Day's Journey, considered by many to be O'Neill's greatest work, was written between 1939 and 1941, and O'Neill asked for it not to be published or produced until 25 years after his death, for fear the strongly autobiographical elements would be an embarrassment. However, his widow, Carlotta, declared that O'Neill had changed his mind in the last few weeks of his life and stated that both production and publication would be allowable under certain circumstances. Thus, despite his earlier wishes, by 1956 the play was not only produced in Sweden, Boston, and New York, but also published, only three years after his death. It won him a fourth Pulitzer and once more elevated him to prominence, albeit posthumously. A subsequent revival of *Iceman* was allowed the critical attention and acclaim it had formerly been denied, and *A Touch of the Poet* was another great success.

PLOT DEVELOPMENT

The play is set one August morning in 1912 at the summer home of the Tyrone family. James Tyrone, retired actor and wealthy landowner, ushers his once-beautiful wife, Mary, into the living room. Despite the surface impression of a happy couple relaxing after breakfast, we sense numerous, unspoken undercurrents: Tyrone's concern with his wife's health, his suspicions against his sons, Mary's disgust at her husband's financial management, concern for her son Edmund's health, and indignation at being too closely observed. As the play unfolds, all of these undercurrents will be explained as we learn more of the family background and their various secrets and fears. For the time being we are left with a mystery we have to piece together.

The sons, Jamie and Edmund, enter, and the tension mounts. Jamie is wary of his mother and picked on by his father, just as he is defended by his younger brother, who seems to have health problems of his own. Edmund amuses them with a comic saga about one of his father's tenants, but Tyrone gets upset at Edmund's socialistic side comments and Edmund leaves. Mary insists Edmund has just a cold, although it is clear she suspects far worse, but Tyrone and Jamie seem not to want to force the issue. We are given more clues to Mary's difficult past, but everyone resists talking further about such things, and Mary leaves to see her house staff.

Tyrone and Jamie now discuss Mary's "illness" and whether or not she should face Edmund's probable consumption, a disease from which her father died. Jamie feels she should face the truth and criticizes his father's choice of doctor. Despite his wealth, Tyrone has a reputation of stinginess. Tyrone returns the attack, complaining of Jamie's proclivity for "whores and whiskey" and bemoaning his lack of ambition and periodic dependency. Jamie agrees he is a failure but feels unable to change. His father then blames him for leading Edmund toward a similar life of dissipation, which has worsened his condition—a charge that deeply upsets Jamie, who sees Edmund as far more independent than himself. We learn that Mary has been home only two months since her last "cure," and the worry is that Edmund's illness may set her back. As the two continue to argue over who is to blame, Mary returns to quiet them, and they exit to work in the gardens.

Mary fusses over Edmund, who has returned. As they chat, we learn that Mary feels isolated; she hates this house and has no friends in town. Edmund points out it is partly her own fault. He is fearful she is falling into old habits (we will later discover she is a morphine addict), but Mary indignantly refutes their suspicions, getting Edmund to back off by making him feel guilty, and sends him outside to join the others and leave her alone.

Act 2 is later that day as they wait for Tyrone to come in for lunch. The maidservant, Cathleen, brings a drinks tray and Edmund and Jamie both sneak whiskeys. Jamie tries to get Edmund to take things easier and prepare him for the possibility he has consumption, but Edmund, too, seems not to want to face this. Jamie is worried that Edmund left Mary alone; they both suspect she has been taking morphine. Mary enters and their suspicions are confirmed by her appearance. They argue as Mary criticizes Jamie for being disrespectful of his father, even as she complains about Tyrone herself.

They accuse her of taking morphine, which she denies, just as their father returns. As Mary starts to ramble, Tyrone sees what is happening, even while Edmund tries to protect his mother. Mary is past caring. Tyrone is angry and distraught, taking another drink before they head in for lunch.

After lunch they sit together trying to avoid their mutual disappointments while Mary continues to ramble about her past and how much she has hated her life since she met Tyrone. The doctor phones, asking Edmund to visit him, which sets Mary off on a diatribe against doctors, whom she blames for her addiction. Agitated, she leaves to take more morphine, and no one tries to stop her. The men bitterly carp at each other in their dismay, and Edmund leaves to change for the doctor's. Tyrone confirms to Jamie that Edmund has consumption and needs to go to a sanatorium to recover. Jamie warns him not to choose a cheap one to save money, and decides to accompany his brother to the doctor's for support. Tyrone also plans to visit his friends at the bar, though Mary asks him to delay. He suggests she go for a car ride, but she hates both the cheap car and poor chauffeur Tyrone has provided, and has nowhere to go. She begins to retreat into memories of the past, to her teenage convent days, before she felt everything went wrong. We learn of their dead second child, Eugene, who died at two from measles he caught from seven-year-old Jamie. Mary suspects this was an intentional act on Jamie's part, and she relates how her difficult birth with Edmund was what started her addiction. Tyrone asks Edmund to appeal to her to stop, but she is too far gone, which they both know. They all leave her, again, alone.

Act 3 begins later that evening, as the fog has started to descend. Mary is high from morphine she has fetched using the car, and chats to Cathleen, to avoid being alone. Mary expects her family to stay out late and not come home for dinner. She tells Cathleen of her past, her dismay over Tyrone's parsimonious character, and how they first met. She builds a picture, not entirely credible, of herself as an innocent, pious convent girl who was misled into loving the wrong man. She is surprised by the return of Tyrone and Edmund, who have been drinking. They sit and watch with a mixture of pity and bitterness as she chatters on about her miserable life, assigning them the blame. They keep drinking and try not to get sucked in, but cannot stop defending themselves on occasion. Each has guilt and a desire to blame the others. Edmund wants Mary to face his illness as he now has, but she refuses, and he storms out. Tyrone tries to comfort Mary and take her in to dinner, but she goes to shoot more morphine, and he eats alone.

Act 4 begins around midnight. Tyrone is very drunk, playing solitaire, as Edmund returns, also drunk. They argue about leaving lights on, Tyrone's Irish Catholic pride, and Jamie—anything to avoid the real issues. Edmund has been walking in the fog, thinking about the transience and degradation of life, and how this has been explored by poets like Dowson and Baudelaire, of whom his traditional father disapproves. Tyrone is nonplussed by his son's cynicism and sense of nihilism. Tyrone offers his version of Mary's youth, which is far less contented and pious than hers. The two drink and play cards while waiting for Jamie, and discuss Mary's addiction. Edmund blames his father for his penny-pinching ways—hiring poor doctors and leaving treatment too late—and it is clear he has always believed his mother's version of events. Tyrone tries to defend himself, but he accepts some blame. Edmund confronts him about the cheap sanatorium he suspects he plans to send him, and Tyrone agrees to choose somewhere better, "within reason." He tells Edmund about his desperately poor upbringing and the way this led him to trap himself in a single, lucrative acting role for the steady income, and so ruining a promising acting career. Edmund feels he better knows his father after this. We see Tyrone is as bitter and trapped in the past as Mary. Edmund shares a series of transcendent experiences he has had at sea and on the beach, in which he has suddenly felt at one with nature and free of earthly concerns, which have made his reality all the more onerous. His father is impressed by his poeticism but worried by its morbidity.

Jamie arrives, also drunk, and Tyrone steps outside to avoid an argument. Jamie and Edmund continue to drink. Jamie has been with a prostitute and is angry at Tyrone's refusal to spend the money on a proper sanatorium for Edmund. Edmund sympathizes while Jamie talks about his own empty life, but when he calls their mother a "hophead," Edmund punches him. Both apologize, before Jamie descends into maudlin self-pity, beginning to jealously rant against Edmund to assuage his own self-disappointment. He drunkenly confesses he has tried to bring Edmund down to make himself look better, and punish him for causing their mother's addiction. He warns Edmund not to trust him in the future and falls into a stupor. Tyrone reenters, voicing disappointment in his oldest son, as Jamie briefly reawakens to send a last few barbs his father's way. As Jamie and Tyrone nod off, we hear Mary playing the piano. They spring awake as Mary enters in a daze, holding her wedding dress. The men fall apart as they witness her reliving her childhood as if it were happening. She no longer recognizes them or listens to their attempts to bring her back, so they return to drinking as Mary re-creates her version of life in the convent.

CHARACTER DEVELOPMENT

While her constant search for her glasses might suggest a desire to look at life clearly, ultimately, Mary prefers to live in an imaginary past. Although she begins the play drug free, as it proceeds, she keeps taking morphine to help her to slip into this past and avoid the unpleasantness of reality, currently the harsh fact of Edmund's life-threatening consumption. Even though it is clear by her occasional outburst that she knows the truth, she tries to believe Edmund has only a cold, thus freeing herself from any need to worry or act. The morphine assists in this aim and offers her a life free of psychological pain, where she can forget about her unhappy marriage, selfish husband, the death of her baby, Eugene, and even her own addiction. As she explains: "It kills the pain. You go back until at last you are beyond its reach. Only the past when you were happy is real." Her idealized past as an innocent convent girl from a happy home, tricked into a disastrous marriage, is a complete fabrication, but the morphine helps avoid the reality of even that, as it totally fogs her mind. Mary ends the play in a narcotic dream in which she relives her past as if it were physically occurring, and it seems a dream to which she is destined to keep returning.

No one in this family expects to be happy, as all are consumed by real or imagined guilt. Tyrone feels guilt over Mary because he has given her a shabby life, hired the cheap doctor who got her hooked on morphine, and delayed in finding her treatment. He feels more guilt over trying to send Edmund to a cheap sanatorium. His guilt all stems from his miserliness, a habit he cannot break. Mary feels guilt over Eugene's death, as she had not been there to stop Jamie from infecting him with the measles, which killed him, and over just giving birth to Edmund, who seems so unhappy. Also her addiction makes her feel guilty, as she knows how much they all want her to stop, and she feels inadequate as a wife and mother. Jamie feels guilt over his own failure in life and in causing Eugene's death. He even feels guilt over Edmund's ill health, believing that his attempts to corrupt him to make himself look better caused it. Edmund feels less guilt, but still sees his life as a waste.

Tyrone's greatest bitterness is for his lost chance at becoming a great actor due to his financial insecurity. Instead of extending his repertoire, he kept playing one popular role until he became so typecast, no one wanted him to play anything else. Tyrone pushes his sons to make something of their lives to compensate, but usually in the wrong direction, exploiting rather than assisting them. Jamie despises acting, and Edmund sees working on a newspaper as a waste of time. All three drink too much to calm their individual sense of failure. Also a chauvinist, Tyrone has always put himself and his career ahead of Mary. He loves her and depends on her for emotional support, but he has never really considered her feelings. He has had a hard life, having to support his mother and siblings since the age of 10 after his father walked out on them, and it is this that has made him so penny-pinching. He tries to break free of this habit, agreeing to let Edmund pick his own sanatorium and he will pay for it, but he cannot resist insisting "within reason."

In many ways, Jamie, named after his father, is a poor shadow of Tyrone, and since he mostly despises his father for wasting his talent, this leads to even greater self-hatred. Having been instrumental in his younger brother's death at the age of two when he was seven years old, Jamie has never recovered—possibly even believing his mother's accusation that he killed his brother out of jealousy. His bitterness is exacerbated by the loss of the guiding hand of his mother to drugs and has resulted in a life of dissipation, filled with alcohol and prostitutes. While exceedingly drunk, he confesses to having misled Edmund out of jealousy, but his evident love for his brother elsewhere should make us suspicious of such claims, which more likely stem from Jamie's entrenched lack of self-worth. While Jamie, like Edmund and Tyrone, drinks to forget, it is clear this does not work for him. Jamie remains the most aware of reality; he is the first to accept Mary's return to drug use, Edmund's illness, and his own uselessness. Jamie is an empty shell of a man, a lost soul with no sense of selfhood. His lifestyle reflects his desperation—for love, direction, and happiness—all of which are precluded by such a lifestyle. When told his countenance has a "Mephisophelean cast," O'Neill does not mean he is devilish, but that he is like Christopher Marlowe's Mephistopheles, because earth has become for him a living hell. We see more of Jamie's life in *Moon of the Misbegotten.*

Edmund's life has been more adventurous than Jamie's, but he seeks something he has yet to find. Effectively a self-portrait of the 23-year-old O'Neill, Edmund seems to know something the others have yet to grasp, and is more accepting and less guilt-ridden over the family's condition. Despite his illness and sensitive nature, he is perhaps the strongest in the family and is certainly the least dependent. Yet Edmund, too, has his moments of avoidance. He is fairly sick but hides from this truth as it rightly scares him, and his excessive drinking only exacerbates his condition. He is also the last to accept his mother's lapse and vainly tries to bring her back right to the end. On his ocean travels he has experienced an "ecstatic freedom" in nature. "The peace, the end of the quest, the last harbor, the joy of belonging to a fulfillment beyond men's lousy, pitiful, grey fears and hopes and dreams!" It is an almost Emersonian transcendental experience, but one that leads him to give up on life rather than embrace it: "I will always be a stranger who never feels at home, who does not really want and is not really wanted, who can never belong, who must always be a little in love with death."

Ultimately, whatever their shortcomings, or perhaps because of them, O'Neill wishes us to understand and pity all four Tyrones, and forgive them, as he did. While the play is intensely personal, it has lasted because it is also a profoundly universal depiction of humankind in all its pain, regret, uncertainty, and love. While the Tyrones hurt each other in an excruciating fashion, it is more from self-defense than any maliciousness, and the saddest aspect, perhaps, is the evident love they hold for each other.

THEMES

The play recounts a bleak day in the life of the Tyrone family on which all their fears and guilts bubble to the surface and are swiftly reburied. As they alternately blame themselves and each other for the sad state of their lives, Tyrone and his sons drink to excess, and Mary gradually recedes into a morphine-induced haze. Tyrone's lost career and penny-pinching ways, Jamie's wasted life and predilection for brothels, Edmund's experiences at sea and current ill health, as well as Mary's disappointments and addiction combine to make us appalled and sympathetic toward the human failings that have brought this family to such a state.

O'Neill saw his own family experience as symbolic of the misplaced values of the whole country in its materialistic fascination and subconscious repression of reality. He wanted to depict the negative effects of this on the quality of people's lives. But although the play might question the American ethic of success, O'Neill is less interested in the larger society than in the individual psyche. The Tyrones are utterly isolated in their fogbound house, from the outside world and each other, so we can study each of them in detail, as if they were bugs in a jar and no more able to escape. By the close, we are left with no sense of hope as this family is trapped and doomed to lives of pain and unfulfillment by their own collective guilt and inability to change. The only relief is that three are marked for early death.

The notion of blame and blamelessness influences all of them. In act 2 Mary tells Edmund: "It's wrong to blame your brother. He can't help being what the past has made him. Any more than your father can. Or you. Or I." Mary likes to see fate to blame, as that releases them all from guilt, but, in direct contrast, Tyrone blames the family entirely, himself included when he is being most honest. The truth lies somewhere in between. Mary was never tricked, but married Tyrone because she loved him, and Tyrone could have been less manipulative toward his children, not pushing them into lives they hated in an attempt to bring them the glory he feels he missed. However, Tyrone's poor upbringing psychologically ensured his later regretted decision to limit his acting career, and Mary could not have helped being subscribed the morphine that led to her addiction by an overzealous doctor after Edmund's birth. Both fate and character are at fault.

At one point Edmund asks his father, "Did you pray for Mama?" Tyrone answers, "I did. I've prayed to God these many years for her." Edmund retorts, "Then Nietzsche must be right. God is dead: of His pity for man hath God died." O'Neill depicts a world in which religion is inadequate and faith an impossibility. Mary used to live in a convent and talks about having once considered becoming a nun, but it becomes increasingly clear that she had never really had this desire and found no comfort, then or now, in faith. Mary is also, significantly, the name of Jesus' mother, and she has a 33-year-old son, Jamie, the same age as Christ when he died; but if this is what has become of Mary and her son in the modern age, O'Neill seems to suggest that we truly do live in a godless world.

O'Neill underlines the power of the past by setting the whole play in the past, to show how these relationships continue to haunt. Mary refers to the whole family as victims of a past that has shaped them and which they cannot change. However, it is a past they do not even try to escape, and one in which Mary, especially, prefers to hide and re-create to her satisfaction. By the end she becomes trapped in this past, unable to escape. The current truth pains her and she cannot face it for more than a fleeting moment (such as when she acknowledges that Edmund is really ill), so she uses her morphine to help her forget about her husband's neglect, her second son's death, and her own addiction by receding into an earlier, idealized time, before the pain. Edmund sees her inability to face her present as destructive, for it reduces her to a ghost, with no more substance than the past she re-creates.

The Tyrones all try to forget their pasts to improve their present, but it is a futile exercise as the past keeps intruding. If they could only face what has happened, it may allow them to be freed of it and move forward, but they can only view it when under the soothing influence of drugs or alcohol, which does not allow them to deal with it honestly. They cannot come to terms with what they have collectively done or not done, and so they allow their memories, or the memories of others, to destroy them, or enrage them to destroy each other. Although they try to blame each other, the Tyrones are each partly responsible for their own destruction.

HISTORICAL CONTEXT

O'Neill refused to have *Long Day's Journey* produced during his lifetime as its depictions were too close to home, being unashamedly autobiographical. On one level it is a profoundly intimate play, a blend of both confession and exorcism. The Tyrones were the O'Neills in nearly every detail and character trait, with all of their addictions, fears, and failings. Such personal experience naturally allowed O'Neill to present detailed and realistic psychological portrayals. In a dedication printed at the front of the first published edition, O'Neill describes it as a "play of old sorrow, written in tears and blood" (7). His depiction of his family appears as shockingly brutal as it appears honest. Such searing openness would allow many writers who followed to tell the truth about themselves and others with far less fear of rejection or disapproval.

Set in August 1912, when its author (and Edmund) was 23, the play is curiously isolated from the many striking events of that year, which may be one reason it seems so timeless. There are no direct references to local or world events, such as workers striking on both sides of the Atlantic, the sinking of the *Titanic*, Woodrow Wilson being elected, Lenin's rise in Russia as he takes over *Pravda*, war in the Balkans, or Scott reaching the South Pole. And on one level *Long Day's Journey* is a very private play, but it does offer some historical insight. Through James Tyrone we get a sense of the theatrical scene prior to O'Neill's own revolution, where touring companies repeated popular melodramas to the masses rather than offer new plays, and actors became typecast regardless of talent. Tyrone's upbringing, through nineteenth-century early-industrial squalor into wealthy landowner; Edmund's wanderlust; and Jamie's life of dissipation each offers interesting perspectives on profoundly American tendencies of that period and beyond.

Written between 1939 and 1941, *Long Day's Journey* was frequently set aside as O'Neill grew too distressed or depressed about the onset of World War II. The sense that the world is a rotten place and possibly marked for imminent destruction is an undercurrent that pervades the play. The house, the family, and the twentieth century are all in the fog, lost, without a way out. *The Iceman Cometh*, written during the same period, shares much of its disillusionment.

LITERARY STYLE AND DEVICES

During his lonely years in boarding school, college, and in recuperating from tuberculosis, O'Neill sought refuge in reading and was drawn to many authors whose works were considered shocking at their time, including Oscar Wilde, George Bernard Shaw, and Henrik Ibsen. Shaw and Ibsen would be especially influential on his own writing, and O'Neill would write his share of shockers, both in style and subject matter. On the surface, *Long Day's Journey* seems a fairly realistic play, no doubt helped by the warts-and-all presentation of its central family. Drug addiction, alcoholism, prostitution, tuberculosis, and loss of faith may all have been common life experiences in the 1940s, but they were rarely discussed in so open a forum. Yet, like so many of Ibsen's dramas, the play is also saturated with symbolism underlining its central themes; the most obvious symbol being its use of darkness and fog.

O'Neill depicts the Tyrones being gradually encompassed in darkness, as night draws in and their home becomes fogbound. The fog is symbolic of the way in which, not just Mary, but each of them has become isolated and insulated from each other and the outside world. They separate themselves through embarrassment or disgust, then complain of their loneliness. The darkness at the close of the play is both external and internal; given their fears and insecurities, these people have no means of escape. Mary and Edmund both welcome the fog, grateful for the opportunity it gives them to lose themselves; its opacity may be restrictive, but they see it as safe. The fog offers them a place to hide, but the foghorn keeps sounding to warn them of the reality lurking outside their dream worlds, always threatening to intrude.

In this play O'Neill perfected his use of language by producing realistic-sounding dialogue that could carry both emotional conviction and poetic eloquence. But the play says as much in what is not said as in what is said, as the Tyrones' inability to articulate to each other is part of their problem. It is most important when reading the play to attend to gesture and expression; look carefully at all the stage directions in which O'Neill guides the actors by pointing out how certain lines should be spoken, where and how characters look when they speak, or how they react to what is said.

The lengthy character descriptions at the play's start also contribute to our understanding of the underlying story that, just like the issues dividing the Tyrones, is never fully verbalized. For example, Mary's paleness and restlessness at the start should warn us that something is awry, and her deformed fingers suggest an inner rot. O'Neill even tells us the names of the authors on this family's bookshelves, informing us that these are well-read people who should be both wise and eloquent. Ironically, they turn out to be neither when it most counts, and squander their learning avoiding truths and honest connections with each other. The alcohol they drink numbs them to truths they cannot escape; it allows them to confess and yet gain no solace, for they know they cannot turn back the clock. They seem caught in a fatalistic grip, unable to go back or forward. In the play, which is based on O'Neill's family history, Tyrone's father committed suicide and Mary's father died of consumption, providing a generational link to Edmund. In the O'Neill family's future, one of the sons will commit suicide, and the other will become a drug addict. One wonders how much O'Neill saw a genetic sense of fate in operation. It is this aspect, perhaps, that gives the play its tragic sensibility.

The play's strength lies less on its physical action than on its psychological insight, which is both intricate and intense. Yet the play is also very carefully structured; even the classical unities of time, place, and action are kept. O'Neill allows all the characters to have at least one scene together, two at a time, with one another. This allows us to witness the different relationships more intensely: the two sons with their father, the husband with his wife, and the mother with each of her sons. Mary, obviously the lynchpin on whom the others' fates depend, is the only one who spends time alone on- and offstage. It is also she who closes the play, and her retreat to her childhood strongly suggests that this family is trapped in the dark night that has descended upon them all.

SITUATION OF WORK

Eugene O'Neill was the first international American playwright, and the only American dramatist thus far, to win the Nobel Prize. Although his reputation was built on plays written in the 1920s and 1930s, it was firmly secured by the later masterpieces. The lengthy, semiautobiographical *Long Day's Journey* has become the jewel in the crown of his oeuvre due to its emotional intensity and realistic psychological portrayal of tragic human nature. It was built on a lifetime accumulation of theatrical and personal experience, and contains all of O'Neill's strengths and few of his weaknesses. Michael Hinden explains how the absence of any overwrought plot, or uneasy connection between action and theme, and the presence of biting honesty, subtle characterization, and crafted language make *Long Day's Journey* "our best American play" (5). He goes on to describe several further reasons why the play is a masterpiece, including the simplicity of its dramatic form; the rich, psychological complexity of its four main characters; the directness of its presentation without sentimentality; the emotional rhythm of the characters' interactions; its intensity of feeling; the quality of the dialogue (both natural and expressive); as well as its deep insights into guilt, vulnerability, and the need for family connection. He concludes, "*Long Day's Journey* simultaneously marks the pinnacle of O'Neill's career and the coming of age of American drama" (6).

O'Neill took note of all that had been developing in American drama prior to his arrival on the scene—the melodramas, comedies, romances, and satires, as well as the stirrings of realism—and did not create anew, but built on aspects of all of these in his many varied plays. O'Neill had been particularly impressed by the work of Edward Sheldon, who had realistically depicted varied social ills from poverty to racism in his plays. O'Neill, too, felt that drama mattered, and that it was the duty of a playwright to explore the sickness of society in order to uncover its roots and try to discover a sense of the meaning of life to help people cope with fears of death. The "sickness" he saw manifest in terms of such issues as materialism, greed, and dehumanizing technology. Not counting the plays he destroyed before his death or left incomplete, he produced 13 major short plays and 24 long ones in which he explored these issues using a variety of avant-garde techniques, including symbolism, expressionism, masks, asides, and stream of consciousness, as well as devising some new techniques of his own. His plays can be seen as a little uneven, but he was always exploring new ways to get closer to those meanings he sought, and it is fair to say that the body of his work revolutionized American theater.

With its roots in Greek tragedy and imbued with the intensity of Shakespeare, O'Neill's work would inspire others that contemporary American theater was an art form worthy of attention and study. O'Neill had tried before to reveal the inner minds of his characters through various techniques, from masks and monologues to having them speak their interior thoughts, but in *Long Day's Journey* he perfected the process. The insecurity, ambivalence, and complexity of all four Tyrones is realistically conveyed though dialogue and character interaction. All four have the potential to be sympathetic and tragic; for although they scramble to assign blame, O'Neill allows his audience to understand their potential innocence. Each is both victim and victimizer. Although the Tyrones' day ends in darkness, ironically, the play's audience can only be enlightened into the intricacies of human nature by what they have witnessed. No longer would audiences be satisfied by the simple characterizations of the past.

CRITICAL RECEPTION

Given O'Neill's initial restrictions on having the play produced or published until 25 years after his death, it caused quite a theatrical stir when the Swedish Royal Dramatic Theater announced it would premiere the play in February 1956, and Yale University Press would publish it a month later. The Swedish Theater had been very supportive of O'Neill in the past, and Carlotta insisted that her husband had agreed to let them produce this play in acknowledgment of that, and the money from the publication would go into a fund to help other playwrights. It was initially performed in Swedish, and there remained no plans to produce it in the United States or Canada. However, pressure to see this new O'Neill work was intense, and by October there had been tryouts in Boston, and a New York opening in November; both were highly successful, despite Carlotta's insistence that the play not be cut and should run as O'Neill had written it, for three and a half hours.

Cyrus Durgin, witnessing the Boston production, called it "one of the splendid dramatic accomplishments of the decade" and "O'Neill's Last, Great Play" (n.p.). Opening-night reviews from New York were even more ecstatic. *Newsweek* declared it "one of the great tragedies of American theatre" ("Triumph" 117); Henry Hewes, "the most universal piece of stage realism ever turned out by an American playwright" (30); and Walter Kerr, "a stunning theatrical experience" (3). John Chapman declared it "O'Neill's most beautiful play" and "one of the great dramas of any time" (1). It ran for 390 performances and won O'Neill his fourth Pulitzer Prize (the first ever to be granted posthumously), as well as a New York Drama Critics' Circle Award, Outer Circle Award, and Tony Awards for both the play and the lead actor, Fredric March.

In 1957 the play was invited by the State Department and the American National Theater and Academy (ANTA) to represent the United States at the International Drama Festival that year in Paris. They moved the entire production to France for a month, where it continued to be a huge success and was given a five-minute ovation on opening night—unheard-of enthusiasm from the French for an American play. On its return to America, a national tour was arranged to capitalize on the play's fame. Cast changes led to a shaky start, but with much critical support, audiences became enthused and the tour made a profit. Indeed, as the play has continued to be produced, one of its strengths has been its amenability to different directorial and acting interpretations.

While initial critics found the play nihilistic, later study suggested it was more existential in outlook. O'Neill had taken the naturalistic theater of Ibsen and Strindberg a logical step forward and produced a play that naturalistically depicted the workings of the inner mind rather than the outward reality. Harold Bloom views *Long Day's Journey* as "the best play in [America's] more than two centuries as a nation" (3), and Robert Brustein feels that it "contains the finest writing O'Neill ever did" (qtd. in Bloom 25). Begun in 1977 as the *Eugene O'Neill Newsletter* by editor Frederick Wilkins, in association with the Eugene O'Neill Society, this compendium of essays, reviews, and information on O'Neill developed into the *Eugene O'Neill Review* in 1988, and has printed countless articles on the play from every imaginable perspective, showing the great popularity of O'Neill within critical circles.

SUGGESTED READINGS

Atkinson, Jennifer McCabe. *Eugene O'Neill: A Descriptive Bibliography*. Pittsburgh: University of Pittsburgh Press, 1974.

Berlin, Normand. *Eugene O'Neill*. New York: Grove, 1982.

Björk, Lennart A. "The Swedish Critical Reception of O'Neill's Posthumous Plays." *Scandinavian Studies* 38 (August 1966): 331–350.

Bliss, Matt. "'So Happy for a Time': A Cultural Poetics of Eugene O'Neill's *Long Day's Journey into Night*." *American Drama* 7.1 (fall 1997): 1–17.

Bloom, Harold, ed. *Modern Critical Interpretations of Eugene O'Neill's* Long Day's Journey into Night. New York: Chelsea, 1987.

Bogard, Travis. *Contour in Time*. New York: Oxford University Press, 1972.

Bryer, Jackson R. *Checklist of Eugene O'Neill*. Columbus, OH: Merrill, 1971.

Cargill, Oscar N., Bryllion Fagin, and William J. Fisher, eds. *O'Neill and His Plays: Four Decades of Criticism*. New York: New York University Press, 1961.

Carpenter, Frederic I. *Eugene O'Neill*. Rev. ed. Boston: Twayne, 1979.

Chabrowe, Leonard. *Ritual and Pathos: The Theater of O'Neill*. Lewisburg, PA: Bucknell University Press, 1976.

Chapman, John. "A Masterpiece by O'Neill." *New York Daily News*, November 18, 1956, sec. 2: 1.

Driver, Tom F. "On the Later Plays of Eugene O'Neill." *Tulane Drama Review* 3 (December 1958): 8–20.

Dugan, Lawrence. "The Tyrone Anthology: Authority in the Last Act of *Long Day's Journey into Night*." *Comparative Drama* 37.3–4 (fall 2003–winter 2004): 379–95.

Durgin, Cyrus. "'Long Day's Journey' O'Neill's Last, Great Play." *Boston Daily Globe*, October 16, 1956: n.p.

Floyd, Virginia. *The Plays of Eugene O'Neill: A New Assessment*. New York: Ungar, 1985.

Gassner, John. *Eugene O'Neill*. Minneapolis: University of Minnesota Press, 1965.

———, ed. *O'Neill: A Collection of Critical Essays*. Englewood Cliffs, NJ: Prentice-Hall, 1964.

Gelb, Arthur, and Barbara Gelb. *O'Neill*. Rev. ed. New York: Harper, 1973.

Griffin, Ernest G., ed. *Eugene O'Neill: A Collection of Criticism*. New York: McGraw-Hill, 1976.

Hewes, Henry. "O'Neill: 100 Proof—Not a Blend." *Saturday Review* 39 (November 24, 1956): 30–31.

Hinden, Michael. Long Day's Journey into Night: *Native Eloquences*. Boston: Twayne, 1990.

Kerr, Walter. "'Long Day's Journey' Actor and Playgoer Share Impact of O'Neill's Drama." *New York Herald Tribune*, November 18, 1956: 1, 3.

Liu, Haiping, and Lowell Swortzell, eds. *Eugene O'Neill in China: An International Centenary Celebration*. New York: Greenwood, 1992.

Manheim, Michael, ed. *Eugene O'Neill*. Cambridge, UK: Cambridge University Press, 1998.

———. *Eugene O'Neill's New Language of Kinship*. Syracuse, NY: Syracuse University Press, 1982.

Martine, James J., ed. *Critical Essays on Eugene O'Neill*. Boston: Hall, 1984.

McDonald, David. "The Phenomenology of the Glance in *Journey*." *Theatre Journal* 31 (October 1979): 343–56.

Meaney, Gerardine. "*Long Day's Journey into Night*: Modernism, Post-Modernism and Maternal Loss." *Irish University Review* 21.2 (fall-winter 1991): 204–18.

Miller, Jordan Y. *Eugene O'Neill and the American Critic*. Hamden, CT: Archon Books, 1973.

Moorton, Richard F., Jr., ed. *Eugene O'Neill's Century: Centennial Views on America's Foremost Tragic Dramatist*. Westport, CT: Greenwood, 1991.

Murphy, Brenda. *O'Neill*: Long Day's Journey into Night. New York: Cambridge University Press, 2001.

O'Neill, Eugene. *The Complete Works of Eugene O'Neill*. 2 vols. New York: Boni & Liveright, 1924.

———. *The Iceman Cometh*. New York: Random House, 1946.

———. *Long Day's Journey into Night*. New Haven: Yale University Press, 1956.

———. *A Moon for the Misbegotten*. New York: Random House, 1952.

———. *Thirst and Other One Act Plays*. Boston: Gorham, 1914.

Orlandello, John. *O'Neill on Film*. Madison, NJ: Fairleigh Dickinson University Press, 1982.

Ranald, Margaret Loftus. *The Eugene O'Neill Companion*. Westport, CT: Greenwood, 1984.

Redford, Grant H. "Dramatic Art vs. Autobiography: A Look at *Long Day's Journey into Night*." *College English* 25 (1964): 527–35.

Selmon, Michael. "'Like . . . So Many Small Theatres': The Panoptic and the Theatric in *Long Day's Journey into Night*." *Modern Drama* 40.4 (winter 1997): 526–39.

Shawcross, John T. "The Road to Ruin: The Beginning of O'Neill's *Journey*." *Modern Drama* 3 (December 1960): 289–296.

Sheaffer, Louis. *O'Neill: Son and Artist*. Boston: Little, Brown, 1973.

———. *O'Neill: Son and Playwright*. Boston: Little, Brown, 1968.

Sinha, C. P. *Eugene O'Neill's Tragic Vision*. Atlantic Highlands, NJ: Humanities, 1981.

"Triumph from the Past." *Newsweek*, November 19, 1956: 117.

Usui, Masami. "Mary Tyrone's Drug Addiction and Quest for Truth in Eugene O'Neill's *Long Day's Journey into Night*." *Studies in Languages and Cultures* 16 (1990): 109–22.

6

Lorraine Hansberry
A Raisin in the Sun
1959

BIOGRAPHICAL CONTEXT

Born on May 19, 1930, in Chicago, Illinois, to Carl and Nannie Hansberry, Lorraine Vivian Hansberry was the youngest of four children. Deeply involved in the black community, her parents taught her from an early age there were two things a person should never betray: family and race. Her father ran a successful real estate agency and was active in the National Association for the Advancement of Colored People (NAACP) and the Urban League, donating large amounts of money to various causes and founding one of the first African American banks in that city. Her mother was also politically active. A concern for black culture, politics, and economics surrounded young Hansberry, as leading black figures including Paul Robeson, Duke Ellington, Joe Louis, and Jesse Owens passed through her home. She also learned much from her uncle William Hansberry, a professor at Howard University and one of the earliest African American scholars to study African history, making notable contributions in the field. It was through him that Hansberry developed her admiration for, and understanding of, the African contribution and connection to African American culture.

In 1938 Carl Hansberry risked going to jail by challenging Chicago real estate covenants, which legally enforced housing discrimination, by moving his family into an all-white neighborhood. His family faced much hostility, as whites gathered outside the house to shout and throw bricks. Young Hansberry was nearly hit in the head by a concrete slab before the mob was broken up by an armed bodyguard. The Hansberrys stayed in their house until the Illinois court ordered them to leave, but Carl, with aid from the NAACP, took the case to the Supreme Court, winning a landmark case in 1940—Hansberry vs. Lee—in which the legal basis for restrictive covenants was struck down, and the family could legally return home. In practice, however, little changed, as housing discrimination continued unabated. Attending an integrated high school, Hansberry suffered frequent taunts and insults. Embittered and discouraged by these and other aspects of American racism and discrimination, Carl planned to move his family to Mexico City, but died in 1946, before the move could be orchestrated.

Although her older siblings had attended Howard University, in 1948 Hansberry decided to attend the University of Wisconsin. There she saw a production of Sean O'Casey's *Juno and the Paycock,* which inspired her to write a play about her own culture that would come to fruition in *A Raisin in the Sun* several years later. Dissatisfied by a number of her courses, Hansberry left Wisconsin in 1950 to head for New York, where she transferred to the New School of Social Research and began work for Paul Robeson's radical black monthly, *Freedom.* She wrote articles about conditions in the black community, as well as reviewing books and plays by blacks. By 1952 she had become an associate editor.

It was in New York that she became personally involved in the racial struggle, marching in public demonstrations, speaking on street corners, and helping black tenants move back into apartments from which they had been evicted. She met Robert Nemiroff, an aspiring writer and graduate student in English and history at New York University, on a picket line against discrimination. They married in 1953. Their joint commitment to social justice is evidenced by the fact that the night before their wedding they took part in a demonstration to save the Rosenbergs from execution for treason.

Hansberry felt her writing was the best means she had to contribute to the fight for civil rights, and so in 1953 she resigned from full-time work at *Freedom* to concentrate on her own work. Both she and Nemiroff took on a series of jobs to make ends meet, but when Nemiroff was offered the chance in 1956 to run a music publishing business by Philip Rose, they became sufficiently wealthy for Hansberry to devote herself to writing full time.

Uncertain whether her first completed work would be a novel, an opera, or a play, she found her interest centering on a play she had tentatively titled *The Crystal Stair,* from a line in Langston Hughes's poem "Mother to Son." In the poem, a black mother asserts that "life for me ain't been no crystal stair," as she describes her struggle to provide a better life for her family and encourages her son to continue the fight. Hansberry later changed the title to *A Raisin in the Sun,* from a line in Hughes's "Harlem," which warns that a dream deferred might "dry up / like a raisin in the sun"—or "explode." She felt this new title better conveyed the bitterness of the social conditions that conspired to defer the aspirations of the black family in the play. The drama would reflect her own experience of housing discrimination, as well as her admiration for the racial pride of working-class blacks.

Impressed by the play, their friend Rose, with his many connections in the entertainment industry, found the backing to produce it. He sent a script to Sidney Poitier, a rising film star, and Poitier agreed to play Walter, recommending his former teacher, Lloyd Richards, as director. Richards also accepted and would become the first black director on Broadway. While hoping for the offer of a Broadway theater, the play tried out in New Haven, Connecticut; Philadelphia; and Chicago. Reviews were sufficiently positive to gain them access to the Ethel Barrymore Theatre, where the play opened on March 11, 1959, for a run of 538 performances. Its success was confirmed when the New York Drama Critics' Circle voted it Best Play of the Year over Tennessee Williams's *Sweet Bird of Youth*, Archibald MacLeish's *J.B.*, and Eugene O'Neill's *A Touch of the Poet*.

Hansberry became an overnight celebrity, appearing on numerous talk shows and using these platforms as an opportunity to speak to a wider audience about the need for black social, political, and economic reform. Selling the play's movie rights to Columbia, she offered a pair of possible screenplays with additional provocative material. Not wanting to be too controversial, the producers stuck with a shortened version of the produced play, but the film, which opened in 1961, was moderately successful.

In 1960 Hansberry had been commissioned to write a television play for NBC, for a series that was subsequently cancelled. The play, *The Drinking Gourd*, a study of the universally dehumanizing social system of slavery, was finally published in 1972, but has not yet been produced. Continuing to divide her time between sociopolitical causes and writing, Hansberry spoke out against the Cuban missile crisis in 1962 and was inspired to write a postatomic war play, *What Use Are Flowers?* (1972), in which she imagines a nuclear fallout and its social consequences, and which has also remained unproduced.

In 1963 she was hospitalized for tests that indicated cancer, but she continued to write and be politically active. A scene from her work-in-progress, *Les Blancs*, set in a mythical African nation, about the radicalization of a white reporter and a black intellectual, was staged at the Actors Studio Writers Workshop. This play was completed after her death by Nemiroff, who staged a short-lived, controversial production in 1970. At the request of James Baldwin in May 1963, Hansberry joined a meeting of prominent blacks and whites with Attorney General Robert Kennedy to discuss the racial crisis, forcefully arguing for better treatment of black Americans and condemning an American society that allowed such discrimination. She also contributed the text for *The Movement: Documentary of a Struggle for Equality* (1964), a book of distressing photographs of the black experience in America prepared by the Student Nonviolent Coordinating Committee. Two operations failed to cure her cancer, and her health would gradually worsen over the final months of her life. She and Nemiroff would also quietly divorce in 1964, though they continued their creative collaboration and friendship.

Hansberry's second produced play, *The Sign in Sidney Brustein's Window*, opened at Longacre Theatre in New York three months before she died. Despite mixed reviews, out of respect, the play was kept running up to her death on January 12, 1965, at 34 years of age. Many critics were dismayed by her choice of a Greenwich Village locale peopled by mostly white characters, expecting her to write another play about black experience, but Hansberry refused to be intellectually limited. Tracking these people's lives, the play comments on the damaging facile judgments people too often make on others.

After her death, Nemiroff worked to bring Hansberry's other writing to public attention. In addition to publishing the unproduced plays and producing *Les Blancs*, he also edited a memoir, *To Be Young Gifted and Black* (1969), and wrote and produced a play based on this, which was later adapted for television, as well as producing an acclaimed musical version of *A Raisin in the Sun* (1972). He died in 1991, shortly before his edited version of Hansberry's original screenplay for *Raisin* was published.

PLOT DEVELOPMENT

Set entirely in the Younger living room, the play takes place in Chicago during the middle of the twentieth century. Three generations of the family live in this crowded space. Ruth rises early to set the apartment in motion, waking her preteen son, Travis, who sleeps on a make-down bed. She sends him to the bathroom they share with other families on their floor, and shouts for her husband to rise. Impatiently waiting for the bathroom, Walter chats with his wife, but Ruth's general weariness makes her short-tempered, even when he tries to be pleasant.

Walter rushes to the bathroom after Travis, while his son eats breakfast. Travis asks his mother for fifty cents he needs for school, but she insists they have no cash to spare. She fusses and he sulks, but he cannot stay angry as she teases him. As he leaves he tells his father about the money, and Walter extravagantly gives him a dollar in defiance of his wife. Walter tries to get Ruth enthusiastic about his dream to open a liquor store with his friends

Bobo and Willy Harris. He hopes that Ruth may be able to influence his mother to loan him the money from an insurance check she is expecting from the death of his father. Ruth appears uninterested, viewing Willy as a "good-for-nothing loudmouth" and Walter's ambition as unrealistic. Walter bemoans his wife's lack of support as his younger sister Beneatha enters. Walter asks her about her decision to go to medical school, knowing a large part of the insurance check will inevitably go to pay for that. Beneatha objects to his attempts to deride her ambition, as Ruth tries to make peace between them. As Walter leaves for work, with embarrassment he asks Ruth for fifty cents for his carfare.

Mama (Lena) enters and shows herself to be the boss in this house, criticizing Beneatha for not wearing a robe, and meddling with Ruth over how she looks after Travis. Beneatha leaves for the bathroom as Mama tells Ruth she does not intend to loan money to Walter to start a business. Mama sees how tired Ruth looks and suggests she call in sick to her housecleaning job, but Ruth refuses, saying they need the money and pointing out that they do not want to rely on Mama's inheritance. Mama plans to pay for Beneatha's schooling, but, to Ruth's delight, would like to use the rest of her check for a down payment on a small house for the whole family.

Mama reminisces about her husband, Big Walter—how he loved his family but worked himself to an early death. Beneatha returns and fills the others in on her relationship with the wealthy George Murchison, whom she sees as too shallow to take seriously. Speaking dismissively of God, Beneatha raises her mother's anger and is put firmly in her place. Ruth tries to comfort them both, but she is also hiding something.

The following morning is Saturday; Mama and Beneatha are cleaning, Walter is waiting for the check to arrive, and Ruth is out seeing a doctor. Joseph Asagai, a Nigerian intellectual, phones Beneatha and is invited over. Ruth returns and, as Mama had suspected, is pregnant. Asagai arrives and gives Beneatha some Nigerian robes. Although he teases and lectures her, he is evidently enamored and she is attracted to him. He leaves and soon after the check arrives. Mama uncovers Ruth's intention to have an abortion rather than add another body to this cramped living space, but she is interrupted by Walter, who comes to plead for money. He is angered at her refusal and gets a lecture from his mother when he turns on Ruth. He tries to make Mama see his frustration, but she is turned off by his obsession with wealth and warns him about Ruth's plan. Unable to react to his mother's intense disgust, he walks out.

The second act begins later that same day, with Beneatha exploring her African roots. Ruth is skeptical, but Walter, returned from drinking, embraces Beneatha's evocation of their African ancestry and bursts into a tribal dance.

George arrives for a date with Beneatha and breaks the mood; he is upset by Beneatha's changed appearance. She accuses him of being an assimilationist, he mocks their African heritage, and Ruth sends her to get changed. George feels out of place as Ruth tries to be hospitable and Walter sounds him out for a loan, then verbally attacks him for his indifference. After Beneatha and George leave, Ruth tries to get Walter to talk; initially antagonistic, he calms and makes up, then Mama returns. She has put a down payment on a house. Walter is exasperated, but Ruth is delighted; then they learn it is in a white neighborhood: Clybourne Park. Walter is horrified, but Ruth refuses to be put off. As Ruth goes to punish her son for staying out late and puts him to bed, Mama tries to explain to Walter her decision, but he berates her for being dictatorial and killing his dream, and goes to bed.

The next scene takes place a few weeks later as the family prepares to move. Beneatha and George enter arguing after another date; he just wants a pretty girl and is getting tired of her intellectuality. He leaves as Mama arrives after a hard day's work. In a scene cut from the original Broadway production but later replaced, Mrs. Johnson, a neighbor, calls round to maliciously gossip, telling them about a black family that has been bombed by whites. Initially, Mama treats her civilly, despite Johnson's evident (jealous) desire to find fault, but she finally balks and sends her packing. Walter's employers call and Ruth learns he has not been to work for the past three days. He has been drinking and wasting his time, having lost his sense of direction. Mama recognizes her fault in this, apologizes, and, to Walter's amazement, offers to put him in charge of the remainder of the money. As Travis retires to bed, his father creates for him a vision of the future in which Walter is a wealthy executive and offers to hand him the world by his 17th birthday.

A week later it is moving day, and Ruth is overjoyed about the prospect. Walter is happy too, as he now feels a man in his own house, and he and Ruth dance together. They are surprised by a white man at the door. Karl Lindner has come to talk to Mama. Beneatha realizes quickly that he has come to warn them away from Clybourne Park. Walter takes longer to understand, but when he realizes Lindner's goal—to buy their new house back to keep the family from moving in—he sends him away. They tell Mama about Lindner, then give her some gardening tools and a hat as gifts. In the midst of their celebration, Bobo arrives. They learn Walter gave his friend Willy Mama's money to get the liquor store, and Willy has absconded. Walter never banked a portion for Beneatha's schooling as Mama had asked, and she is scornful toward Walter for the loss.

The play moves to an hour later, where the family remains stunned by their loss. Asagai calls to see Beneatha, who has lost her dream to become a doctor. He castigates her for her lack of independence, depending on money gained only through the death of her father, and asks her to go with him to Nigeria. She is uncertain and asks for time to think. Walter, meanwhile, searches for a small white card and leaves. Mama is preparing to give up on the house, but Ruth is desperate to move and pleads for them to try. Walter returns and admits he has called Lindner and plans to let him buy back the house. The women are all disgusted by his decision to demean himself in front of this man, but when he leaves, Mama defends him against Beneatha's disownment, insisting that they must continue to love Walter and "measure him right," for he has made poor choices that have hurt himself as much as them, but he had the best intentions. Lindner returns and Mama challenges Walter to go through with his plan in front of his son. He cannot, and defiantly tells Lindner they intend to move to Clybourne Park, and the family prepares to move, Mama and Ruth overjoyed at Walter's psychological growth. Filled with emotion, Mama is last to leave, as she exits with her sickly plant underarm toward their new home.

CHARACTER DEVELOPMENT

The differences between Joseph Asagai and George Murchison are important, as is Beneatha's choice between them. While Asagai is the complete African, George is the assimilated American. George is not a character to emulate, as he refuses to recognize either the equality of women, wanting Beneatha as his little woman, or the importance of his African heritage, dismissing it as irrelevant. He knows facts about Africa but has lost touch with its spirit and strength. Because of his wealth he is satisfied with the status quo and so selfishly refuses to change. Such individual selfishness is antagonistic to African American development as a whole. George may have wealth, but he has no real identity of his own, and he lacks the vibrancy we see in Asagai's firm ethnic identity. Asagai is showing the rich tradition of Africa not just to Beneatha, but also to the audience. In the 1950s, when this play was first produced, his sophistication would have been at odds with many people's limited perception of Africans as savages. Yet we should recognize that Asagai is unable to recognize what might be seen as American aspects of Beneatha's character, for his experience is entirely African. Asagai cannot accept Beneatha's drive for personal fulfillment, although he admires her spirit. In his own way he wishes to dominate her as much as George does. Beneatha needs to find her own identity, which will lie somewhere between the Americanness of George and the Africanness of Asagai.

Beneatha has education, but she seems uncertain as to what she intends to do with it. She has lessons to learn beyond her academic education, including a need for tact and a respect for her elders and their beliefs. Her ambitions rely heavily on financial support from her family, and their sacrifice, if made, should be acknowledged. Walter limits her by her gender, feeling she should be satisfied with being a nurse or a wife rather than being a doctor. Her spirit allows her to rise above his opinion. Beneatha wants to be independent, and it is this aspect of her dream that places her even beyond the understanding of Mama and Ruth. Mama and Ruth are not against female independence, but they do not see how it can be practically possible at this time, and it is a question Hansberry leaves open to debate. Mama and Ruth do teach Beneatha an important lesson about love that, in her immaturity, she has not realized: love is not necessarily peaceful or easy, but like life itself, it is a constant struggle if it is to have any meaning.

At the start, Ruth seems prematurely aged and tired, ready to give in and accept the meager life she has. She has momentarily lost her passion to strive further up the social ladder. Ruth dislikes risks and wants a safe life—but safety allows for little progress. Though the rest of her family still have the energy and desire to want more, she has been worn down by hard work. She has borne a large burden, nurturing and providing for her family with little reward. Ruth's resignation is in direct contrast to Walter's intensity—a fire burns within him, even if it is still immature and its flames are only nervous and fitful. His "erratic" quality sets him apart, differentiating him from the ordinariness and predictability that are beginning to crush Ruth's spirit.

Ruth and Walter are at odds; she has given up and become indifferent to the outside world, while Walter refuses to give up his desire to be a part of that wider society. This is indicated by his interest in the newspaper. Ruth's dormant strength returns, however, as she refuses to give up the house Mama buys. We learn that this has been her dream as much as Mama's, and she is able to reinforce Mama's slipping spirit. Evidently, some advances need more than individual strength, which underlines the importance of family connections. The Youngers live in a ghetto neighborhood, and Mama and Ruth's desire to move is valid—the children chase rats in the street, and the apartment is not only cramped but infested with cockroaches. A better home will allow them more room to grow. The urgency of this move is emphasized by the discovery that Ruth will be having another child.

Mama's key attributes are her strength and her clear sense of direction. It was her and her husband's combined strength that has brought the family this far. Hansberry is fully aware that black progress in America will not happen overnight, but will be a lengthy process, just as it is for any social group forced to begin with next to nothing. Equality will take generations of struggle—each generation contributing a little bit to the progress. Having provided a house, Mama now needs to give her family space to grow. She initially declares, "We working folk not business folk," and so dismisses Walter's business dreams without fair consideration. She wants the family to progress, but may selfishly want to be the instrument of change. Mama must allow her children control of their own lives. Yet, though Mama is the head of the family at the start, it may not be so much a role she demands, as one she must take, since Walter has yet to grow into it. Beneatha calls Mama a tyrant, but after putting a deposit on the house, Mama soon gives her son control of the family fortune, which he consequently wastes. This underlines the important lesson that control or respect cannot be given, but must be earned.

Whether Walter is the central character of the play is debatable. Though his growth toward manhood is important, so too is Beneatha's search for selfhood. In a way, privileging Walter's development over Beneatha's is an acceptance of the very male supremacy Hansberry questions. The check that Walter hopes for is not his, but his mother's: an insurance policy paid out on his father's death. Taking this money will not assert his manhood, for this is something he needs to achieve by his own resources. It is, perhaps, hard for him to live under his mother's roof, but he must earn his own way out. At the start of the play, Walter is more talk than action, and Ruth is wise not to get sucked into his dreams; she has heard them too often, seen too little done to achieve them, and she has little time for dreams. Walter's early assertions of control seem ridiculous as he still thinks like a boy, without regard for his responsibilities. He defies his wife by giving Travis money, but then has to borrow money from his wife for his carfare. Walter's view of Africa is a romanticized one, as he performs his tribal dance, but it allows us to see the inner potential in Walter, which has become buried by so much empty talk.

Karl Lindner interrupts Walter's naïve optimism and provides a reality check. Lindner's characterization is subtle—awkward and soft-spoken, by himself, he seems to offer little threat. However, we should recognize the larger community and power behind such a figure. His discomfort ensures we realize that what he is asking is wrong. Even he seems to realize this, but he cannot surmount his own prejudices. He uses platitudes to mask what he is doing, but no one is ultimately fooled. His commentary on empathy is ironically something of which he is incapable. How, we should ask, is the Youngers' hardworking background any different from those folk in Clybourne Park? How can Lindner be anything other than a complete racist? Walter's instinct to eject this man from his home is right, and this action will be more empowering than the money he got from Mama. Walter begins his second confrontation with Lindner fairly sheepishly, but he draws strength as he continues—partly from within himself and his own pride, and partly from his family and a recognition of the dignity he owes them for their sacrifices. It is at this moment we see the man in Walter—now he can give orders to others and expect them to follow as he has finally earned their respect.

THEMES

Growing up in Chicago, Hansberry had seen firsthand the growing tension between wanting to assimilate and maintaining pride in one's own culture. *A Raisin in the Sun* celebrates the wonderful diversity of black culture as well as black resistance to white oppression, as the Youngers demand to be treated as equals by the Karl Lindners of this world. But the play is about a lot more than that, exploring a variety of topics from family dynamics and the generation gap to personal identity and women's rights.

Nemiroff rightly describes the play in his introduction to the 25th anniversary edition, as presaging a "revolution in black and women's consciousness." He insists that the play has not grown less relevant with the passing of time, since the issues with which it deals remain prevalent in American society. However, Hansberry's cast does not just depict relationships defined by race and gender, but it includes characters of different classes, ages, and nationalities, so that we may consider universal issues surrounding class, generations, and national development, besides the more obvious issues of race and gender. It is the play's ability to both maintain and go beyond its author's racial identity that makes it so effective.

Hansberry deliberately pits the idea of Africanness against that of what it means to be an American in the play. By this she emphasizes the bifurcated experience of many African Americans who are not wholly at home in either culture but need a balance of the two, denying the importance of neither and adopting elements from each. Despite his Afrocentricism, Asagai points Beneatha toward a central truth of the play—every individual must make his or her own life. If you do not use your own resources, then what you receive will never truly belong to you. The future is never guaranteed, but to maintain your dignity, you must strive to pursue what you feel is right. The play offers no happy ending as the future for the Youngers is full of danger and risk, but they face this unflinchingly, and, perhaps more importantly, together.

Asagai wants to take Beneatha to Africa, but his impulse is selfish. Beneatha's home is in America, and America needs her spirited input. We never learn if she accepts his invitation to go to Africa, but we should hope she refuses. Beneatha will not find her identity solely in Africa, because she is also American. Beneatha dresses as a Nigerian and adopts an Afro haircut, but she has no idea of what being a Nigerian means—it takes more than clothing and hairstyles to become assimilated. We may ask how much of Beneatha's interest in African culture is just a fad—as were her excursions into photography, acting, horseback riding, and the guitar. Yet we can view each of these hobbies not as a waste, but as a part of the necessary process of finding and expressing oneself. Beneatha is right to suggest that blacks need a better understanding of Africa as an important part of their heritage, but she must not ignore the fact that they live in America, and this too is a part of their heritage. Beneatha's and Walter's exhibitions of their African roots show an important pride, but they also need to have pride in their American-born family and to recognize what their strength has achieved in six generations.

In the Youngers' home, though their furniture seems ordinary and worn, it also evokes a sense of hope and pride. The audience should realize that even this moderate apartment has been a hard-won achievement. Life, for the Youngers, is a constant struggle to keep ahead and to keep up appearances as they scramble to become part of the middle class, while being restricted to low-paying and frustratingly demeaning servant jobs. However, the danger of becoming so involved with appearances, Hansberry warns, is that we neglect what lies beneath—qualities of love, dignity, and unselfish sacrifice. These are concepts Walter and Beneatha, especially, need to understand. All the characters in the play are so centered on their own dreams that their vision is restricted, and they fail to recognize each other's dreams. As the play progresses we see the Youngers learn to recognize and accept each other's dreams, and so strengthen the family as a unit.

There are dark aspects of the play that should not be overlooked. One such aspect is Hansberry's controversial depiction of how little black solidarity exists, with the inclusion of such unhelpful characters as Willy Harris and Mrs. Johnson. While Willy runs off with Walter's money, Mrs. Johnson's appearance as a gossipy, unhelpful neighbor further underlines the inability of many blacks to assist each other. Mrs. Johnson seems motivated by jealousy, not wanting the Youngers to rise above her, and Beneatha is right to compare her with the Ku Klux Klan: both are destructive to black development in America.

Hansberry also ensures that we realize how potentially dangerous it will be for the Youngers to move to Clybourne Park. It would be a mistake to see this play as having a happy ending. Hansberry purposefully leaves us uncertain as to what will happen next. Even Mama's emotion at the end, being inarticulate, remains ambivalent: is it from pride of her son's growth, or could it indicate an element of fear toward the dangerous unknown into which her family is going? What will Beneatha decide to do with her life, and will her gender restrict her choices? What indignities might the Youngers be forced to suffer in Clybourne Park, where it is clear they are not welcome? In early drafts Hansberry had included an additional scene showing the family facing white aggression in their new home, but this was later dropped. What these stage characters have achieved so far is only a fragment of what they will need to ensure true equality in American society for both blacks and women.

HISTORICAL CONTEXT

Hansberry was writing during a complex and troubled period of American history. The country faced political uncertainty, the threat of atomic warfare, and a modern world full of fear and an apparent lack of values. The response of the Theatre of the Absurd was to laugh in the face of despair, but Hansberry strove for something more meaningful. She refused to view life as absurd or futile. She was willing to face the truth, but sought ways to rectify the overwhelming problems the world faced rather than laugh them away. The lessons of self-pride, responsibility, and hope that *Raisin* conveys, in the face of all the difficulties the Younger family encounters, and will continue to encounter, speak to everyone.

Hansberry wrote about black experiences prior to the turbulent civil rights movement in the 1960s, portraying black life accurately and realistically. She challenged common stereotypes by the very complexity of her characters. As with most ethnic groups in America, blacks have faced what W.E.B. Du Bois coined a "double-consciousness." Affected by two different cultures, they find themselves unable to ignore either without sacrificing a part of their identity. An effective value system for blacks becomes problematic as they seek a balance between African tradition and American experience. This double-consciousness creates some of the apparent contradictions within *Raisin*, such as the conflict between Mama's matriarchal rule (African) and Walter's patriarchal expectations (American). Hansberry never asks us to take sides, but to consider the potential within each tradition.

Facing the American black experience unflinchingly, Hansberry was willing to point out both strengths and weaknesses, trying to explain past behaviors, and offer hope for a potentially greater future given the positive qualities her characters imbue. At the beginning of *Raisin*, the head of the Younger household, Big Walter, has just died from overwork and strain, prompted in part by his grief over the death of his third child lost "to poverty" years before. This points out the high infant mortality rate in the ghetto and its devastating effects on families. And yet through his death, Big Walter has left an inheritance that will allow his family to grow, once they have worked out how. It is a legacy that turns out to be more rooted in pride than cash, as Walter sends Lindner packing and the family moves to Clybourne Park.

Hansberry was also extremely dedicated to women's rights, with her whole life as a forceful, intellectual, public figure being a repudiation of the social limitations she saw being set on women. Her plays depict empowered female characters, such as Beneatha, who embattle the sexism they encounter, with expedience rather than dogmatically demonizing all men. As a lesbian at a time when gays were social outcasts, Hansberry saw the need for tolerance as a priority. Her writing insists that the devaluation or suppression of another person because of gender, sexuality, or color is always wrong.

LITERARY STYLE AND DEVICES

Written in a realistic style, *Raisin* was not so much a sensation for stylistic innovation as for its racially charged subject matter. Hansberry, however, makes careful use of metaphor through the play's physical setting and use of props and imagery—not the least, the title, from Langston Hughes's poem, "Harlem," which centers our attention on the potential dangers to the wider society of ignoring and holding back the dreams of people like the Youngers. Walter's stirring speech in the guise of tribal leader, despite his drunkenness, tells us much about his potential, as does his job as a chauffeur—he is a man capable of sitting in the driving seat; he just needs a sense of the right direction in which to head, which he achieves by the play's close. Mama's plant, which she so doggedly preserves, underlines both her desire to grow and her refusal to give in. It also represents her dream—to have a house with a garden. The Scarlett O'Hara hat that Travis gives her is an indication of Mama's progression—in owning property, she has become akin to the mistress of the plantation, rather than one of the slaves who worked there.

The play's sense of realism is more than that of a traditional kitchen-sink drama. Hansberry's sense of reality has a gritty and truthful air, and her characters all the more human by their evident flaws. Her desire to portray characters so truthfully that an audience cannot help but identify is to draw them into facing the same class, gender, and race problems the characters encounter. *Raisin* also boasts moments of spectacle, such as Walter's spear-wielding speech, which have their roots in expressionism. Hansberry's ear for dialect is precise, displayed in the contrasting speech patterns of Mrs. Johnson, Mama, Beneatha, Lindner, and Asagai. Having Walter deliver his speech to Lindner in black English about why he intends to move his family to Clybourne Park makes it more of a direct challenge to the white man, just as the intelligent and often lyrical speech of blacks like Beneatha and Asagai challenge expectations of whites in the audience. By instilling a poeticism into the speeches of both black Chicago maid and African intellectual, Hansberry indicates a wide-ranging culture with dignity and wisdom at every level.

There is also a strong critique of money throughout the play, played out in contrasting images of wealth and poverty. Walter is obsessed with money and getting on, and he is slow to realize what manhood really requires. Though Walter seems at first to be empowered by money, we come to realize that his true empowerment comes from his denial of money and insistence on dignity. Like Arthur Miller, Hansberry suggests that capitalism gets in the way of the real system of love under which people should live their lives. Walter erroneously believes that life is money, but Mama knows that freedom is more important, having been closer to a generation that had none. It is what one does with that freedom that will determine one's life. Walter needs to respect the past and his parents' achievements, but it is now his turn to achieve, and Mama must allow him the freedom to develop self-respect. It is Mama's self-respect that provides the roots of her strength. Mama allows Walter real control not when she gives him money, but when she allows him the freedom to choose what to do about the house. If Walter were to accept Lindner's money, it would be a major regression for the whole family. He would be playing the black stereotype from which they are striving to escape, and ruin any chance of self-respect for the future.

SITUATION OF WORK

Hansberry's writing has had a tremendous influence on subsequent black playwrights, and *Raisin* is a major landmark in black American theater. According to Nielsen ratings, the 1989 American Playhouse television production of *Raisin* had the largest black viewership of any program in the entire history of the PBS network, and the highest overall viewership of *American Playhouse*. As a play that speaks to and for the black American community, this is testament to the play's lasting appeal, but it is also a play that has provoked spirited opposition.

The aspirations, relationships, and desires of the Younger family are universal and make the Youngers recognizably human to an audience who would have been unused to seeing blacks realistically depicted onstage. A number of critics, however, have seen color as almost irrelevant to the plot and declare Hansberry to be a universalist rather than a racial activist: she is, in fact, both. If Hansberry had been overtly radical, it is likely the play would never have been produced. By submerging her racial commentary, Hansberry was able to get the play performed and prove that blacks have a place on Broadway and should no longer be dismissed. She writes about a black family who is specific—we can only universalize them because they are so realistic. But it is wrong to downplay the Youngers' race, because it is central to their existence. The Youngers are not just middle class, but African American middle class, and the stakes in their struggle to make good are intensified by this fact. The diversity of the dreams of the Younger family run the gamut from business to education to domesticity and are testament to the diverse culture from which they spring. Through the family history, the Youngers represent six generations of resistance to white oppression, and they are not interested in integration so much as equality.

When critics accuse Hansberry of embracing white middle-class ideas and advocating assimilation, as has often been the case, it is being grossly unfair to Hansberry and her play. The play is as wary of assimilation as it is of finding all the answers in Africa. Hansberry's racial commentary may be subtle, but color is integral to the play. *Raisin* anticipated many of the mounting concerns for blacks and women of its day. It was a trailblazer whose success enabled other blacks to get their plays produced. Its profound affirmation of black life in all its diversity and creativity, along with its depiction of black strength through generations of struggle, makes the play a firm classic. Through it, Hansberry gained historical importance as the first black woman to have a play on Broadway, as well as being the youngest American, first black, and only the fifth woman to win the New York Drama Critics' Circle Award.

CRITICAL RECEPTION

Raisin opened in New York at the Ethel Barrymore Theatre on March 11, 1959. Its success was unprecedented and forever changed the way African American artists were perceived by mainstream theater. It drew positive reviews from all seven of the crucially influential New York newspaper critics and began a highly successful run of 538 performances. Its critical success was confirmed by its winning the New York Drama Critics' Circle Award for Best Play, but not all the critics, then or now, reacted so positively. Some viewed it as too soap-operatic, while Tom F. Driver of the *New Republic* argued that the play was "old-fashioned," adhering to the "over-worked formulas ... of the 'domestic play,'" insisting that Hansberry had merely presented white stereotypes in blackface (21). Others felt that the play promoted black materialism through the Youngers' drive to advance socially, thus depicting blacks whose only desire was to be like whites, which would be of no service to true black advancement.

The central argument has been over whether *Raisin* is truly a black play. Despite being often misquoted on the issue, Hansberry herself saw the play as about black experience before anything else, but Henry Hewes of the *Saturday Review* suggested that the fact that the central characters "are colored people, with all the special problems of their race, seems less important than that they are people with exactly the same problems everyone else has" (28). Such opinions implied that the play, therefore, did not particularly speak to black audiences. But given that *Raisin* was so strongly supported by the black community, this seems disingenuous, as blacks came in droves to see the play because it did so closely represent their experience. Perhaps, the best proof of this came in 1975 when Woodie King, Jr., began to prepare a documentary on the black theater. He called his film *The Black Theater Movement: "A Raisin in the Sun" to the Present* after discovering that more than two-thirds of the numerous people he interviewed admitted to being influenced or aided or both by Hansberry and her work. As he wrote in a later article for *Freedomways*, "To mention all of the artists whose careers were enhanced by their encounters with Hansberry and *A Raisin in the Sun* would read like a *Who's Who* in the black theater" (221).

SUGGESTED READINGS

Abramson, Doris E. *Negro Playwrights in the American Theatre: 1925–1959.* New York: Columbia University Press, 1969.

Ashley, Leonard R. "Lorraine Hansberry and the Great Black Way." *Modern American Drama: The Female Canon.* Ed. June Schlueter. Rutherford, NJ: Fairleigh Dickinson University Press, 1990. 151–160.

Barthelemy, Anthony. "Mother, Sister, Wife: A Dramatic Perspective." *Southern Review* 21 (1985): 770–89.

Bates, Randolph. "Teaching Film and *A Raisin in the Sun.*" *Louisiana English Journal* 4.2 (1997): 62–67.

Bernstein, Robin. "Inventing a Fishbowl: White Supremacy and the Critical Reception of Lorraine Hansberry's *A Raisin in the Sun.*" *Modern Drama* 42.1 (spring 1999): 16–27.

Brown, Lloyd W. "Lorraine Hansberry as Ironist: A Reappraisal of *A Raisin in the Sun.*" *Journal of Black Studies* 4 (March 1974): 237–47.

Carter, Steven R. *Hansberry's Drama: Commitment and Complexity.* Urbana: University of Illinois Press, 1991.

Cheney, Anne. *Lorraine Hansberry.* Boston: Twayne, 1984.

Cooper, David O. "Hansberry's *A Raisin in the Sun*." *Explicator* 52 (1993): 59–61.

Driver, Tom F. "Theatre." *New Republic*, April 13, 1959: 21.

Effiong, Philip Uko. *In Search of a Model for African-American Drama: A Study of Selected Plays by Lorraine Hansberry, Amiri Baraka, and Ntozake Shange*. Lanham, MD: University Press of America, 2000.

Hairston, Loyle. "Lorraine Hansberry: Portrait of an Angry Young Writer." *Crisis* 86 (April 1979): 123–24, 126, 128.

Hansberry, Lorraine. "An Author's Reflections: Walter Lee Younger, Willy Loman, and He Who Must Live." *Village Voice*, August 12, 1959: 7–8.

———. *The Collected Last Plays*. Ed. Robert Nemiroff. New York: Random House, 1972.

———. *The Movement: Documentary of a Struggle for Equality*. New York: Simon & Schuster, 1964.

———. A Raisin in the Sun *(Expanded 25th Anniversary Edition) and* The Sign in Sidney Brustein's Window. Ed. Robert Nemiroff. New York: Plume, 1987.

———. A Raisin in the Sun: *The Unfilmed Original Screenplay*. Ed. Robert Nemiroff. New York: Plume, 1992.

———. *To Be Young, Gifted, and Black: Lorraine Hansberry in Her Own Words*. Adapted Robert Nemiroff. Englewood Cliffs, NJ: Hall, 1969.

Hewes, Henry. "A Plant Grows in Chicago." *Saturday Review* 42 (April 4, 1959): 28.

hooks, bell. " '*Raisin*' in a New Light." *Christianity and Crisis*, February 6, 1989: 21–23.

Kaiser, Ernest, and Robert Nemiroff. "A Lorraine Hansberry Bibliography." *Freedomways* 19.4 (1979): 285–304.

Kappel, Lawrence. *Readings on* A Raisin in the Sun. San Diego, CA: Greenhaven, 2001.

King, Woodie, Jr. "Lorraine Hansberry's Children: Black Artists and *A Raisin in the Sun*." *Freedomways* 19.4 (1979): 219–21.

Kodat, Catherine Gunther. "Confusion in a Dream Deferred: Context and Culture in Teaching *A Raisin in the Sun*." *Studies in the Literary Imagination* 31.1 (spring 1998): 149–64.

Leeson, Richard M. *Lorraine Hansberry: A Resource and Production Sourcebook*. Westport, CT: Greenwood, 1997.

McKelly, James C. "Hymns of Sedition: Portraits of the Artist in Contemporary African-American Drama." *Arizona Quarterly* 48 (1992): 87–107.

Mutalik-Desai, A.A., ed. *Indian Views on American Literature*. New Delhi, India: Prestige, 1998.

Parks, Sheri. "In My Mother's House: Black Feminist Aesthetics, Television, and *A Raisin in the Sun*." *Theatre and Feminist Aesthetics*. Ed. Karen Laughlin and Catherine Schuler. Madison, NJ: Fairleigh Dickinson University Press, 1995. 200–228.

Scheader, Catherine. *They Found a Way: Lorraine Hansberry*. Chicago: Children's Press, 1978.

Seaton, Sandra. "A Raisin in the Sun: A Study in Afro-American Culture." Midwestern
    Miscellany 20 (1992): 40–49.
Washington, J. Charles. "A Raisin in the Sun Revisited." Black American Literature
    Forum 22 (1988): 109–24.
Wilkerson, Margaret B. "Lorraine Hansberry: The Complete Feminist." Freedomways
    19.4 (1979): 235–45.

7

Edward Albee
Who's Afraid of Virginia Woolf?
1962

BIOGRAPHICAL CONTEXT

Born to Louise Harvey in Washington, D.C., on March 12, 1928, Edward was given up for adoption two weeks later as his mother had been abandoned by the father and felt unable to raise a child. Days later, New York millionaires Reed and Frances Albee came forward as foster parents and brought him to their Westchester home, officially adopting him the following year and naming him Edward Franklin Albee III after the paternal grandfather. He grew up with servants, private tutors, and plenty of culture and travel. A child prodigy, Albee began writing poetry at the age of 6, and at 12 wrote a three-act sex-farce set on an ocean liner, *Aliqueen*. Reed's father had owned a profitable chain of vaudeville theaters, which allowed the young Albee to meet many playwrights, including Thornton Wilder, who would suggest he try writing plays.

Reed Albee was stern and quiet, totally dominated by a wife who was considerably younger and taller than her husband, and neither one showed much affection toward their son. Although he felt no resentment toward them, Albee never felt comfortable with either one, viewing them as self-absorbed snobs and seeing himself as an outsider. He would later come to satirize their small-minded prejudices in many of his plays. Albee preferred the company of his nanny and his maternal grandmother, Grandma Cotter, who came to live with them. It was she to whom he dedicated *The Sandbox* (1960), produced the year she died, about a family's callous reaction to the death of a grandmother.

Hating the authoritarian aspects and academic pressures of the various schools to which he was sent, Albee was expelled or dropped out from several until he arrived at Choate School in Connecticut. Here he stayed until graduation and found much encouragement for his writing. In 1945 his first published poem appeared in the literary magazine *Kaleidograph*, and in 1946 *Choate Literary Magazine* published a short play called *Schism*, an anti-Catholic, naturalistic drama about an eloping couple.

Attending Trinity College, he published in the literary magazine and did some acting, but was expelled in his second year for not attending required courses and chapel. Shortly afterward he argued with his parents over his late-night drinking and left home for good. He would have no further contact with his father, who died in 1961, and would not see his mother again until 1965. He moved to Greenwich Village and concentrated on becoming a writer, writing short stories and plays, but mainly poetry. A trust fund from his paternal grandmother paid the rent, and he supplemented this with odd jobs, including office boy, record salesman, barman, and messenger for Western Union. Despite some heterosexual experience and an earlier unofficial engagement to a socialite of whom his parents had approved, Albee had realized he was homosexual since his teenage years. In 1952 he moved in with music critic William Flanagan, beginning his first long-term relationship. Flanagan became an artistic and intellectual mentor over the next eight years as they traveled together and attended cultural events.

In 1959, approaching 30, without having published or produced a thing in the previous 10 years, Albee borrowed an office typewriter and wrote himself a play: *The Zoo Story*. This would be his breakthrough, although no American company would produce it. *Zoo Story* was first performed in Berlin, Germany, where it shared the bill with Samuel Beckett's *Krapp's Last Tape*. It tells the story of a loner who acts out his own murder with the unwitting aid of an upper-middle-class editor and shocked audiences with its subversive nature and attack on the complacency of contemporary American life. Returning to New York, Albee separated from Flanagan, although they remained friendly. He lived for the next few years with Terence McNally, then an actor, but later a successful playwright. In 1960, Provincetown Playhouse agreed to give *Zoo Story* an Off-Broadway premiere, where it won mixed reviews but ran for 582 performances, winning an Obie and other awards. It has become one of Albee's most anthologized and studied plays, and launched Albee's career as a playwright.

Along with other early works such as *Sandbox* and its more fleshed out version, *The American Dream* (1961), the success of *Zoo Story* effectively gave birth to American absurdist drama, even while the plays themselves, containing elements of hope, do not wholly reflect the nihilistic absurdist vision created by European playwrights. The less popular *Fam and Yam* (1960), a scathing attack on the theatrical establishment (based on an interview he had been granted by playwright William Inge), and *The Death of Bessie Smith* (1960) showed that Albee was a playwright willing to experiment with subject matter and form. The latter used the events of the blues singer's death to explore racism and unfulfilling relationships, presented through an episodic structure and doubled plot.

Although it had been difficult finding backing, Albee's first full-length play, *Who's Afraid of Virginia Woolf?* eventually ran for two years on Broadway and had successful productions abroad. Depicting two warring couples, the play considers the troubles of love and marriage in both particular and universal aspects. It is about the problematic relationships of those we witness, and the general decline of Western society as a whole. It won many awards, but was denied the Pulitzer and had mixed reviews. With profits from the play, Albee bought a house on Long Island and helped establish Playwrights 66, to workshop and finance productions by new writers, including Terence McNally, Lanford Wilson, Sam Shepard, and LeRoi Jones (Amiri Baraka). He became a public figure, lecturing at universities, even traveling abroad on behalf of the State Department and being invited to the White House to meet President John Kennedy.

His 1963 adaptation of Carson McCullers's *The Ballad of the Sad Café* (1963) was negatively reviewed, and his second full-length play, an exploration of religious faith, *Tiny Alice* (1964), fared little better; critics found it dramatically and philosophically confusing. Albee called a press conference to explain the play, and precipitated a war between himself and the critics. His adaptation of James Purdy's novel *Malcolm* (1966), about the sad fate of an abandoned boy, which closed after seven performances, did little to help. The critics remained wary of Albee for the next 30 years, until the major success of *Three Tall Women* (1991), which depicts his mother at three stages of her life, based on stories she told him after their 1965 reconciliation. She died in 1989 and this play was Albee's means of coming to terms with their complex relationship.

In the interim, *A Delicate Balance* (1966), about alienation and the breakdown of a dysfunctional family, had finally won Albee his first Pulitzer, although reviews remained mixed. He continued to experiment and produce both adaptations and original plays, including the abstract Beckettian double-bill *Box* and *Quotations from Chairman Mao Tse-Tung* (1968) and *All Over* (1971), set during a wake shortly after the real-life demise of his friend Flanagan. All closed early and were hated by the critics, but here we see a turnaround in Albee's life. He met Jonathan Thomas, a Canadian artist, who became the longest and most stable relationship of his life and helped him kick a serious drinking problem he had developed in the 1960s. *All Over* had been conceived as a double bill with a companion play about life. Produced four years later, this companion piece, *Seascape,* won a second Pulitzer, despite closing after 65 performances. An exploration of evolution, in which human-size lizards converse with a retired couple, *Seascape* was directed by Albee himself.

The 1980s were marked by a series of critical and commercial failures, as Albee, seemingly unperturbed, continued to experiment in his writing. *The Man Who Had Three Arms* (1982) closed on Broadway after only 16 performances, and many critics saw its tale of a man famed for having three arms but who then lost one as an analogy of the playwright's own fear that he was losing his talent. After this, New York productions became scarce, and the decade culminated in his mother's death and the discovery that Albee had been virtually disinherited in her will. He also discovered details of his adoption and a freedom to write about his past now that both parents were dead. Producing *Three Tall Women,* which premiered in Vienna, he rekindled his popularity with critics and the public alike, gaining him a third Pulitzer after its 1994 Off-Broadway production, as well as New York Drama Critics' Circle and Outer Critics' Circle awards. In 1994 he was granted an Obie for Sustained Achievement in the American Theatre.

In 1993 Signature Theatre offered a season of Albee plays to a mixed reception, and the rest of the decade, aside from *Three Tall Women* and a 1996 revival of *Delicate Balance,* proved similarly mixed. Albee's return to Broadway in 2002 with a play about the mercurial nature of love, *The Goat, or Who Is Sylvia?,* proved he was not yet finished. *The Goat* won Tony, Drama Desk, New York Drama Critics' Circle, and the Outer Critics' Circle awards. Ostensibly about a man who falls in love with a goat while trying to come to terms with his son's homosexuality, it is a rare inclusion by Albee of the issue of homosexuality. Albee has written nearly 30 plays and continues to write, so a final assessment cannot be made, but he has greatly contributed to American theater through both his own work and his commitment to experimentation, as well as by his strong support of younger artists struggling to be heard. His numerous prestigious awards include the Margo Jones Award (1965), an American Academy Medal for Drama (1980), and the William Inge Award (1991).

PLOT DEVELOPMENT

Act 1 is titled "Fun and Games," but the play begins in darkness with a crash, drunken laughter, and Martha cursing her husband, George, as he tries to placate her. At two o'clock in the morning they are arriving home from a faculty party run by Martha's father, the president of the university at which George teaches history. Martha is drunk and agitatedly tries to recall the name of a Bette Davis movie in which Davis played a discontent housewife, a role Martha feels like playing. To George's dismay, Martha has invited another couple to join them for drinks, a couple whose name she cannot remember. She carps at him, reprising a song she sang at the party, "Who's Afraid of Virginia Woolf," to mock him. He holds his own, teasing her about her laugh, her teeth, and the fact that he is six years younger. Before their guests arrive, he asks her to behave and warns her not to mention their "kid."

As Martha screams "SCREW YOU!," George opens the door to welcome Nick and Honey. Nick is uncertain they should have come, but Honey settles in as George arranges drinks and teases both wife and guests. Martha responds with brash vulgarity, Nick with coldness, and Honey with a giggling attempt to break the tension. Nick has been hired by the biology department, and the party was to introduce him and his wife. Martha accompanies Honey to the bathroom, leaving George and Nick to talk. Nick tries to remain polite while George riles him in the guise of small talk, making denigrating remarks about faculty life. When Nick fights back, George apologizes. Nick tries to keep up as George mocks his own lack of advancement, compares their wives, voices his suspicions of biologists, asks if Nick has children (which Nick does not), and mocks his father-in-law.

Honey returns announcing that Martha is changing. George learns his wife has been telling Honey about their son. His angry response scares Honey, and Nick asks George to tone it down. Martha returns, dressed to kill, and she and George continue to spar. Martha turns her attention to Nick, deliberately flirting. She finds out about his boxing exploits, compliments his body, and he begins to respond. While Martha relates an embarrassing story of how she once knocked George down, he fetches a shotgun, which, to everyone's horror, he shoots at Martha. It is a joke gun and a parasol comes out of the barrel. Having enjoyed the joke, Martha tries to kiss George, but he hurts her by breaking away.

They continue to drink, and Nick heads for the bathroom while George and Martha argue over which department Nick is in. When Nick returns, George conjures up a derisive vision of Nick involved in eugenics, trying to create a master race, at which Martha delights and Nick gets angry. Honey, who is getting drunk, mentions George and Martha's son again, and George and Martha argue over their son's appearance and whether George is the real father. When George goes to get more booze, Martha talks about her domineering father and how he had her annul a previous, rash marriage. She explains how she met George, but he gets annoyed at her explaining she had planned for him to take over from her father, but he had been unsuitable. He breaks a bottle in anger and starts singing "Who's Afraid" until Honey breaks it up, declaring her need to vomit.

The second act, "Walpurgisnacht," continues with Nick apologizing for his wife. George jokes back, but then tries again to rile Nick, who is uncomfortable with his host's behavior. When Nick threatens to hit him, George backs down. Nick suddenly explains how he married Honey because he thought she was pregnant, but it was a hysterical pregnancy. George responds with a story about a boy he once knew who had accidentally shot his mother, who ordered "bergin" instead of bourbon at a gin joint, then on a later occasion crashed the car and killed his father. They discuss pregnancies again and George mentions Martha does not have them, until Nick reminds him of his son.

Martha reports Honey is feeling better. George starts to tell Nick his version of his college career, but Nick interrupts explaining how he and Honey got together. They had been childhood sweethearts and marriage had been expected, and she also had money from her father, an evangelical preacher; he confesses it was not a love match. Now drunk, Nick describes an intent to insinuate himself into the college and sleep with the wives to get on; he even suggests he should sleep with Martha to see George's reaction. George takes it calmly, annoying Nick, and tries to offer Nick advice, which he vehemently refuses. Honey and Martha join them, and the conversation turns to throwing up.

Martha and George try to hurt each other by talking about their son, and who he hates the most. Nick suggests Honey stop drinking and she snaps at him. On learning George had not yet told his story, Martha mentions a book he had tried to publish. She also makes an aside implying George was the boy who had ordered "bergin." Honey asks if they can dance and George puts on classical music, then Martha changes this for jazz so she and Nick can dance provocatively together. While dancing, she describes George's book—an autobiography about a boy who killed his parents—which her father had not allowed him to publish. George cries, "THE GAME IS OVER," but Martha keeps talking until he physically attacks her. Nick pulls him off and throws him down, while Honey enjoys the violence.

Trying to regain his composure, George suggests they change the game from "Humiliate the Host" to "Hump the Hostess." Nick refuses involvement, so George changes the game to "Get the Guests," which makes Nick and Honey nervous. George relates an unflattering version of all Nick has told him about his relationship with Honey. Nick tries to stop him before Honey realizes who this story is about. When she understands, she runs off to be sick again, angry with Nick for telling secrets. Nick is angry, although his concern is only for himself, and as he follows after Honey, he threatens to get George back.

Martha berates George for going too far. He complains she is being hypocritical, as she constantly tears into him, but she shouts back, "YOU CAN STAND IT!" She even implies he needs it. He calls her deluded and she threatens him as Nick had. Each mentions the 23 years they have struggled against each other, but now they declare total war and seem rejuvenated at the prospect. Nick returns to say Honey is lying down in the bathroom. Martha sends George to get more ice and seduces Nick. They do not see him, but George sees them embrace and smiles; this is part of the contest. Martha breaks away, uncertain she wants this. George returns and infuriates Martha by calmly sitting down to read a book. To goad him, she and Nick fondle each other, but George refuses to react. She sends Nick out to wait for her and gives George a final chance to stop her, but he tells her to get on with it, so she leaves. After she is gone, he reads a passage from Oswald Spengler's *Decline of the West*, but then hurls the book down in fury against the door chimes.

His noise wakes Honey, who enters half dreaming and lets slip the fact she does not want children, because she is afraid of pain. George realizes she has been taking something to prevent pregnancies and mocks her, trying to make her realize her husband is having sex with his wife. She is too upset to focus, and fixates on the bell noise she heard. He tells her it was a messenger coming to announce his son is dead, and then plans how he will tell Martha this obvious lie.

The final act, "The Exorcism," begins with Martha alone. She drinks and talks about her sadness, then Nick enters to say his wife is behaving strangely, lying in the bathroom, drinking. Nick had been unable to get an erection. Martha tells Nick, to his mocking disbelief, that George is the only man who has ever made her happy, and she feels remorse for how she treats him. Nick views George as spineless, but Martha knows better. She orders Nick to be her houseboy, and he kowtows, opening the door when it chimes. George enters with flowers, and he and Martha clown around before teaming up to tease Nick. Then George and Martha begin arguing with each other, and Martha pretends she and Nick had made love. George talks of being able to recognize truth from illusion as he sends Nick to fetch Honey for one final game he calls, "bringing up baby." Martha pleads for him to stop, but he goads her into fight mode again.

George declares his intention to peel away the layers and get down to the "marrow." He gets Martha to tell the story of their son. It is a recitation they both know by heart, though George breaks off into a requiem mass. Honey suddenly declares she wants a child. Martha turns on George, suggesting he was jealous of their child; he retorts, saying the child was embarrassed by his mother, and she insists he was ashamed of his father. They begin to talk over each other until Honey screams for them to stop. George announces to Martha their son is dead, she attacks him in a fury, and Nick holds her back. Martha complains and Nick realizes the child has only ever been in George's and Martha's imaginations. The couple are barren. Nick and Honey leave feeling stunned, as George and Martha prepare to go to bed. George tells Martha "it was ... time" and sings "Who's afraid" as Martha admits she is afraid. The curtain falls with them together, fearful of what will come next.

CHARACTER DEVELOPMENT

We change our ideas about the characters during the play, and no one ends how he or she first appeared, proving that appearances do continually deceive and we should be wary of them. George begins an apparently emasculated wimp but grows in stature, taking on more control, becoming, for a time, quite menacing. George is actually in control from the start—it is he who first mentions their son by subtly telling his drunken wife not to mention it, as if intentionally provoking that very outcome by the warning. It is also George who works toward making them all, including himself, recognize the illusions under which they have been living and move toward starting afresh without such protection. Martha, meanwhile, starts out a loudmouthed drunk who seems to dominate and castrate her husband, but becomes more sympathetic as we learn of her problematic past with a domineering father who controls everything she and George do.

Of the guests, Nick begins the All-American boy, but his attraction is diminished as we learn of his ambition to sleep his way to the top, and witness his callous treatment of his wife. In fact, for all his athletic build and threats of force, Nick actually fits the emasculated male figure better than George, for in the course of the play he shows subservience to all three of the other characters, following their instructions even to the point of playing the role of houseboy. Even Honey, who initially appears so sweet and innocent, shouts with joy at signs of violence, shows firm control of her husband when he tries to restrict her, and turns out to be aborting her pregnancies without any qualms.

Although we see some echoes of George and Martha in the way Nick and Honey are heading, the characters complement each other in terms of personality and desire. Both Martha and Honey are emasculating to a point, but while Martha is an alcoholic who desperately wants a child, Honey rarely drinks and has been refusing to have a child. Honey is also mostly warm, open, and friendly toward others, against her husband, who is grimly polite and coldly ambitious. Also, while Nick married Honey for her father's money and because he thought she was pregnant, it becomes clear that George and Martha's marriage is one of passion, despite the fact that Martha accuses George of marrying her for money and position. Despite the surface antagonisms, they still have moments of mutual laughter, which implies a deeper connection. They know each other so well, even down to who has more teeth; Nick and Honey are by comparison virtual strangers to each other. The only thing they all share is a desire to avoid the truth.

George and Martha's relationship seems grounded in masochism. Each invites the other to attack, so each can have an excuse for revenge. By describing what they do as "games," they create a socially acceptable ritual of abuse, an abuse in which they revel to release their bitterness and self-loathing. Both feel they have wasted their lives and blame the other. Some of their games are deeply personal habits with rigid rules; others they invent on the spur of the moment. All of their games are spiteful, intended to damage. Yet, George and Martha end the play together, as George tries to calm his wife's fears, and they present an image of an intimate couple who desperately need one another.

Their underlying passion is partly what fuels their games, which, to some degree, give them a thrill in their otherwise dull lives. On a number of occasions Martha asks George to kiss her, usually when delighted at some witticism he has made, and she insists to Nick, who cannot sexually satisfy her, that George is the only man who ever has. Although George pretends to be unconcerned when Martha leaves with Nick, his anger is displayed when he throws his book and then revenges himself. At the center of their relationship seems to be the fact that they have no children. Whether a child would really have helped their marriage remains debatable, but both claim a need for that child, and their duel commitment to the illusion of their invented child seems a means by which they have remained close.

Nick and Honey are the next generation, and George tries to warn Nick of where he could be heading, but Nick is contemptuous of his advice. George is, after all, a teacher, and he tries to teach the younger generation how to be better and not make the same mistakes he has made. Though unable to be a biological father, he adopts at times a fatherly stance to Nick in particular. But each generation, apparently, insists on making its own mistakes. With his kinship to the college president, George could help Nick in his career, which is the only reason Nick suffers his company. Nick is a careerist in the way George was expected to be, but was unable to pursue. That Nick and

Honey are each so self-obsessed, and innately indifferent toward the other, bodes ill for the future unless they change their ways, and the horrors of the relationship between George and Martha become almost preferable, for at least they are connected.

Martha's father, the president of the university, never appears, although his controlling hand is apparent on both couples. All dance to his tune—Martha allowing him to annul her romantic marriage to a gardener, then following whatever orders he gives. It is to satisfy him that she invited Nick and Honey back in the first place. Because of this man's disapproval, George was not allowed to publish his book and has not been deemed the right material for promotion. Nick is sensitive from the start that this is the man to please, hence his tolerance for George and Martha, the daughter and son-in-law. In the wider social picture such a figure represents such overcontrolling, intolerant social leaders Albee sees at work in the nation, whose callous control helps distort further the lives of those under them.

THEMES

Its realistic veneer makes it seem different from Albee's earlier plays, but *Who's Afraid?* is very typical of his work, with its focus on confrontation presented through verbal duels, and death in both a physical and psychological sense. At the heart of most of Albee's writings are concerns with the fear of abandonment, betrayal, the hope for love, and the feeling of not belonging, which are rooted in his own upbringing. Anger is a common reaction in his characters, and his plays are in one sense an attempt at anger management, as he works through these demons from his own past. He is also perennially interested in the relation between truth and illusion, and the ineffective ways people communicate with one another.

George and Martha are an older couple who seem trapped in an abusive and uncomfortable relationship, with no divorce in sight. In many ways they are a kind of fleshed-out version of Mommy and Daddy from *American Dream*. Yet we are left with the impression that this couple needs each other, and may even love one another, despite the antagonism and the bitterness. Meanwhile, the much younger couple who visits them, Nick and Honey, although initially appearing comfortable and loving, turn out to be quite the opposite, as he sleeps around and she is secretly stopping her pregnancies. In the spirit of the absurdist movement, Albee wishes to strip away surface presumptions to reveal the true inadequacies, fears, and longings behind these people's relationships, yet he does it in an almost realistic style and without the absolute pessimism of true absurdism. There remains the hope that things could get better; Nick extends his hand to Honey, who has declared her decision to have a child, and George and Martha hold each other in the growing darkness, having exorcised the reductive dream of their fake child.

Albee told William Flanagan that the play's title came from a slogan scrawled on a mirror in a Greenwich Village bar, which he took to mean, "Who's afraid of life without false illusion" (103). The title highlights Albee's concern with the way people use fictions in their lives and relationships with others to allay fears and hide from truths; it also carries a suggestion of danger. The "wolf" is revealed to be George, whose masculinity Martha has been bringing into doubt by feminizing the phrase, yet he turns out to be not as toothless as we, and Nick, suppose. Despite an ineffectual appearance, he is the one who elicits people's confessions and largely directs the increasingly unpleasant games.

Act 3's title, "The Exorcism," at one point was a working title for the whole play, but at least two things are exorcised in the final act: Honey's fear of having a baby, and George and Martha's imaginary son, whom Nick and Honey, and the audience, have assumed was real. George peels off layers until the marrow has been reached, and an agreed truth is revealed. Albee seems to suggest that by stripping away the fictions with which we live, in marriage as in life, and by accepting who we really are, we may see more clearly what has gone wrong and be able to fix it, or at least live better with it.

When Martha sings the title song to George, it seems an attempt to belittle him, offering a slur on his masculinity and calling him weak and effeminate. It's not the "Big Bad Wolf" but "Virginia Woolf." However, the play reverses this by having George sing it to Martha at the close. Woolf was a writer who courageously battled the Victorian image of the Angel in the House to try and gain some independence as a woman. Though she ended unhappily, committing suicide, it was without compromising her ideals. Martha has never had the courage to escape the dominance of her father, who even now still dictates her life. At the play's close, Martha admits it is she who is afraid, and we are left to guess at what—perhaps of the type of independent woman Virginia Woolf was, but she could never hope to be? Or just simply of her life ahead as an alcoholic, without the fiction of the son to bring release.

Who's Afraid? asserts Albee's belief in the need for individuals to acknowledge the nature of reality and the necessity for compassionate human relationships to provide the support that people need to survive an often-hostile world. They have all been using illusions to survive, but Albee shows how false this survival is; it is, in fact, more of an anesthetization and only puts their problems on hold rather than cure them. George and Martha created their fantasy child as an attempt at consolation, being unable to conceive one of their own, but it only exacerbates their despair and isolation as they must keep it a secret from everyone, and so it holds them back from the real contact they need and crave. It is, however, always difficult to face the truth, especially when it rests in admitting one's own failures. It is not only Martha but also George who feels insecure at the play's end.

George has also failed in his inability to get his book published, which has been his sole attempt to break out and make something of his life. His effort to face his past in this book may be indicative of a willingness to face the truth, but, if Martha is to be believed and he really intended to kill his parents, then this, too, has been just another avoidance. Just like Nick, George bows to the authority of his father-in-law and so demeans himself and has wasted his potential. In admitting their failures, all George and Martha have left is each other, and that is what they cling to desperately at the play's end.

Although it is tempting to view Nick and Honey as younger versions of George and Martha, despite the pain George and Martha inflict on one another, their relationship is actually more honest and caring than Nick and Honey. A number of times Martha tries to kiss George, and it is implied by both that they married for love; Nick and Honey fall short in both these areas. While both couples are childless, it is by Honey's choice that she and Nick have no children, whereas George and Martha were infertile, again making them a more sympathetic couple. The theme of sterility also works on a symbolic level, with George and Martha representing not only the older generation but also the United States itself, as their names—echoing George and Martha Washington, another barren couple—suggest. Albee sees America as a whole suffering from the same delusions and difficulties these two couples encounter, diverted from meaningful lives by either complacency or the race for material advance.

HISTORICAL CONTEXT

American society in the 1960s was marked by a political climate in the midst of a cold war with the Soviet Union and an increasing fear and embrace of new technology. The cold war was characterized by mutual distrust, suspicion, and misunderstanding between the United States and the Soviet Union, a similar relationship we see existing between the characters in the play. Ironically, three days after the play opened, there was a major clash between the Soviet Union and the United States over the Soviet deployment of nuclear missiles in Cuba, which some feared might lead to World War III; fortunately, conflict was circumvented. Nick's name is derived from

Nikita Khrushchev, the ruthless premier of the Soviet Union at the time. Khrushchev, who was thought to represent the cold wave of the future in his hard political stance, determines Nick's characterization. Nick is a personification of the corruption of ideals of progress that have been supplanted by materialistic and technological advances; he represents science led astray, just as America felt threatened by the Soviet nuclear weapons program.

Nick is actually a scientist, a biologist, and George connects this to totalitarian modes of thought, accusing him of eugenics and associating him with Hitler's vision of a master race by referring to his wife by the German term *frau*. George's jeremiad against Nick's genetic engineering research, though exaggerated, warns of the dangers to individualism in the face of social-scientific determinism, such as that created by the totalitarian state in the Soviet Union. Nick's value system stinks of all the worst aspects of the corrupted, materialistic American Dream with his belief in expedient morality. Ironically, of course, he is ultimately as impotent as George, indeed, more so, if Martha is to be believed.

For Albee, the breakdown between husband and wife was meant to be indicative of what he saw as the larger communication breakdown of society in general. The pervasive image of male sterility—both men being emasculated to varying degrees by their wives, and neither able to bear children (whoever is at fault)—becomes symbolic of the sterility and stagnation of the larger society. While absurdists saw in this a nihilistic future, Albee refuses to give in. Just as sterility suggests failure, in the same way, fertility, once embraced, would imply the possibility of progression. *Who's Afraid?* is less a critique of marriage than of society as a whole, a society that has lost the ability to allow individuals to humanly contact one another. George and Martha—named after the first First Family of America, the Washingtons—represent all of America and its skewed value system. The Washingtons, despite their public appearance, were also reputed to have had a tumultuous private relationship, further highlighting the danger of judging by appearance.

LITERARY STYLE AND DEVICES

As an artist, Albee closely examines American society and tries to expose its false and artificial values and the damaging complacency he sees infecting middle and upper classes. The people in his plays are also often cruel, almost deliberately vacuous—the women emasculating and the men misogynistic. When Albee peels back the layers of domesticity, family, and relationships, we see that all is not well. That he manages to do this so often with such good humor is partly due to what fellow playwright Harold Pinter has called his "mischievous streak" (qtd. in Page) Some of that humor comes from ironic reflection, but in a play like *Who's Afraid?*, it is also evident in moments of slapstick as well as clever wordplay, which is informed by the wit and intellect of the playwright.

For a writer with such a meager academic background, Albee is nonetheless eclectic and knowledgeable about a great range of topics from politics and science to literature and history. References to varied fields of study pepper George's speech. His words and the play as a whole are filled with metaphor and symbolism. Imagery of entropy and decline are particularly prevalent, with numerous assertions of the decline of Western civilization. We frequently hear of Carthage and Gomorrah, fallen cities of the past, and of tragic and destructive figures like Oedipus and Medea. George reads a passage from Oswald Spengler's *Decline of the West* (1918), and all of the characters are revealed to have gone from promising beginnings to empty materialism. When George enters with his flowers, he intones, "Flores para los muertos," meaning "flowers for the dead," which is also a line from Tennessee Williams's *A Streetcar Named Desire,* spoken as Blanche is losing her grip. George's playful declension—"Good, better, best, bested"—suggests a world that has outdone itself, just as his assertions about the battle between history and biology bodes ill for the future. But Albee suggests it is possible to reverse that direction.

Countering the imagery of decay, there is also much religious symbolism in the play's language and action that point to a redemptive reading. Recalling the underlying Christian elements in *Zoo Story,* some scholars interpret George's killing off the imaginary son as a crucifixion that will bring about the resurrection of George and Martha's marriage, as well as the possibility for new life with the exorcism of Honey's fear of childbearing. The son, like Jesus, has died to allow others to lead better lives. George's role of priest as he reads the requiem mass in Latin during Martha's recitation is also crucial to this explication of the play. We should note that the play ends on Sunday morning, the time for religious contemplation and a day religiously connected to the image of the rising sun/son.

Albee views his writing as a kind of music. He designs the language of his characters to incorporate points of rest where there is silence to balance the sound of them talking, as well as passages that are loud and soft, in the same way a musician composes any performance piece. When two characters talk at the same time, as do George and Martha, it emulates an instrumental duet, as each aurally complements the other. The whole structure of his play is similarly precise. The different acts, each with its own title, illustrate the three stages of Albee's stripping away the layers of deceit among these four people. We begin with a lighthearted movement called "Fun and Games," in which the four make jokes at each other's expense, then move forward to "Walpurgisnacht," named after a German festivity that takes place on the night of April 30. Originally a witches' celebration of mischief while awaiting the devil, under Christian influence it became a series of rituals to ward off evil—Albee's version could easily fit either reading. We end with "The Exorcism," which sums up both the action and the theme of the whole play and exorcises those demons brought to life in "Walpurgisnacht."

SITUATION OF WORK

Many critics and scholars would credit Edward Albee as virtually single-handedly reinventing American theater in the 1960s, and *Who's Afraid?* was the play that gave him the exposure and impetus to do that. As *Village Voice* critic Michael Smith realized at its premiere production, here was a "new kind of play" that significantly advanced American drama beyond the dominant naturalistic conventions, largely by making all four of its characters so unpleasant and leaving no one with whom the audience can easily sympathize (17). Drama scholar Matthew Roudané declares that *"Who's Afraid?* unquestionably certified Albee's place in American literature" (*Understanding* 65) and was "an epochal Broadway debut" (*Understanding* 85).

The 1960s were a quiet decade for American masters Arthur Miller and Tennessee Williams, and Albee's only other major rival for attention at this time was Neil Simon, whose idealistic comedies were incredibly popular but lacking in literary merit. In many ways, it seemed that Albee may have just been the right playwright at the right time. But his continued contributions over nearly five decades, three Pulitzer Awards, and erstwhile commitment to taking risks with serious and often experimental drama in a nation that has forever been at odds with such forms suggest a far more lasting talent.

Very much a part of the beginnings of Off-Broadway theater in the 1960s, Albee had been hailed as the iconoclastic leader of a new theatrical movement and labeled as the successor to Arthur Miller, Tennessee Williams, and Eugene O'Neill in that he took drama seriously. He is, however, more closely related to the likes of such European playwrights as Beckett and Harold Pinter. Although a play like *Who's Afraid?* may seem at first glance to be realistic, its surreal nature is never far from the surface. George and Martha's child turns out to be nothing more than a figment of their combined imagination, a pawn invented for use in their twisted psychological games. In one sense Albee creates a hybrid style that incorporates both European and American technique, and a work like *Who's Afraid?* becomes a flawless blend of European experimentation and American realism, which, on the other hand, also refutes the nihilism of European absurdism as well as the pat resolution and assurance of many American plays.

One of Albee's greatest contributions to American theater is the sheer cleverness and sharpness of his language, which simultaneously animates his themes and entertains. John Guare, Adrienne Kennedy, Megan Terry, and Sam Shepard are just a few of the playwrights who have felt inspired by the acerbic originality of Albee's dialogue. David Mamet acknowledges Albee as one of his main influences, and a play like *American Buffalo* (1977), with its small cast, claustrophobic setting, apparently realistic surface built on a lie, and profane language, could be seen as a direct homage to *Who's Afraid?* and was equally, controversially received.

Despite the harsh pictures Albee portrays, his work is neither depressing nor nihilistic as some critics have claimed, for like David Mamet, there is an underlying compassion at work, which insists that the endemic spiritual malaise he depicts can be combated if only the characters—and by extension, those watching—would become more self-aware and engaged. Although Albee has continually experimented with theatrical styles and techniques, his artistic purpose has been consistent throughout: to reveal the truth about the complacency and evasions he sees abounding in American society and ask that something be done to counter this.

Early in his career he was labeled as part of the Theatre of the Absurd, the postwar European movement that includes such dramatists as Eugene Ionesco, Samuel Beckett, and Harold Pinter; however, this classification is inaccurate. Although Albee's dramaturgy and theatrical style in certain plays have resembled Ionesco's and Beckett's, the worldview expressed in his plays is never as fatalistic and nihilistic as theirs. Rather, he espouses an existentialist vision from which he criticizes individuals and American society as a whole, with biting satire, but also with hope for change. Albee has always viewed himself as an "affirmative existentialist" (Roudané, *Necessary Fictions* 1) rather than an absurdist, though critics such as Martin Esslin and Nelvin Vos have argued otherwise.

Admittedly influenced by Eugene O'Neill's *The Iceman Cometh, Who's Afraid?* continues O'Neill's fascination with the lies (or pipedreams) we tell ourselves to survive in an antagonistic environment, and the speculation as to whether such lies are ultimately harmful or necessary. While O'Neill would say they are necessary, Albee comes down on the other side, suggesting it is healthier in the long run to face the truth squarely on. This is what George and Martha do at the close of the play, and because both are uncertain and scared, it is important that they do so together.

CRITICAL RECEPTION

Despite initial admiration from the critics for his early work, the fact that Albee had not staged a full-length play on Broadway was beginning to suggest that here was just a promising new writer who would never rise beyond small venues. Albee's response to such criticism was to write a caustic article for the *New York Times* in which he accused Broadway, with its commercial obsession, of being the real Theatre of the Absurd. He then sought to stage a play there that would not follow the usual formulas and would show America the possibilities of serious drama. The premiere of *Who's Afraid?* on October 12, 1962, caused a sensation just in the fact that here was a nonmainstream play opening in a Broadway theater to tremendous commercial success; it ran for 664 performances.

Although *Who's Afraid?* has become recognized as one of the great American plays, the critics' early reviews were mixed, and those who enjoyed it did so with some guilt. In part, its reputation as a controversial play alternatively reviled and praised by critics helped boost attendance and extend its Broadway run. Criticisms objected to the play's risqué language and the outright bitterness of the characters, and found the imaginary child concept implausible. Critic John Chapman talked about its "depravity and obscenity" ("For Dirty-Minded" 1), calling it a "sick play about sick people" ("A Play Lies" 46), and scholar Andrew Harris relates how prior to the play being allowed to open in Boston during its 1963 road company tour, the head of the city's licensing division, Richard J. Sinnott, declared it would be a "mortal sin" to let the play run as written, calling it a "cesspool" (as had Chapman) and complaining about its abuse of the Lord's name (88). Prior to its 1964 London opening, much of its language had to be toned down to satisfy the censor. The resulting play still caused *Guardian* critic Philip Hope-Wallace to describe it as "hateful and shamefully funny and hideously watchable" (11).

Those who championed the play enjoyed its theatricality, emotional power, biting satire, and humor. The reviewer for *Theatre Arts* called it a "brilliant exercise in theatrical craftsmanship that is devastatingly funny, emotionally shattering and intellectually provocative" (Rev. of *Who's Afraid* 10), and *Variety*'s Hobe insisted it established "Albee as a gifted playwright" (n.p.). A few critics, put off by the play's success, felt that Albee had betrayed his aesthetic principles by producing a conventional Broadway play, but this seems ingenuous as *Who's Afraid?*, with its intentionally claustrophobic set, brutal language, and emotional power, was scarcely the usual bland Broadway fare.

Despite winning the New York Drama Critics' Circle Award for Best Play and five of the six Tony Awards for which it was nominated, *Who's Afraid?* did not get the Pulitzer for which it had been nominated, because the board of directors did not want to give the award to a "dirty" play. John Gassner and John Mason Brown, the widely respected drama critics who recommended *Who's Afraid?* for the prize, resigned from the Pulitzer committee in protest, and no award in drama was given that year. Critics aside, the play remained a major commercial success and had even greater success in 1966, when Ernest Lehman adapted it for the screen, and Mike Nichols directed the hit movie with Richard Burton and Elizabeth Taylor. It was the highest-grossing movie for Warner Brothers that year. Albee felt Hollywood had done a good job on the movie, which actually gained a greater consensus of positive reviews, but felt it lacked some of the humor of his original play.

SUGGESTED READINGS

Albee, Edward. *The Plays*. 4 vols. New York: Atheneum, 1981–1982.

———. *Selected Plays of Edward Albee*. Garden City, NY: Nelson Doubleday, 1987.

———. *Three Tall Women*. New York: Dutton, 1995.

———. "Which Theatre Is the Absurd One?" *American Playwrights on Drama*. Ed. Horst Frenz. New York: Hill & Wang, 1965. 168–74.

Amacher, Richard E. *Edward Albee*. Rev. ed. Boston: Twayne, 1982.

Baxandall, Lee. "The Theatre of Edward Albee." *Tulane Drama Review* 9 (1965): 19–40.

Bigsby, Christopher. *Albee*. Edinburgh, Scotland: Oliver & Boyd, 1969.

———, ed. *Edward Albee: A Collection of Critical Essays*. Englewood Cliffs, NJ: Prentice-Hall, 1975.

———, ed. *Twentieth Century Views of Edward Albee*. Englewood Cliffs, NJ: Prentice-Hall, 1975.

Bloom, Harold, ed. *Edward Albee: Modern Critical Views*. New Haven, CT: Chelsea House, 1987.

Bottoms, Stephen J. *Albee: Who's Afraid of Virginia Woolf?* Cambridge: Cambridge University Press, 2000.

Chapman, John. "For Dirty-Minded Females Only." *Sunday News*, October 21, 1962, sec. 2: 1.

———. "A Play Lies under the Muck in *Who's Afraid of Virginia Woolf?*" *New York Daily News*, October 15, 1962: 46.

Cohn, Ruby. *Edward Albee*. Minneapolis: University of Minnesota Press, 1969.

Debusscher, Gilbert. *Edward Albee: Tradition and Renewal*. Trans. Anne D. Williams. Brussels, Belgium: American Studies Center, 1967.

De La Fuente, Patricia, ed. *Edward Albee, Planned Wilderness: Interviews, Essays, and Bibliography*. Edinburg, TX: Pan American University Press, 1980.

"Edward Albee: Special Issue." *American Drama* 2.2 (spring 1993).

Esslin, Martin. *The Theatre of the Absurd*. Garden City, NY: Doubleday, 1961.

Flanagan, William. "The Art of the Theatre IV." *Paris Review* 39 (1966): 92–121.

Giantvalley, Scott. "Albee's Titles." *Explicator* 46 (1988): 46–47.

———. *Edward Albee: A Reference Guide*. Boston: G.K. Hall, 1987.

Gussow, Mel. *Edward Albee: A Singular Journey*. New York: Simon & Schuster, 1999.

Harris, Andrew B. *Broadway Theatre*. New York: Routledge, 1994.

Hayman, Ronald. *Edward Albee*. New York: Ungar, 1971.

Hirsch, Foster. *Who's Afraid of Edward Albee?* Berkeley, CA: Creative Arts, 1978.

Hobe. "Shows on Broadway: *Who's Afraid of Virginia Woolf?*" *Variety*, October 17, 1962: n.p.

Hope-Wallace, Philip. "*Who's Afraid of Virginia Woolf?*" *Guardian*, February 7, 1964: 11.

Kolin, Philip C., ed. *Conversations with Edward Albee*. Jackson: University Press of Mississippi, 1988.

Kolin, Philip C., and J. Madison Davis, eds. *Critical Essays on Edward Albee*. Boston: G.K. Hall, 1986.

Mann, Bruce J., ed. *Edward Albee: A Casebook*. New York: Routledge, 2003.

McCarthy, Gerry. *Edward Albee*. New York: St. Martin's, 1987.

Page, Chris. "America's Premier Playwright Reflects on 45 years of Surviving in a 'Tough Racket.'" *East Valley Tribune*, November 14, 2004: n.p.

Paolucci, Anne. *From Tension to Tonic: The Plays of Edward Albee*. Carbondale: Southern Illinois University Press, 1972.

Roudané, Matthew. *Understanding Edward Albee*. Columbia: University of South Carolina Press, 1987.

———. *Who's Afraid of Virginia Woolf?: Necessary Fictions, Terrifying Realities.* Boston: Twayne, 1990.

Rutenberg, Michael E. *Edward Albee: Playwright in Protest*. New York: Avon, 1969.

Sisko, Nancy J. "Comic Strategies in *The Tempest* and *Who's Afraid of Virginia Woolf?*" *English Language Notes* 28.4 (June 1991): 63–67.

Smith, Michael. "Theatre Uptown." *Village Voice*, October 18, 1962: 11, 17.

Stenz, Anita Marie. *Edward Albee: The Poet of Loss*. New York: Mouton, 1978.

Tyce, Richard. *Edward Albee: A Bibliography*. Metuchen, NJ: Scarecrow, 1986.

Vos, Nelvin. *Eugene Ionesco and Edward Albee: A Critical Essay*. Grand Rapids, MI: Eerdmans, 1968.

Wasserman, Julian N., ed. *Edward Albee: An Interview and Essays*. Syracuse, NY: Syracuse University Press, 1983.

Rev. of *Who's Afraid of Virginia Woolf?*, by Edward Albee. *Theatre Arts* 46 (November 1962): 10–11.

8

Sam Shepard
Buried Child
1978

BIOGRAPHICAL CONTEXT

Born on November 5, 1943, in Fort Sheridan, Illinois, to Elaine and Samuel Rogers, Sam Shepard Rogers III (called Steve) was named after his father, a military man. When Shepard was a small child, the family moved frequently until his father left the army, settling in the small town of Duarte, California, to try his hand at farming and ranching; his efforts, however, were unsuccessful. Eventually the father left and became an alcoholic hermit living in the desert, like the father in *True West* (1980). The impoverished agrarian life in which Shepard grew up lies behind *Buried Child* and many other of his plays. After a delinquent adolescence, including alcohol, drugs, drag racing, and fighting, with its typical rebellion against authoritarian parents and mainstream values, Shepard graduated high school and began training in animal husbandry. Dissatisfied, he auditioned for a touring theater group, the Bishop's Company Repertory Players, hoping to escape rural life.

Staying with Bishop's Company until they reached New York, by 1963 Shepard had joined the growing artistic counterculture scene he discovered in Greenwich Village. Dropping his last name to become Sam Shepard and break fully from his past, Shepard hedonistically embraced the sex-and-drugs revolution taking place. Ralph Cook, head waiter at Village Gate, the jazz club where Shepard bused tables, was given the use of a local church that he converted into Theatre Genesis, and invited Shepard to get involved.

Shepard's earliest work was largely improvisational and marked by an intent to shock. In 1964 Cook directed two short plays—*The Rock Garden*, an exposure of the inadequacies of family life, and *Cowboys*, an episodic piece in which two city dwellers act out cowboy scenarios—to give Shepard his first public airing. Though the plays were ignored or berated by most, one critic, Michael Smith, wrote a glowing review that described Shepard as a playwright with "an intuitive approach to language and dramatic structure" (13), which encouraged audiences and gave Shepard the positive feedback he needed to continue.

The timing was perfect: Off-Off-Broadway was beginning to flower, and Shepard had just the voice and style they wanted to promote. He had a succession of rapidly composed one-act plays produced at such establishments as La MaMa, Edward Albee's Playwrights Unit, and Caffe Cino, which established his position as their foremost writer. These plays, among which *Chicago* (1965), *Icarus's Mother* (1965), *Red Cross* (1966), *La Turista* (1967), and *Melodrama Play* (1967) all won Obies and growing respect from critics, typically dispensed with traditional ideas of character and plot, appearing almost as abstract collages of movement, image, and sound. *Melodrama*, which experimented with the conventions of melodrama in an exploration of false heroics, was one of his first plays to feature rock and roll as a central metaphor.

Switching gears, in 1968 Shepard worked on the screenplay of the movie *Zabriskie Point*, a project from which he later withdrew to play drums and tour with the Holy Modal Rounders. Shepard's style changed in his next plays: *The Unseen Hand* (1969) used more complex language and was grounded in myth, while *The Holy Ghostly* (1970) moved from simply depicting a cultural wasteland to investigating strategies of personal survival. However, these were less well received. In 1969 Shepard married O-Lan Johnson, an actress from Theatre Genesis, and the couple had a child, Jesse Mojo, in May 1970. Also in 1970, after some protest over its stereotyped representations of black men, Lincoln Center produced *Operation Sidewinder,* a symbolic and satirical piece exploring issues of Vietnam, military duplicity, and consciousness, involving drugs, a giant snake, advanced technology, American Indian myth, black militants, and a divorcing couple. Shepard had disliked the production, and reviews were universally scathing.

In 1971 Shepard wrote *Cowboy Mouth* with Patti Smith, seemingly a poeticized documentary of their brief affair. Intending to perform it with Smith, Shepard pulled out after one preview soon after, leaving for England with his wife and son. His next play, *The Tooth of Crime* (1972), a darkly humorous confrontation for dominance between Hoss and Crow, the old and the new, which many consider his first major play, premiered in London but fared better in its 1973 American production. Shepard was developing more distinctive characters, a clearer sense of plot, and his mythic and symbolic elements were better controlled. The year 1974 was a creative year as Shepard, remaining in England, experimented with the less wordy *Geography of a Horse Dreamer*, a metaphoric exploration of artistic dilemmas; wrote a revue for his wife and her friends about childbirth, *Little Ocean*; and penned the more oblique *Action*, in which he explored the concept of action without motivation between two couples during Christmas dinner.

Returning to America in 1974, Shepard won another Obie in 1975 with the American production of *Action* and its companion play, *Killer's Head*, which considered the psychology of the condemned. The following year he directed *Angel City* at the Magic Theatre in San Francisco, one of his favorite venues. Filled with music, imagery, and lyricism, *Angel City* was Shepard's disappointed but creative response to having toured with Bob Dylan in the fall of 1975, exposing what he saw as the ethical incapacity of Hollywood. The year 1976 continued with the pulp-fiction improvisation *Suicide in B-Flat* and the operetta *The Sad Lament of Pecos Bill on the Eve of Killing His Wife*.

Curse of the Starving Class (1977), with its depiction of America in decline, marked a new stage in Shepard's writing, and is the first of what have become known as his "family plays." More realistic in style, these plays are a mix of Shepard's trademark monologues, visual images, and distinct stage actions with more-traditional characters and plot. *Starving Class* won a controversial Obie based on its publication alone, and its production proved problematic. Scathingly received in London, it was not produced in America until the following year, where it had only moderate success. It was the family play that followed that really brought Shepard into the mainstream; *Buried Child* (1978) won both Obie and Pulitzer awards, had a successful run Off-Broadway, and won Shepard both critical and popular approval to continue his exploration of the darker side of the American psyche.

The year 1978 also marked Shepard's film debut, in Terrence Malik's *Days of Heaven*, and the first collaboration between Shepard and director/actor Joseph Chaikin in *Tongues* and *Savage/Love*, two pieces designed for voice and percussion, which were well received by critics. In 1980 Shepard presented *True West*, the first play Shepard admits to having spent time rewriting until he felt it was right, and perhaps his most accessible, with its simple plot of two brothers at loggerheads. It had an initially troubled production history and did not meet huge success until the 1982 Steppenwolf Company production in Chicago, with John Malkovich and Gary Sinise, which transferred to a lengthy Off-Broadway run (762 performances) and a PBS *American Playhouse* production in 1984.

In 1982 Shepard left his wife, O-Lan (their divorce would be finalized in 1984, the same year his father died), to move in with Jessica Lange, whom he had met on the set of Graeme Clifford's film *Frances*. The couple would go on to have two children, Hannah Jane and Samuel Walker. Shepard's new play was *Fool for Love* (1983), about the tempestuous and incestuous relationship between siblings Eddie and Mary. It was made into a movie in 1985 with Shepard himself playing Eddie. The year 1985 was also the year of *A Lie of the Mind*, another family saga and Shepard's first play to premiere in New York since the early 1970s. A big-name cast and great reviews seemed to put Shepard once more in the theatrical public eye, but Shepard seemed more interested in his film career, after an Oscar nomination in 1983 for *The Right Stuff* and the positive reception of his screenplay for *Paris, Texas* in 1984. He was elected to the American Academy of Arts and Letters in 1986 and awarded its Gold Medal for Drama in 1992.

Shepard produced nothing new for the theater until 1991, with *States of Shock*, an absurdist response to the Persian Gulf War with all of its jingoism and false heroism. This was followed by *Simpatico*, for which Shepard struggled to find a producer and finally directed an unsuccessful production with the Public Theater in 1994. It related a tangled web of relationships and blackmail against a background of horse racing to show the unavoidable interrelationships that exist between people and their pasts. He also continued to collaborate on performance pieces with Chaikin; they had worked on *The War in Heaven* in the late 1980s, and in the 1990s on *When the World Was Green: A Chef's Fable*, but Chaikin's failing health restricted production. Throughout the 1990s, Shepard continued to balance theater with a successful film career. In 1994 his mother died.

In 1995 Shepard substantially revised *Buried Child* for a new performance by Chicago's Steppenwolf Theater, which successfully transferred to New York in 1996 and marked Shepard's first appearance on Broadway. In 1996, the Signature Theater dedicated a whole season to Shepard, for which he wrote a revised version of *Tooth of Crime*, subtitled *Second Dance*. In 1998 *Eyes for Consuela*, based on Octavio Paz's short story "The Blue Bouquet," was produced. It explored the problematical nature of love through its relation of an encounter between an American traveler and a Mexican bandit. The year 2000 saw *The Late Henry Moss*, another play about problematic father-son relationships, premiering at the Magic Theatre with an all-star cast, then opening in New York the following year. Shepard continues to successfully balance careers in both film and the theater. His latest play, *God of Hell* (2004), is a political piece about a cattle-raising couple harassed by a government official.

PLOT DEVELOPMENT

Set in a dilapidated family home in Illinois farm country, *Buried Child* begins with the lights rising to show Dodge, wrapped in a blanket, staring at a silent television. In his seventies, he is momentarily roused by the sound of rain and drinks from a bottle of whiskey he hides under the sofa cushions. Beginning to cough, he stops as his wife, Halie, calls down from upstairs. Asking if he needs a pill, she mentions that it is un-Christian, and we realize she is suggesting he commit suicide to put himself out of his misery. She remains offstage as they shout to each other about the rain, television, and horse racing. She recalls a trip she took with a man before she and Dodge met, when she won money on the horse races, but shuts up when Dodge questions whether she slept with him.

Halie tells him their eldest son, Tilden, is in the kitchen should he need anything, and another son, Bradley, will be coming over later to cut his hair. She is meeting Father Dewis, a local minister, for lunch. Dodge is upset because last time Bradley cut his hair while he was asleep, and did a bad job. She insists Tilden will protect him, but Dodge holds little respect or feeling for either son. Dodge calls for Tilden, who enters with arms full of corn and stares at his father while Dodge coughs. Tilden says he picked the corn outside, but Dodge says this is impossible because he has not planted corn in over 30 years, and tells him to put it back from wherever he took it. Tilden dumps the corn in Dodge's lap.

In his forties, Tilden has come home because of some trouble in New Mexico. He goes to get a stool to sit on while he shucks the corn, and Dodge takes another swig of whiskey. Tilden returns and talks about having been lonely in New Mexico, asking for some whiskey as he shucks corn and leaves the husks strewn on the floor. Dodge refuses as Halie calls again, wanting to know what Tilden is doing. Tilden refuses to answer. Halie warns Dodge not to let Tilden drink and mentions he has been in jail. We learn Tilden used to be an All-American but has fallen down since then, and Bradley is an amputee, having chopped off his own leg with a chainsaw. Halie talks about another son, Ansel, now dead, whom she views as the only one to show promise.

Halie finally enters, dressed in black. The men sit as she talks disjointedly about Ansel—playing basketball, being a soldier, and dying on his honeymoon with his Catholic wife. Jealous of the wife she says cursed him, Halie seems to have deeply loved Ansel. She notices the mess, gets worried by Dodge's crazy-sounding speech, and is bemused by Tilden's insistence that there is corn outside—she has seen none from her window. She demands he tell them where he got it from. He says the back lot and cries when she threatens to kick him out of the house. Dodge defends him and he and Halie argue. She gets upset as Dodge speaks disparagingly about Bradley, and cryptically announces, "He's not my flesh and blood! My flesh and blood's buried in the back yard!" and swiftly leaves, telling him to keep close watch on Tilden.

Tilden tells Dodge he should not have said what he did, and Dodge refuses to talk further. Tilden warns him if he does not talk, he will cease to exist, so Dodge criticizes him for coming back home. Tilden goes back outside, but Dodge begins a coughing fit for which he needs medication. Once Dodge is subsided, Tilden suggests he sleep and promises to stay. As Dodge falls asleep while recalling getting the game ball at a baseball match, Tilden steals his whiskey, covers his father with the corn husks, then leaves. Bradley, on a wooden leg, clumsily enters, and, taking off Dodge's baseball cap, proceeds to cut his father's hair. The sound of the electric clippers mingles with that of the rain.

Act 2 begins later that night, while still raining. The mess has been cleared, Dodge still sleeps, and Tilden's son, Vince, arrives on the porch with his girlfriend, Shelly. Vince is on edge and annoyed at Shelly for making fun of his family home. He has been away for six years. He calls but gets no response and enters; neither notices Dodge. Shelly puts on Dodge's cap, while Vince goes to look upstairs. Dodge wakes and takes his cap as Shelly backs away nervously. She explains how she and Vince have stopped by on their way to New Mexico to see Tilden. Vince joins them, and Dodge initially acts as if his grandson is Tilden, then seems not to know who Vince is. When Vince asks where Halie is, Dodge grows increasingly threatening and looks for his whiskey. He insults Shelly, who wonders if they have the wrong house, and tries to leave, but is stopped by Vince. Tilden enters, his arms full of carrots.

Dodge shouts at Tilden for taking his whiskey, but Tilden is unresponsive. When Shelly asks Tilden if he recognizes Vince, he replies, "I had a son once but we buried him." Dodge tells him to shut up, saying this happened before he was born. Shelly offers to take the carrots, and handing them over, Tilden suggests they cook them. Dodge asks Vince to buy him more whiskey, and Vince tries to get him to lie down. Dodge refuses, pointing out that bad things happen when you lie down—including his hair, and murdering of children. Shelly suggests Vince get the whiskey, and he gets angry, trying to knock the carrots down. Tilden brings a knife and a stool, and in defiance of Vince, Shelly sits and prepares the carrots while Dodge and Tilden watch. Vince tries to get them to recognize him, but both seem oblivious.

Vince decides to get Dodge his whiskey, taking the two dollars he offers. Shelly is nervous, but stays when he leaves. She talks to Tilden, who seems to want to tell her something. He asks to touch her rabbit-fur coat, and she gives it to him. He puts it on and recalls a youth when he felt more liberated, then he tells Shelly about Dodge drowning a baby. Dodge tries to quiet him and falls helplessly on the floor. Tilden ignores him, adding that no one knows why Dodge killed the baby or where he buried it, then offers Shelly her coat back. She is too stunned to take it. Bradley enters, takes the coat, aggressively asks who Shelly is, and wonders if she is with Tilden. He belittles his brother, who runs away. Fearful of Bradley, Shelly suggests they help Dodge, but Bradley suggests killing him instead. Seeing himself in charge, he orders Shelly to open her mouth and puts his fingers inside. Then he drops her coat over Dodge's head.

Act 3 begins in the morning. The rain has stopped. Bradley is asleep on Dodge's sofa under his blanket, his wooden leg removed, while Dodge sits weakly on the floor. Shelly brings him a cup of broth, which he refuses. He thinks Vince is not coming back, though she insists he will. Feeling like this is her house, she questions Dodge about the family pictures she saw in Halie's room, where she slept the night, after escaping from Bradley. Dodge refuses to be drawn and talks only of corpses and graves. She asks about the baby, but he changes the subject. He begs Shelly to stay as he hears Halie returning.

Halie is now dressed in yellow, even carrying yellow roses, and Father Dewis is with her. Both are tipsy and joke on the porch before coming in, while Dodge hides under Shelly's coat. Halie enters, moves the coat to cover Bradley's wooden leg, and when Dodge complains, takes the blanket off Bradley for him. Bradley wakes and tries to get the blanket back, but obeys Halie when she stops him. She asks Shelly, who sits quietly drinking Dodge's broth, what she is doing, and threatens her. Halie flirts with Dewis, who feels increasingly uncomfortable here, drinks from his flask, and talks about a commemorative statue being made of Ansel, while berating the nation's current youth. Speaking of the importance of belief, she throws a rose at Dodge. Shelly rises to explain why she is there, but Halie appears uninterested and is more worried where Tilden might be.

Bradley grabs the blanket and returns to the sofa as Dodge and Halie shout at him. Annoyed no one is paying her any attention, Shelly smashes her cup. Bradley suggests she is a prostitute, so she retrieves her coat and takes his leg. As Bradley weakly whimpers, Halie angrily asks Dewis to intervene. He tries to calm Shelly, but she threatens them, saying she knows they have a secret. Dodge offers to confess, despite Bradley and Halie wanting him to stop and Shelly's reluctance to listen. He tells how their farm used to be prosperous and that they had enough boys when Halie got pregnant again, six years after he had stopped sleeping with her. She gave birth, and unsettled at the way Tilden was spending time with the boy, Dodge killed it.

As Halie complains to Bradley for not stopping Dodge from telling, Vince crashes onto the porch, drunk, and begins smashing bottles while singing the Marine Battle Hymn. He imagines he is in a battle. Dodge and Halie both acknowledge their grandson, Dodge demands his money back, and Vince pretends he does not know them. Halie asks Dewis again for help, but he feels out of his depth. Bradley tries to grab Vince, but misses. Shelly declares her need to leave, but Vince will not let anyone out. He pulls a knife and starts to cut the porch screen. Dewis drops the roses next to the wooden leg and takes Halie upstairs, as she happily reminisces about Vince as a baby.

Vince climbs inside onto the sofa, through the hole he has cut, and pushes Bradley to the floor. Shelly has gone outside and looks in, watching Bradley crawl after his leg as Vince knocks it away and smells the roses. Dodge declares his last will and testament, leaving the house and contents to Vince, his carpentry tools to Tilden, and asking that his body be burned on a fire made from his farming equipment. Shelly insists they leave but Vince wants to stay. He had driven all night, not intending to come back, but had a vision of his family connection and returned. Shelly leaves. Vince tosses Bradley's leg offstage to send him after, and he takes the blanket as he passes. Dewis comes to ask Vince to help Halie, but Vince send him packing, saying no one is in the house.

Dodge has died, so Vince covers him with the blanket and roses, then lays himself on the sofa, ignoring all that next takes place as the lights fade. From offstage, Halie speaks to Dodge about the vegetables she now sees growing outside, suggesting the rain has brought them on. Tilden appears, muddy and carrying a child's corpse, which he takes upstairs, as Halie wonders about the relationship of rain, growth, and the sun outside, and the stage turns dark.

CHARACTER DEVELOPMENT

Shepard's quasi-autobiographical collection of fiction, *Motel Chronicles* (1982), recounts a cross-country trip he made when he was 19 to visit the Illinois home of his grandparents. He later drew on this experience for *Buried Child*, and Vince is an alter ego of the playwright, reflecting his own ambivalence toward family and upbringing. His characters are not direct portraits, but his grandparents had been plain dirt farmers, Dodge was a family name, and Shepard had an uncle with a wooden leg like Bradley. Scholar Stephen Bottoms talks of the "sadomasochistic vacuum" of the Dodge family existence (164). They all need each other, and because of this, they can express only contempt for one another. Family life becomes intensely competitive as each needs to talk and is unable to find anyone who will listen. Shelly, as an outsider, becomes the necessary ear to facilitate their speech, but what she uncovers is not pretty.

Unwilling to move on, Dodge tries to deny the possibility of new growth, even as Tilden covers him with the corn he has picked. Dodge's drinking is a classic reaction to guilt, as a person attempts to obliterate the memory of his or her past with alcohol. Dodge has become a parody of the patriarch, with his baseball cap crown, sofa throne, and blanket mantle, over which the younger generations fight. His sons battle weakly, having lost their promise and seeming almost as debilitated as their father.

What Dodge has done—drown his wife's illegitimate child—we do not learn until near the close of the play. There is an implication that the child may have been the result of an incestuous relationship between Ansel and Halie, who seems to have idolized her youngest son. She fondly recalls how he kissed her, and how she was devastated by his marriage to another, after which he soon died. It is more likely, however, that the father was Tilden, who was so solicitous of the child while it lived, and talks of having lost a son. Some critics have suggested there is an uncertainty about Ansel's reality, thinking he may be Halie's creation to help her deal with all that has happened, but Bradley and Dewis both seem to recall him, although Bradley questions his mother's idealization of him.

Halie's emotional estrangement from her family is shown both by what she says and by the fact that she frequently speaks from offstage, creating as great a distance from her family as possible. Her black garb at the start suggests mourning, and she talks at length about her dead son, Ansel, but it is more than he for whom she mourns. Her change to yellow clothing and the armful of yellow roses she carries in the final act contribute to the possibility of hope as the burden of death seems to have lightened, but Halie is drunk and ends the play offstage as she began, so progress remains ambiguous. Also, yellow could represent not happiness but the jealousy that lies at the heart of this family's difficulties. Dodge has never trusted his wife, and their sons have been made to compete with one another for attention.

Dodge's oldest son, Tilden, displays no current affection for his parents or for his own son, Vince, but his care for the land and the dead son seems to have rejuvenated the farmland. It is he who embraces the body of the buried child, by which action he acknowledges the family crime, allowing them to move on. Tilden originally liked to travel, enjoying the flight of a fast car ride and moving to New Mexico to escape the family; however, he ended up lonely and in trouble, and came home to find roots, just as Vince now does. Although both Dodge and Halie suggest Tilden is useless and needs constant watching, it seems less about what he does than about what they fear he might do. When

Dodge leaves Tilden his carpentry tools, it implies a possibility that he recognizes Tilden as a potential savior of this family.

Bradley, Dodge's next son, tries to dominate his father by cutting Dodge's hair, but is displaced in turn by Vince, who throws away Bradley's false leg (indicative of Bradley's own impotence) and takes Dodge's place on the sofa, which Bradley had tried to inhabit. Each of Bradley's attempts to dominate end in failure with him whimpering for aid. Dodge wills Vince his house, land, and furnishings, disinheriting his own sons in preference for a grandson he hardly knows, and one assumes this can only be a decision based on spite. The only inheritance he leaves Bradley is shown in Bradley's inability to feel appropriate emotional responses—thus he intimidates his father and symbolically molests Shelly by sticking his fingers in her mouth. Tilden too is silently abusive toward his father, and his play with Shelly's coat can be read as a kind of rape.

Vince left this "home" at 16, and this is his first return in six years, echoing the six years Dodge had not slept with his wife before she had her final child, which links Vince to the symbolism of the unearthed child at the close: Vince too had been lost to the family but is now restored. To his annoyance, Dodge and Tilden affect not to recognize Vince when he first arrives, and this has been his greatest fear—that he will be neither remembered nor accepted by the family. He had planned to leave, but after his vision of connection decides to stay and rebuild the farm—in taking Dodge's place on the sofa after his death, Vince clearly takes on the role of leader of this household, though without Dodge's "crown" and "mantle," for Vince wants to start afresh.

When Vince thoughtlessly leaves his girlfriend without protection, Shelly is manipulated by Tilden, Dodge, and Bradley, who play out a competitive game of confession and hostility toward each other and her. But Shelly survives and even shows an ability to care as she tries to understand their strange behavior and slowly draw out the truth. Shelly's wearing of Dodge's cap, her impulse to call him "Grandfather," and the feeling that she somehow belongs in this house suggest a potential female connection here, but like Halie, she remains on the periphery, for this is a male kingdom. She leaves at the close, suggesting that possibilities do lie elsewhere, and this may not be the whole picture.

THEMES

Shepard depicts three generations of a family within a home in which the furnishings and the family seem equally worn. The dark secrets this family keeps subvert the myth of small-town wholesomeness and show how

Shepard views the American agrarian ideal. The characters' bizarre behavior and outwardly exaggerated defects symbolize inner psychological defects and archetypal generational conflicts, which have shaped their lives. We watch how the family farm passes from one generation to the next and goes through cycles of decay and regeneration. The play also tells a mythic family story of guilt and betrayal in which the older generations have abdicated their responsibility, handing down an inheritance of emotional sterility that the younger generation needs to recognize, understand, and transcend.

This family constantly argues over minor things to avoid having to face their own failures and complicities. The number of times characters cover themselves or each other with blankets, coats, or corn husks symbolizes the extent to which all are complicit in hiding from the truth, and each other. This is a family so buried in guilt they have lost the power to communicate even on a daily basis. And as Tilden warns, if you stop talking, you cease to exist. Halie's infidelity (past and present) and Dodge's drinking have greatly contributed to the family's breakdown, and they should bear the brunt of the guilt. Dodge is evidently worn out from the start, a picture of ill health, showing how the effects of guilt wear a person down until there is hardly anyone left. His impotence (and eventual death) is evident from his prone positions throughout the play and his burial under Tilden's corn husks.

Shepard uses doubling to underline his themes, both in character and plot, to create a tangled web of relationships. The concept of the son's return is repeated several times. It implies the possibility of a return to a simpler past, the initial Edenic vision of America, which seems natural to seek on a farm. The first son to return is Tilden, a high school sporting star just like his father had been, who subsequently lost his way, went wandering, lived in New Mexico for some years, then returns home to assuage his loneliness. He seems bewildered and out of touch with reality, but has reconnected to the land, discovering bumper crops in the back field. This is the field where Dodge has buried the child he killed, whom we can assume was the result of an incestuous relationship between Tilden and Halie. The blood of the dead child has seemingly nourished these crops, suggesting America's frontier promise rests on the blood of the innocent. Yet Tilden's obsession with what grows there also implies a renewed connection between him and his child, reinforced by Tilden entering at the close with the body of this dead son.

Tilden's earlier entrances with crops reflect on his final entrance with the corpse: all connect to suggest fertility and progress. Darkness and rain are replaced by bright sun; the rain, having created new growth, suggests that death can be replaced by new life. Significantly, the play takes place on a Sunday, and the epigraph from a poem by Pablo Neruda sets the scene for the conflation of human and vegetable growth we witness—as well as conjuring up images of decay and resurrection in its references to falling and flying. The "sun," which has brought out the crops, is echoed by the "son" Tilden carries in his arms at the close. If the buried child has been the source of the family curse, then its exhumation may signify the end of that curse and an expiation of the sins of the previous generation. The dead son whom the family has avoided and denied has been brought to light and faced, and the murderer, Dodge, has died, allowing the living son, Vince, to take charge with a clean slate.

The second son to return is Vince, who has also been absent for some years and who looks so like his father that Dodge even supposes he is Tilden at first. Vince also was a sporting hero at high school but has subsequently gone roving, we may assume to follow a musical muse, given the saxophone he carries. He too has become fearful of losing his roots and returns to check that connection. As his grandfather and father refuse to acknowledge him, he leaves, intending never to return. His second return is more forceful. Having had a vision on the road of a connection that transcends him as an individual, he comes to claim his place in the family line. However, there remains the danger that Vince will not follow the loving embrace Tilden represents at the play's close and may instead fall into the violent, unloving ways of his grandfather. He assumes Dodge's posture at the close and seems about to lose his partner, Shelly, who has left without him.

Shepard is deliberately ambiguous, balancing the myth of Osiris against that of Oedipus. In the myth of Osiris, often linked to the ritualized death of the corn king, the king dies to return the land to life with his sacrifice—so Dodge, the family patriarch, dies, and the new blood, Vince, inherits the land. Tilden brings in the child as an act of atonement, confronting past sins that can now be healed. These are images of renewal. But Shepard balances these against the story of Oedipus, in which son sleeps with mother to devastating effect, and in which Vince becomes the (grand)father-killer who may be doomed to repeat the mistakes of his forebears. His only real inheritance is that of inherent male violence, a violence he has exhibited out on the porch. He inherits not just the farm, but the emaciated corpse—a symbol (and warning) of the inevitable end of such violence. Family too remains ambiguous for Shepard, a site of potential love and/or betrayal, passion and/or violence; to grab the former, one must risk the latter, for in Shepard's world, the two cannot be separated.

HISTORICAL CONTEXT

Growing up in the 1950s, Shepard would have been open to the increasingly narrow gap between high and low culture and the trend toward expressionism that allowed the artist greater freedom to simply create. Art no longer demanded formal training or traditional form; it was simply an expression of self. On one level, Shepard's plays pretty much document contemporary American history since the counterculture rumblings of the 1960s. The Beat Generation, led by writer Jack Kerouac and poets Allen Ginsberg and Lawrence Ferlinghetti, with their drug-induced riffs on contemporary life, clearly had an influence, just as the rise of improvisational jazz, rock music, and movies in the national culture. Shepard's work is filled with subversive pop-culture images and grotesque satire of the society in which he grew up. The loners and drifters in his plays, each doppelgangers for Shepard himself, try to make sense of the detritus of American society and its unfulfilled potential.

As T. E. Kalem declared on reviewing *Buried Child*, "If plays were put in time capsules, future generations would get a sharp-toothed profile of life in the U.S. in the past decade and a half from the works of Sam Shepard" (146). Shepard's plays deal with how Americans have chosen to identify themselves in the latter half of the twentieth century, and the picture is not hopeful, being filled with images of alienation, miscommunication, and violence. His portraits are not without hope, but it is a kind that is very muted. He both celebrates and pines over the decay of many American national myths, including that ever-elusive American Dream. *Buried Child* is constructed around Shepard's take on numerous homegrown American myths, from the idealized agrarian life to the violence and alienation underpinning both patriarchal and frontier mentalities.

America's experimental theater circuit came to fruition in the 1960s at the start of Shepard's career, and his subsequent rise to stardom maps many of the developments of that theater. Dedicated to saving the American theater from stagnation, and in efforts to remain artistically apart from Broadway and Off-Broadway, the playwrights of Off-Off-Broadway and beyond have embraced many non-American theatrical forms and techniques. Shepard owes clear debts to European playwrights Luigi Pirandello, Harold Pinter, and Samuel Beckett, among others. But his plays, nevertheless, remain intensely American in his choice of character, theme, and subject, and maybe partly because of this, Shepard has become the best-known experimental dramatist in the United States.

LITERARY STYLE AND DEVICES

Buried Child is built on a classic theatrical topic—the intricate and changing relationships between family members seeking roots and a sense of identity—but it relays this in a distinctly postmodern fashion, with discontinuity, pastiche, and what seem to be unresolvable tensions. Disinterested in mainstream respect, Shepard uses this high-profile opportunity to show the mainstream what experimental drama is all about; there is a spontaneity and dark humor about his writing that are highly distinctive. This is not domestic realism, though more realistic than most of Shepard's earlier plays, but a careful blend of the surreal with the superreal to create an exciting kind of theater that has greatly influenced contemporary theater. The play has all the force of a mystery as the audience, along with Shelly, tries to unravel the secrets within Dodge's household, but it is also a mythic exploration of family guilt and betrayal, conveyed by a complex web of symbols.

Such items as the sofa, blanket, corn, baseball cap, rabbit-fur coat, wooden leg, and yellow roses all carry symbolic resonance that grows louder as they switch possession. Tilden's entrance with the dead child at the close has caused much controversy; some even view its ambiguity as a representation of the contemporary confusion of American life. The child's symbolic value is simultaneously negative and positive, representing both the unpleasant past and a hopeful future, with Tilden willingly embracing the horror. The cumulating litter of the set in each act is a comment on the messiness of life itself. The characters' actions often seem brutal and without meaning, until we get enough information to put them into context and they begin to resonate. None of these relationships have evolved in a vacuum, but each is tied to past experience. Vince's aggressive stance, as he delights in smashing his bottles and slashing through the porch screen, echoes the violence underpinning Dodge and Bradley's words and actions, and reflects, for Shepard, the frustration of the American male with the loss of the romantic pioneering frontiers through which they had formerly proven their manhood.

Like Arthur Miller, Shepard is similarly fascinated with issues of betrayal and guilt and the inevitably related issues of blame and responsibility. He too sees the American tendency toward denial as self-destructive and suggests that it is better for people to accept their guilt in order for life to go on. But he does so in a very different fashion. In *Buried Child* the fragmentation of character and speech we witness points to the psychological fragmentation these family members have experienced, having been raised in such an abusive home. Expressionistic exaggerations of character, event, and behavior result in an almost gothic sense of horror, although the set is intentionally naturalistic by contrast. Vince and Shelly's arrival is the needed catalyst to reveal what has too long been buried, having seemingly seeped into the groundwater to destroy the fertility of the land itself for the past decades. But the land reasserts itself, and the crops spring up, without any planting, and the world outside this barren household teems with new life. It suggests the potency of the agrarian roots of America's past, which have not been lost, but remain vibrant once acknowledged.

The influence of jazz and rock music is clear in much of Shepard's work, not just in the songs he included in his earlier work, but in his use of a stage language that is assertively edgy and jumpy as a rock lyric, full of jargon and argot. Aside from a rare speech such as Vince's monologue of discovery, Shepard tries to go beyond conveying direct thoughts or ideas to creating a sequence of images—speaking to the eye and ear before the mind. The disjunction in *Buried Child* seems to increase as the play progresses, with act 3 almost dissolving into chaos, because that is the nature of life. Shepard asks for a setting in which the stairs lead into darkness, the television has no sound (or picture that the audience can see), and we hear constant offstage rain in the first two acts—all is meant to keep the audience guessing and on edge. He provokes the audience to find meaning through such vivid gestures and his elusive symbolism, finally taunting our need for firm answers by refusing to provide any. His revised version eradicates some of the play's ambiguity, but retains plenty of uncertainty as to the best way to live life in a culture addicted to nostalgia, violence, and secrecy.

SITUATION OF WORK

Shepard established his career through Off-Off-Broadway and was one of America's first major playwrights to come so far from the fringe. His career has had its ups and downs, but since his 1964 debut at Theatre Genesis, his work has led the Off-Off-Broadway, regional, and university theater circuits. Despite rare Broadway appearances, he has worked with most of America's leading directors and actors. His increasing connection to films, as with David Mamet, shows the growing contemporary connection between film and stage, as each brings the techniques of one genre to the other. Although acknowledging that Shepard is not the only American postmodern playwright, theater scholar Matthew Roudané views Shepard as "the preeminent playwright of the postwar American theatre" (5) and suggests that Shepard "conferred upon the American stage its modernity in the 1960s" and "interjected a youthful, exuberant, and experimental voice that extended our appreciation of a postmodern aesthetic" (1). Shepard had a string of provocative experimental plays through the 1960s and 1970s, but it was not until *Buried Child*, with its 1979 Pulitzer Award, that his talents were fully acknowledged. This remains a defining play of his oeuvre, which consists of more than 50 stage plays and screenplays.

Buried Child is fundamentally American in its embedded allusions to numerous well-known American family plays from Eugene O'Neill to Edward Albee. Like O'Neill's *Long Day's Journey*, *Buried Child* deals with homecomings and the teasing out and revelation of family fears and secrets that have long contributed to that family's crippling emotional dysfunction. Both also have a woman at the center of this revelation. The dark elm trees outside the house link it to another O'Neill play—his tale of the gothic farming family in *Desire under the Elms*, with their incestuous secrets. Shepard also pays clear allegiance to Tennessee Williams (Halie, dissatisfied with her current life, disappointed in her husband, and hiding in remembrances of past beaus recalls several of Williams's heroines from Amanda Wingfield to Blanche duBois), Arthur Miller (like Biff Loman, Tilden is a high school football star who failed to live up to expectations, and here is a family like the Kellers, the Lomans, or the Carbones, who suffer from a secret long buried), and Edward Albee (with the same violent repartee culminating in infanticide we saw in *Virginia Woolf*), even while his work remains uniquely his own.

Alongside David Mamet, Shepard was one of the most significant and powerful voices in American theater during the 1970s and 1980s. In terms of style, Shepard seems the opposite of David Mamet, whose writing is taut, precise, and pared down to the bone. Shepard's writing, by contrast, follows each random impulse as he constructs plays out of disparate fragments, creating sprawling collages of imagery and spectacle. Yet both are provocative in their exposure of the failings of American culture. Like Mamet, Shepard also seems to balance his skepticism against hope. In *Buried Child*, the myths of Oedipus and Osiris battle it out with no clear winner, making it uncertain if the play is about inevitable destruction or potential rebirth; it is, of course, about both.

While Leslie Wade views Shepard as the "latest Great American Playwright" (1) of the twentieth century, in 1980 Stewart McBride quoted Martin Esslin as declaring "Sam Shepard *is* contemporary American theater" (B2). Richard Gilman, in an introduction to *Sam Shepard: Seven Plays* (1981), declares, "Not many critics would dispute the proposition that Sam Shepard is our most interesting and exciting playwright" (xi). Wade also points out that after *Buried Child*, Shepard was no longer a writer of the avant-garde, becoming instead one of the country's most widely produced playwrights. What is most striking in Shepard is his use of imagery and language in an atmosphere both satiric and tense, and the powerful myths behind his vision that he nostalgically embraces and cynically explodes.

CRITICAL RECEPTION

The play's initial six-week run, directed by Robert Woodruff, began June 27, 1978, at San Francisco's Magic Theatre, an environment friendly to Shepard's work. It was well received, and both a New York opening and a regional production at Yale Repertory were planned for the following year. The New York show had another limited run, this time three weeks, at Theater for the New City, a small Off-Off-Broadway theater. Success there led to the play being transferred to a larger Off-Broadway theater. It ran at Theatre de Lys for four months, then closed as audiences slackened off. The day after it had closed it was announced to have won a Pulitzer Award, which led to the production being revived at Circle Repertory Theater to run for another year. Given the conservative reputation of the Pulitzer committee, which had refused to consider Edward Albee's *Who's Afraid of Virginia Woolf?* for a prize because of its alleged indecency, it caused quite a stir when they awarded the Pulitzer to *Buried Child*. It brought Shepard immediate national media attention, and his work, cultural approval.

Reviews of the play were mostly positive; Jack Kroll described the play as having "a haunting, wounded beauty, strong, sweet, sad and totally dramatized" (147). Clive Barnes insisted that Shepard was "one of the most brilliant" of America's young dramatists at that time, and although he was uncertain if *Buried Child* was his best work, still it "has a certain clarity of construction and provenance to it that should secure it, at the very least, a useful place in the scholastic record" (148). There were some detractors, such as Walter Kerr, who attacked the play as an incohesive pretense at dramatic substance (D3). Douglas Watt disliked what he saw as its improbabilities and blurred vision, despite finding it a powerful work. But Shepard has often been problematic for critics, who are frequently uncertain how to respond. They recognize the power of his work, yet are distracted or repulsed by its brutality, grimness, and oddity.

In 1995 the Steppenwolf Theater, which had successfully revived Shepard's *True West* in 1982, decided to tackle *Buried Child*. The director, Gary Sinise, invited Shepard to rehearsals. Since Shepard had never been entirely happy with the play as originally written, he offered to revise the script to make the play more accessible. It transferred to Broadway in 1996, becoming Shepard's first Broadway production and drawing lavish praise from critics, including Ben Brantley, who declared it a "bona fide classic" and a "spectacularly funny revival" (475). In his revision, Shepard purposefully tried to eliminate some of the more disruptive ambiguous aspects of the prior script, to make paternity clearer and the whole family tale more credible. Dodge's recital of his will and Halie's remembrances of Ansel are truncated, and Vince's bewilderment at his family's refusal to recognize him is emphasized. It becomes clear that the father of the dead child is Tilden, and the themes of denial and responsibility are foregrounded, even while retaining the same essential plot.

SUGGESTED READINGS

Auerbach, Doris. *Sam Shepard, Arthur Kopit, and the Off-Broadway Theatre*. Boston: Twayne, 1982.

Barnes, Clive. "Menace, Mystery in Shepard's *Buried Child*." *New York Post*, December 6, 1978. *New York Theatre Critics' Review* 39 (1978): 148.

Bottoms, Stephen J. *The Theatre of Sam Shepard: States of Crisis*. Cambridge: Cambridge University Press, 1998.

Brantley, Ben. "A Home Where No One Finds Comfort." *New York Times*, October 9, 1995. *New York Theatre Critics' Review* 56 (1995): 475–76.

Coe, Robert. "The Saga of Sam Shepard." *New York Times Magazine*, November 23, 1980: 56–58, 118–24.

Coen, Stephanie. "Things at Stake Here." *American Theatre*, September 1996: 28.

Demastes, William W. "Understanding Sam Shepard's Realism." *Comparative Drama* 21.3 (fall 1987): 229–48.

DeRose, David. *Sam Shepard*. New York: Twayne, 1992.

Dugdale, John, ed. *File on Shepard*. London: Methuen, 1989.

Falk, Florence. "The Role of Performance in Sam Shepard's Plays." *Theatre Journal* 33 (May 1981): 182–98.

Gilman, Richard. Introduction. *Sam Shepard: Seven Plays*. By Sam Shepard. New York: Bantam, 1981: xi–xxvii.

Hart, Lynda. *Sam Shepard's Metaphorical Stages*. Westport, CT: Greenwood, 1987.

Kalem, T. E. "Crazy Farm." *Time*, December 18, 1978. *New York Theatre Critics' Review* 39 (1978): 146.

Kerr, Walter. "Sam Shepard: What's the Message?" *New York Times*, December 10, 1978: D3.

Kroll, Jack. "Bucking Bronco." *Newsweek*, October 30, 1978. *New York Theatre Critics' Review* 39 (1978): 147.

Marranca, Bonnie, ed. *American Dreams: The Imagination of Sam Shepard*. New York: Performing Arts Journal Publications, 1981.

McBride, Stewart. "Sam Shepard—Listener and Playwright." *Christian Science Monitor*, December 23, 1980: B2–3.

McGhee, Jim. *True Lies: The Architecture of the Fantastic in the Plays of Sam Shepard*. New York: Lang, 1993.

Mottram, Ron. *Inner Landscapes: The Theater of Sam Shepard*. Columbia: University of Missouri Press, 1984.

Nash, Thomas. "Sam Shepard's *Buried Child*: The Ironic Use of Folklore." *Modern Drama* 26.4 (1983): 486–91.

Orbison, Tucker. "Authorization and Subversion of Myth in Shepard's *Buried Child*." *Modern Drama* 37.3 (fall 1994): 509–20.

Oumano, Ellen. *Sam Shepard: The Life and Work of an American Dreamer.* New York: St. Martin's, 1986.

Patraka, Vivian M., and Mark Siegel. *Sam Shepard.* Boise, ID: Boise State University Press, 1985.

Perry, Frederick J. *A Reconstruction Analysis of* Buried Child *by Playwright Sam Shepard.* Lewiston, NY: Edwin Mellen, 1992.

Porter, Laurin. "Teaching *Long Day's Journey* and Shepard's *Buried Child*." *Eugene O'Neill Review* 25.1–2 (spring-fall 2001): 80–84.

Putzel, Steven. "Expectation, Confutation, Revelation: Audience Complicity in the Plays of Sam Shepard." *Modern Drama* 30 (June 1987): 147–60.

Rabilard, Sheila. "Sam Shepard: Theatrical Power and American Dreams." *Modern Drama* 30 (March 1987): 58–71.

Roudané, Matthew. *The Cambridge Companion to Sam Shepard.* New York: Cambridge University Press, 2002.

Schiff, Stephen. "Shepard on Broadway." *New Yorker,* April 22, 1996: 84.

Shepard, Sam. Fool for Love *and Other Plays.* New York: Bantam. 1984.

———. The Late Henry Moss, Eyes for Consuela, When the World Was Green: *Three Plays.* New York: Vintage, 2002.

———. *A Lie of the Mind.* New York: Plume, 1987.

———. *Motel Chronicles.* San Francisco, CA: City Lights, 1982.

———. *Sam Shepard: Seven Plays.* New York: Bantam, 1981.

Shewey, Don. *Sam Shepard.* 2nd ed. New York: Da Capo, 1997.

Smith, Michael. Rev. of *Cowboys* and *The Rock Garden,* by Sam Shepard. *Village Voice,* October 22, 1964: 13.

Stacy, James R. "Making the Grave Less Deep: A Descriptive Assessment of Sam Shepard's Revisions to *Buried Child*." *Journal of American Drama and Theatre* 9.3 (fall 1997): 59–72.

Su, Tsu-chung. "The Double in Sam Shepard's *Buried Child* and *True West*." *Studies in Language and Literature* 8 (December 1998): 65–83.

Taav, Michael. *A Body across the Map: The Father-Son Plays of Sam Shepard.* New York: Lang, 1999.

Tucker, Martin. *Sam Shepard.* New York: Continuum, 1992.

Wade, Leslie. *Sam Shepard and the American Theater.* Westport, CT: Greenwood, 1997.

Watt, Douglas. "Slightly Blurry Vision." *Daily News,* December 6, 1978. *New York Theatre Critics' Review* 39 (1978): 147.

Wilcox, Leonard, ed. *Rereading Shepard.* New York: St. Martin's, 1993.

Yim, Harksoon. "Myths Revisited: Sam Shepard's Fatalistic Vision in *Buried Child*." *Journal of Modern British and American Drama* 15.1 (April 2002): 237–58.

9

David Mamet
Glengarry Glen Ross
1984

BIOGRAPHICAL CONTEXT

Born on November 30, 1947, in Chicago, Illinois, to Leonore and Bernard Mamet, David Alan Mamet grew up alongside his sister, Lynn, in a Jewish enclave on Chicago's South Side. His mother, a teacher, divorced his father, a labor lawyer with a fascination for semantics, in 1958, when she decided to leave him for one of his colleagues. Mamet recalls his father at the dinner table, encouraging his children to use words more precisely. This early obsession with the nature of language would evolve into one of Mamet's greatest strengths as a playwright. After the divorce, Mamet gained a stepfather who would become a violent and abusive figure in the family's life, and a half brother, Tony. At 16, Mamet chose to live with his real father and attend private school, where he first took drama classes. During his high school years he worked as a busboy at the Second City comedy cabaret, where he soaked in more of the ways speech and action could be used to varying effect.

His early writing was all dialogue, so playwriting seemed a natural choice. Studying literature and drama at Goddard College in Plainfield, Vermont, he wrote his first play, a revue called *Camel*, to fulfill the thesis requirement. Taking a year off in 1968, Mamet studied acting at the Neighborhood Playhouse School of the Theatre in New York, under Sanford Meisner. Meisner was an original member of the Group Theatre and staunch advocate of Stanislavsky's method acting, whereby the actor is encouraged to develop a character from the inside out, which clearly influenced Mamet's technique. Mamet returned to Goddard to graduate in 1969, then took

a one-year position teaching at Marlboro College. One of the job requirements was to provide a play that could be produced. He wrote *Lakeboat,* a
one-act about life on board a freighter in the Great Lakes, which was staged
by his students in 1970.

Back in Chicago, Mamet took on a series of temporary jobs, including cab-
driver, short-order cook, factory worker, and real estate sales. In 1971 he returned
to Goddard College as drama instructor and artist-in-residence. Finding it easier
to write scenes for his students than search for suitable published ones, he
continued honing his dramatic skill. Forming an ensemble acting group, the
Saint Nicholas Company, with the best of his students, Mamet directed them
in modern classics and his own material.

Returning to Chicago in 1972, some of his plays, including *Duck Variations*
(1972), a series of vignettes featuring two old Jewish men sitting on a park
bench, and *Sexual Perversity in Chicago* (1974), were selected for production at
smaller experimental theaters. *Sexual Perversity,* featuring 34 scenes from the
sexually confused lives of swinging singles, gained Mamet recognition as the
winner of the Joseph Jefferson Award, given annually to the best new Chicago
play. Later in 1974, Mamet, along with William H. Macy and others, founded
the Saint Nicholas Players. They performed several Mamet plays, including
an early version of *American Buffalo,* which would become Mamet's breakthrough play, about three low-life city toughs plotting to steal a coin collection. It would become the first American play produced in England's National
Theatre. Although Mamet resigned from the Players in 1976 because of artistic differences, they would continue to produce his work.

All the while, Mamet had been submitting scripts to New York producers,
and in 1975 a double bill consisting of *Duck Variations* and *Sexual Perversity*
had been produced Off-Off-Broadway. This showcase led to an Off-Broadway
production that opened the following year. It ran for 273 performances and
was listed in *Time* as one of the 10 best plays of 1976. Meanwhile, in 1977,
a revised version of *American Buffalo* opened on Broadway, having gone
through a series of tryouts in Chicago and Off-Off-Broadway. All talk and
little plot, the play challenged people's expectations in the same way his
predecessor Edward Albee had done. Mamet admits to being influenced by
Albee, and in this play used the same small cast, claustrophobic setting,
apparently realistic surface built on a lie, and profane language witnessed in
Who's Afraid of Virginia Woolf? (1962). His highly stylized rendition of speech
has become a marked aspect of his dramatic work. The play's putatively naturalistic study of dialogue and character disturbed and delighted critics, who
recognized the play's characters as archetypes of modern man struggling for
survival in a hostile world full of misleading and destructive myths.

In 1976 Mamet had won an Obie for distinguished playwriting based on *Sexual Perversity* and *Buffalo*, and *Buffalo* then won the New York Drama Critics' Circle Award for Best Play in 1977. Such recognition secured Mamet a place in contemporary theater and a seeming license to continue his creation of a unique American theatrical language. The year 1977 also saw the transfer of *A Life in the Theater*, Mamet's treatise on the history of twentieth-century acting, from Chicago to Off-Broadway; Mamet's marriage to the actress Lindsay Crouse (with whom he would have two daughters, Willa and Zosia); and the offer of a teaching fellowship in drama at Yale University.

In 1978 Mamet was named associate director and playwright-in-residence of the Goodman Theatre in Chicago, and his second Broadway production, the joint bill of *The Water Engine* and *Mr. Happiness*, opened. *Water Engine*, about an inventor who discovers how to run an engine on water and is subsequently destroyed by big business, had initially been broadcast on National Public Radio in 1977. *Mr. Happiness* is a monologue by a self-righteous and unhelpful male agony aunt. Several plays and the first of his screenplays would swiftly follow, to varying success, but they would consolidate Mamet's growing reputation. Some earlier plays were reproduced, and others were performed at regional theaters or in New York, varying with the expected response. They include *The Woods* (1977), about a couple having communication problems on vacation in a remote family cottage, *Lone Canoe* (1979), an exploration of the myth of the noble red man, and *Edmond* (1982), an allegorical tale of self-discovery, which won another Obie, as well as a series of one-acts, the most performed being *Reunion* (1976), *Dark Pony* (1977), and *The Sanctity of Marriage* (1979), the first two depicting relationships between fathers and daughters, and the latter between a married couple about to separate.

Glengarry Glen Ross, Mamet's most successful play, was first produced in London in 1983 under the guidance of British playwright Harold Pinter, another clear influence, and it won the Olivier Award. It moved to Broadway in 1984 and won, among others, New York Drama Critics' Circle, Dramatists Guild, and Pulitzer awards. Telling a story of dehumanizing, materialistic American business, it follows the exploits of a group of real estate agents, based on some of Mamet's own experiences working in a sleazy real estate office that tried to sell worthless tracts of land to old people who could scarcely afford it. More short plays followed, including monologues, sketches, one-acts, and children's plays, which continued to explore Mamet's fascination with the relationship between language and character. He also added to his oeuvre a number of television plays, screenplays, and several adaptations of Anton Chekhov's major plays.

In 1988 audiences were treated to another longer play, *Speed-the-Plow*, which satirizes the Hollywood film industry, and won Mamet his first Tony Award.

In 1991, he divorced Crouse and married Scottish actress Rebecca Pigeon, with whom he later had another daughter, Clara. His next play, *Oleanna* (1991), caused quite a sensation with its controversial study of sexual harassment and power relationships between a student and her professor. Mamet continues to experiment, such as in *The Cryptogram* (1994), which relates its partially autobiographical story of the emotional abuse a young child faces in a family breaking apart from the point of view of the 10-year-old protagonist. It won Mamet another Obie. *The Old Neighborhood* (1997), set in Chicago, also dipped into Mamet's abusive past in its portrayal of a man returning to his roots, and *Boston Marriage* (1999), in its exploration of close female relationships from late Victorian times, counters critical opinion that Mamet only writes good parts for men. His most recent stage creation has been an adaptation of Christopher Marlowe's sixteenth-century classic, *Dr. Faustus* (2004).

Mamet has also had possibly the greatest success of any contemporary playwright within television and film, contributing episodes to NBC's *Hill Street Blues* and *L.A. Law*, and screenplays for hit movies from *The Verdict* (1982) and *The Untouchables* (1987) to *Hoffa* (1992) and *Wag the Dog* (1997). *Vanya on 42nd Street* (1994) was an insightful adaptation of Chekhov's *Uncle Vanya*, depicted as if during a rehearsal of the original play, with additional dialogue by Mamet, and showing Mamet's evident feeling of connection to his fellow naturalist. There is also the movie version of *Glengarry Glen Ross* (1992; to which Mamet added the character Blake) and films of other plays, including *The Water Engine* (1992), *Oleanna* (1994), and *American Buffalo* (1996), for which he provided screenplays. Mamet, too, has directed his own movie material, including *House of Games* (1987), *Homicide* (1991), *The Spanish Prisoner* (1997), *State and Main* (2000), *Heist* (2001), and *Spartan* (2004), most of which, in contrast to his plays, contain highly complex plots.

Author, too, of numerous novels, children's books, poetry, and essay collections, Mamet has been, and continues to be, amazingly prolific. His plays, especially, are finely nuanced and demand much skill from the actors involved. Committedly experimental and willing to risk failure, his body of work may seem uneven, but he was elected to the American Academy of Arts and Letters in 1994 and continues to push boundaries. His stylized dramas have significantly influenced contemporary American drama.

PLOT DEVELOPMENT

Prefaced by a sales maxim, "Always Be Closing," the play has Mamet indicating at once the perennial pressure on the characters he is about to introduce. If they are not closing, that is, completing a sale, then they will not last long in this capitalistic society. The play begins in the middle of a frantic discussion between aging salesman Shelly Levene and the younger office manager, John Williamson. They are in a Chinese restaurant across the road from their real estate office. Levene is trying to persuade Williamson to give him better leads—contact information for prospective customers—to help him make a sale; for if he does not improve, he will lose his job.

Some premium leads have been given to a younger salesman, Ricky Roma, who has been making sales, but Levene indicates Roma is wasting them, and he could do better. Williamson is unconvinced, for although Levene has done well in the past, lately he has done poorly, and he is not allowed to give premium leads to anyone not making sales. Williamson offers to sell Levene leads for cash and a percentage of his profit, and although Levene accepts, he has no money to pay up front, so the offer is retracted. Levene begs for the sake of his daughter, but Williamson ignores the plea and makes to go. Levene asks for just one lead, but Williamson refuses, and Levene has to be satisfied with the regular leads.

In another booth in the restaurant, fellow salesmen David Moss and George Aaronow are bitterly complaining about business. Like Levene, they too are in their fifties. Moss sympathizes with Aaronow, who has just lost a sale. They pass racist comments on various customer groups, reminisce about better times, and complain about this month's office competition, in which the leading salesman wins a Cadillac, and the two weakest get fired. They admire and envy another salesman, Jerry Graff, who bought his own leads and went into business for himself. Moss suggests they steal the leads to pay back the bosses, Mitch and Murray, for their callous treatment, and sell them to Graff. At first Aaronow is unsure how serious Moss is, but then Moss openly asks him to commit the robbery that evening, before the leads are moved, for a share of the profit. Aaronow is reluctant. Moss feels they will suspect him, having complained so much, so he needs someone else to do the job. To force Aaronow to help him, Moss tells him he will name him as an accomplice if he has to do it himself and gets caught.

In two more booths we see Roma and James Lingk. Each was by himself, but Roma has initiated a conversation to try and make a sale. Roma makes his pitch indirectly, philosophizing about life, buying Lingk a drink, and only then pulling out a map of Glengarry Highlands. Lingk hardly has a chance to speak as he gets sucked in.

Act 2 begins the next day in the ransacked office, with Detective Baylen investigating the robbery. Roma rushes in, panicked that thieves may have stolen contracts from deals he had closed, including one with Lingk. Williamson assures Roma he filed most of them, including Lingk's, which would win the competition for Roma. While Baylen goes off to talk to Williamson, Roma chats with Aaronow, who has lost all confidence as a salesman, and keeps asking whether they were insured. Roma tries to cheer Aaronow up, then assesses the damage to his own sales from the lost contracts and leads. He cannot phone anyone, as the telephones have been stolen, but Williamson wants him to continue working.

The detective plans to interview each of the salesmen, and Aaronow is nervous. To Roma's disgust, Williamson gives him older leads to try, but promises Murray will get any missing contracts re-signed. Levene enters in high spirits, declaring he just sold eight units of Mountain View to a couple all had thought a waste of time. They congratulate him as Aaronow is called in to be interviewed. Levene seems amazed at the burglary. Moss comes out from his interview in a foul temper, insulting Levene. Levene relates how he made his sale, and Roma gets Moss upset by pointing out how few sales he has made lately. Moss is uneasy about what Aaronow might be saying, angry at everyone, jealous of Roma's success, and storms off.

Roma gets Levene to continue his story, and Levene re-creates the whole scene. Roma compliments Levene, saying he has learned from him. Levene is skeptical but accepts the compliment. Feeling buoyed by success, Levene calls for more leads and tries to force praise from his manager. Williamson is unimpressed and tells Levene he will be surprised if the sale sticks. Levene insults him, suggesting he knows nothing about sales, and recounts more of his past experiences to show what he has achieved. Williamson is more worried about how Mitch and Murray, his bosses, are taking the burglary.

Roma sees Lingk approaching and asks Levene to pretend to be a client to distract him in case Lingk tries to cancel their deal. They create a smoke-screen, which includes Roma having to take Levene to the airport and accompany him out of town. Lingk finally gets a chance to declare that his wife wants the sale cancelled. Roma offers various excuses as to why that is a bad idea and promises to talk the following week. Lingk refuses, knowing they have only three days to get their money back. Roma tries to fool him over the timing, saying the check has not been cashed. Baylen has finished interrogating Aaronow, who barges in incensed by his treatment, and Baylen asks for Levene. Levene tries not to let Lingk see this means him, and goes in with the detective, while Williamson insists Aaronow calm down in front of a client. Aaronow leaves to find Moss.

Spurred on by fear of his wife, Lingk is not accepting Roma's delays and talks of calling the state attorney if his money is not refunded. Baylen interrupts, asking for Roma to come in. Roma desperately tries to get Lingk to stay with the deal, pretending friendship and saying the deal is off to give him more time to turn Lingk around. He suggests going for a drink, but before they can leave,

Baylen calls for him again. Lingk gets nervous realizing the police are there, and Williamson, misinterpreting this, assures him his contract was sent and check cashed. Lingk leaves, asking Roma to forgive him. Roma scathingly turns on Williamson for losing him the deal, before he goes to be interviewed.

Levene takes the opportunity to criticize Williamson further, but says too much. Williamson notices Levene tells him off for making something up to help Roma. He realizes the only way Levene could have known the contract had not been sent was if he had been the one who robbed the office. Williamson offers to stay quiet if Levene tells him where the leads are. Levene tells Williamson he sold them to Graff through Moss; Williamson, realizing the leads are lost, goes to turn him in. Levene offers all the money he received, plus half his future earnings, but Williamson refuses. He does not like Levene, and tells him that his deal that morning was fake; the couple have no money and just like talking to salesmen.

Roma returns, complaining about events, but offering to team up with Levene, saying he likes the way he backed him up. Saying he will meet him at the restaurant when Levene is taken back into the office, Roma then lets Williamson know he plans to use Levene to make more sales and take half his commission. Aaronow comes back to ask if they have found the burglar, and Roma tells him he does not know as he heads back to the restaurant where the play began. Aaronow sits, declaring, "Oh, God, I hate this job."

CHARACTER DEVELOPMENT

The play introduces us to a collection of real estate salesmen, each totally preoccupied with work. Any semblance of private life has been eradicated—these men are defined by what and how they sell. They sell worthless scraps of land by lying, bullying, and appealing to their customers' most negative emotions, from greed to feelings of inadequacy. Levene twice mentions his daughter as a final attempt to promote sympathy for his plight from Williamson, and both times the reference is not even acknowledged. A humane response is impossible for people who no longer recognize each other's humanity. All they are concerned with is being the best salesman on the block, regardless of whomever they have to tread on to get there, and Levene is no exception.

Levene is in his fifties and losing his edge. Like Willy Loman, he continually harps on how well he has done in the past, while his current sales are nonexistent; he is not even on the board that shows what each salesman has sold that month. Also, like Willy, it is hard to say if Levene's recollections are anything more than exaggerations. Roma appears to like him, twice suggesting he can learn something from him, but by the close we can see this is just another of Roma's deceptions; he will be friendly to Levene only for as long as he feels Levene might be of use to him. By the close of the play Levene is a broken man, no longer even having the capacity to pull off a simple burglary without giving himself away.

Dave Moss, we suspect, will remain combative whatever happens, strengthened by his hatred and envy. He is, throughout, an openly embittered man. Ironically, although he is the criminal mind who initiates the robbery, tries to blackmail Aaronow, and cheats Levene on the eventual sale of the leads, he is possibly the most honest when it comes to what he says. He never pretends friendship, is an out-and-out bigot, and shows undisguised antagonism to everyone. It is hard to sympathize with someone so callous and brutal, and there is some satisfaction in knowing Levene sells him out, and Moss will be charged as an accessory. Aaronow is a gentler version of Moss, less brutal and consequently a less successful salesman, though maybe a little more likeable. He hates his job and seems on edge throughout the play, even though he does nothing wrong. His future looks bleak, as he has lost his confidence to sell and cannot last long in this cutthroat world.

It is implied that Williamson got the job as office manager through nepotism, and his inexperience certainly lets Roma down as he ruins his chance of a deal with Lingk, but he is savvy enough to know from the start that Levene's deal was a fake. The fact that he gave a lead to Levene, which he knew would go this way, shows how much he has detested Levene from the start. He has no patience with the older man who is no longer an effective salesman, offering civility only to Roma, who brings in the goods.

The lonely, henpecked Lingk is a figure of pathos. He even apologizes to Roma for refusing to be duped by him, so desperate is he for the friendship Roma pretends. It is no wonder the Romas of the world can be so successful given that so many people like Lingk exist. They hope for the great deal but are too timid to think for themselves, leaving them prey to anyone with a stronger personality.

Detective Baylen, as a representative of the law, is someone who shows little respect to individuals, and certainly no compassion. He treats all of the salesmen harshly, regardless of their innocence or guilt, and nearly every one comes away from his interview/interrogation incensed by the way he has been grilled. Levene, ironically, since it is he who did the burglary, is the only exception. His own guilt, perhaps, makes him calmly acquiesce to whatever Baylen insists.

James Lingk is the only other character here who is not a salesman. Clearly desperate for friendship and henpecked by his wife, he even apologizes to Roma as he pulls out of a deal he knows was shady. If such men are part of the general public, then no wonder these salesmen have been able to rule the roost for so long. However, the fact that all the salesmen complain that sales are getting harder suggests that times are indeed changing, and the capitalist movement may be on its way out.

Mitch and Murray, two men on the next rung up in the company, are talked about but never seen. They are as faceless as they are careless of the men who work for them. Their judgment is based entirely on the bottom line, and even Williamson is fearful of their anger when things go wrong. The threat of instant unemployment they constantly offer is what spurs on most of these characters to sell, with the possible exception of Roma.

Youthful and handsome, Roma is in a different league from his colleagues, with a personal style and flair that are attractive but insidious. While the others need to talk about past conquests and dream about increasing their current sales, he gets on and makes those sales. His friendly chat with Lingk quickly turns to business, and he soon persuades him to invest in property. When Lingk comes to the office to cancel the deal on his wife's insistence, Roma tries every trick he can to prevent him from pulling out, resorting to a series of lies, including professing to Lingk that he values friendship over business. This is just a pretense of human compassion designed to allay Lingk's fears and keep him on board, and Roma nearly succeeds, were it not for Williamson's unwitting interference.

When Levene pleads with Williamson for better leads to help him recover from his slump, Williamson is unmoved. Like his bosses, he is interested only in sales and not with the messy humanity of the men who do the selling. Indeed, it becomes swiftly evident that the business response necessarily cancels out the human in the dealings of all of these people. Even the supposed friendship and mutual admiration indicated between Levene and Roma is undercut, from both sides. At the start Levene is telling Williamson that Roma is wasting leads, and by the close Roma is planning on using Levene to make more sales and take half of his commission.

THEMES

Although there is a robbery about which there is some mystery as to the perpetrator, the play is not so much a whodunit as a why-he-dunit. Mamet explores the social and economic pressures that lead Levene and Moss to crime, and Roma to such deceitful lengths. Mamet throws us right into the center of a frantic discussion between salesman Shelley Levene and his office boss, John Williamson, to keep his audience as bewildered as someone like James Lingk, who falls prey to Roma. At its heart, *Glengarry* is a play about power, of all kinds and at all levels. It also explores the ways in which men seek power over one another in their striving to get ahead. Set in the all-male environment of a particularly male business world, the play also explores what it is to be a man, with the constant pressure of competition, in a world full of deceit and violence. It is a harrowing vision, revealing the depths of depravity to which men will go to survive: tricking people out of their savings, pretending friendship while sharpening the knife, and playing relentlessly on other people's emotions and potential weaknesses.

Mamet told the *New York Times:* "To me the play is about a society based on business ... a society with only one bottom line: How much money you make" (qtd. in Gussow 19). Thus he encapsulates the play's evident focus on the nature of capitalism, a movement Mamet believes has worn itself out. He draws heavily on the myth of the American Dream, and the play owes a clear debt to Arthur Miller's *Death of a Salesman* in the way it depicts the salesman figure as both victim and perpetrator in the moral corruption of a nation. The only difference is that Mamet's salesmen seem to have grown more cutthroat over the intervening 35 years. Mamet sees Americans, however much they deny it, as obsessed with wealth and the promise of getting something for nothing. This play depicts just how empty and dehumanizing such ambitions have become. For all of his talk about the beauty of moral relativism, for Roma it is a one-way street; while suggesting men like Lingk can get ahead by exploiting others, it is Roma doing all of the exploiting as he closes on a shady land deal. Salesmen are a unique breed, as Miller also showed, as their chatter deliberately creates alternate realities. But when they stop talking, the dream crumbles. By the end of the play, Levene is driven to silence and we are left with the image of Aaronow, too depressed to continue.

The characters create illusions not only for others, but also for themselves to try and bolster their spirits. They constantly blame other things—poor leads, customers, land, and management—to cover up their own ineffectiveness. Levene and Roma, especially, like to play roles, and both feel freed by their desire to sell from owing any allegiance to the truth. Levene cannot accept the fact that he is old and cannot sell anymore, and is constantly trying to create his next sale. Roma, meanwhile, explains the soft-sell illusion he creates, where he pretends he is not a salesman and the land is not worthless, and comes close to believing his own sales pitch. The audience is also continually deluded, as Mamet misdirects them to believe the wrong man stole the leads, that Levene actually sells something, and that Roma's contracts have gone through.

Driven by an uninhibited competitive spirit they see as key to democratic capitalism, these salesmen rationalize every deceit that might close a sale, distorting language and ethical principles to justify what they do. They are selling themselves as well as the land, manipulating people's obsession with the American Dream of a Promised Land to generate more sales. Mamet wants us to know that such selling takes a heavy toll on the human spirit, and a total preoccupation with self-interest inevitably leads to an amoral society. When selling defeats them, men like Dave Moss and Levene resort to crime. Levene cannot even do this efficiently, and when his crime is discovered, he is utterly defeated.

The salesmen deal with a very American vision: the Promised Land—the idea of unspoiled territory just waiting to be grabbed. Land has a sense of permanence and solidity, which offers greater hope and promise than stocks and commodities; it can almost be seen as romantic. Yet in this play such a vision only brings out people's greed. The world of *Glengarry* is a cold one in which those that have, receive more, and the have-nots are discarded without compunction. But as drama scholar Christopher Bigsby points out, *Glengarry* is more than an attack on American business ethics, it also explores people's will to believe, an impulse Bigsby suggests Mamet sees as potentially redemptive.

The power of the salesmen's fictive creations, even though misdirected, offers people a vision in which they can believe. Perhaps this is the real reason why Lingk is prepared to let Roma talk him back into his deal. Mamet's unsentimental, ironic approach to his subject matter may seem caustic at times, yet it refuses to deny the possibility of a better future. Bigsby sees this as evidenced in the characters' continued "need for faith" (*David Mamet* 112), despite having been cheated and betrayed, whether it is Lingk apologizing to Roma, or Levene insisting on his own efficacy as a seller. Capitalism may continue to thrive under Roma, who heads back to the same Chinese restaurant in which he began, but Aaronow's reaction allows us to see the true emptiness of Roma's endeavors.

HISTORICAL CONTEXT

The 1970s had been a difficult time for American businesses as the Japanese made substantial inroads into their territory. Convinced that Japanese success emanated from a corporate model of doing business, the 1980s saw a corporate culture boom on American shores. Asserting a need to be more competitive, many corporations restructured and saw ideological manipulation and control as an essential management strategy. American business culture of this period is enacted by all the characters, but most personified by the offstage characters Mitch and Murray, who ruthlessly rule from the top. As office manager, Williamson must answer to them, and he has little feeling for those who work below him. He shows grudging respect for Roma's sales ability, but he is outright hostile to everyone else.

While best-selling business management texts of the period, such as Thomas J. Peters and Robert H. Waterman's *In Search of Excellence: Lessons from America's Best-Run Companies* (1982), advocated that the best corporate culture was one that loves the customer, loves its employees, loves the company's products, and loves loving the company, businesses remained more concerned with success than love. In a way, Mamet satirizes such books by showing the unethical reality of the hierarchic model of American business rather than such airy ideals. When formulating new management strategies to optimize profits, the idea of love is one that can be used only to manipulate—we see this in *Glengarry* with the cutthroat relationships between the salesmen, fed by the cruel and divisive competition Mitch and Murray devise to keep them on their toes. Aaronow sums up the efficacy of such a strategy when he cries, "Oh, God, I hate this job."

The 1980s were very much the era of the "Me" generation, in which it became fashionable to put the individual first, at the expense of whomever needed to be trampled on to get what was wanted. Everyone was interested in profit, and few cared how that profit was achieved. Mamet saw around him a declining morality reflecting his view of society as a spiritual wasteland, which he tries to convey in the action and characters of *Glengarry*. With the onset of home computers, which at least gave the impression of access and knowledge, coupled with a bull market, many people felt empowered to make great profits. It was in many ways reminiscent of the 1920s and ended just as surely when the financial bubble burst the following decade.

While some critics have been quick to label Mamet's work misogynistic, most likely because of the blunt male characters found in his plays, we should remember that these characters are meant as warnings, not ideals. *Glengarry* features an all-male cast because this is largely reflective of the gender demographic of American sales-type business in the 1980s. The play is meant as a searing indictment of how he saw America in the 1980s, as defining manhood in terms of ruthless and remorseless competition. He shows the cost of that on society in general, but most specifically on men. The distorted belief that one can succeed only at the cost of someone else necessarily destroys all community bonds and leads to a very isolated existence. Ultimately, we should feel sorry for these salesmen, as they have become monstrous largely through social pressures they cannot control.

LITERARY STYLE AND DEVICES

Although the play is networked with complex imagery, Mamet is best known for the way his characters speak, since referred to as "Mametspeak."

It is language that is difficult to read on the page: halting, repetitive, abruptly staccato, and peppered with obscenities and racial slurs. The dialogue of *Glengarry* simultaneously captures the cadences of urban American speech and indicates something of the dissolution of that same culture in its fractured nature. The salesmen's incessant chatter is undercut by their actual inability to communicate anything of meaning. For Mamet's language is beyond naturalism, as it has complex and determined rhythms that are purposefully crafted to underscore characters' development, such as Levene's literal loss of the ability to speak as he breaks down. Bigsby points out how in such a moment Mamet appears to share Edward Albee's belief that it is only through the collapse of speech that the truth can appear (*David Mamet* 124). Like Albee, Mamet sees speech as a kind of subterfuge that only ever masks reality and that needs to be stripped away for any honest realization to take place. The salesmen use language less for communication than as an attempt to wield power, and as a means of control over others.

The play's language is not an attempt at realism, it is so clearly exaggerated. Mamet reveals, through such violent language, both the intense desperation of his salesmen, trapped in an endless cycle of selling, and the negative influence that such selling exerts on their characters. The overly cluttered and drab office setting of the second act further underlines the barren spiritual state of these men. After the crime has been solved, rather than end with any epiphany, the play closes with Roma heading back to the restaurant and the men continuing as before. Mamet has depicted not only a highly competitive, capitalistic world, but also the morally stultifying effect such a world has on business and the men it employs.

The salesmen in this play are consumed by their work and will try and sell to anyone, regardless of a client's need or the quality of the property they sell. Duplicitous and desperate to make a sale at any cost, they lie, wheedle, and trick their clients in their efforts to clinch a deal. All the men begin with energy, garbed in business dress, but as the play progresses we see their outfits become increasingly disheveled, and they take on a haggard appearance as the pressures on them to sell mount. The conversation is constantly of land and travel, and yet we never see any land, but only the narrow and rather sleazy world in which these salespeople live, in which no one really moves or goes anywhere.

The play's title contains an indication of the illusory world of salespeople, a world that seems to force one to sacrifice truth and humanity in order to be considered successful. Glengarry Glen Ross is an illusion, showing how salespeople often offer their clients false images of whatever Promised Land they seek. The name sounds pretty, but is made up of two worthless pieces of land without any merit, created by putting together the misleading names of the two main areas these people peddle: Glengarry Highlands (a place in Florida that has no hills) and Glen Ross Farms (a wooded area without any farmland). The Highlands are being sold by younger salesmen like Roma and represent the present, while the Farms, which Levene has been selling, are the past, which is where Levene has been left, as selling property has become a young man's game.

SITUATION OF WORK

Glengarry marks a major transition in Mamet's work. His previous plays had been predominantly episodic, many no more than an extended single act. They had intrigued and won him some attention, but it would be *Glengarry* that would place him firmly on the theatrical map, evidenced by its winning the Pulitzer Award, among others. *Glengarry* showcases the fully matured strength of Mamet's innovation and originality, illustrating his use of language, complex vision of the darker corners of American society, and forceful characterization. While the first act of the play remains episodic, with its three tightly distinctive duologues, the second act is more conventional in structure, showing Mamet's ability to incorporate plot when necessary, and a playwright in charge of his craft.

With hardly a single complete sentence in the play, and few speeches without an ethnic slur or other obscenity, Mamet redefines contemporary drama in terms of his language and subject matter. Looking at the underbelly of American life and its antiheroes has become an increasingly popular venture since Mamet's successful forays into such material. More importantly, his highly stylized Mametspeak has influenced numerous younger playwrights who continue to search for the right tone to best convey the complexities and pitfalls of twenty-first-century life. Writing for the *New York Times*, Frank Rich fervently describes how Mamet makes "all-American music—hot jazz and wounding blues—out of his salesmen's scatological native lingo. In the jagged riffs of coarse, monosyllabic words, we hear and feel both the exhilaration and sweaty desperation of the huckster's calling" (334).

While we can see *Glengarry*'s exploration of a world where business comes first, as an updated version of Miller's *Salesman* (a comparison no doubt exacerbated by the fact that a major revival of *Salesman* took place the same season *Glengarry* opened) it does more than copy or even pay homage to that earlier play—it builds on its concepts and offers a 1980s correlative to that earlier work. Salesmen continue to strive for success in a business where the rules keep changing, but Mamet's characters are more cutthroat, their language is fouler, and the outlook seems bleaker. Willy Loman's counterpart, Shelley Levene, may not commit suicide at the close, but he faces prosecution and a ruined life, while the world continues on in its mindless pursuit of wealth.

Theater scholar Leslie Kane has written extensively on Mamet and admires *Glengarry* for its "breadth, theatricality, imagination, and complexity" (*Text and Performance* xiii); he considers it "one of the finest post-war American plays" (xviii). He describes Mamet as a "seminal American playwright whose sensitivity to language, precision of social observation, communal and moral vision, theatrical imagination, and continuing productivity account for his broad and deserved critical respect" (xvii).

Mamet is a writer who might be seen as an actors' playwright, for actors have been drawn to the challenges of his roles, allowing Mamet to work closely with many formidable talents, including Joe Mantegna, William H. Macy, Al Pacino, and Dustin Hoffman. The ability to easily draw such star power has helped keep Mamet in the limelight and ensure that his complex plays are seen.

CRITICAL RECEPTION

Mamet had been uncertain if he could get *Glengarry* performed after the relatively poor reception his previous play, *Edmond*, had received. Luckily, it was sent to British playwright Harold Pinter, who declared that all the play lacked was a production, and helped arrange for the National Theatre in London to take it on. Its 1983 production at the Cottlesloe Theatre, directed by Bill Bryden, won many accolades, including the West End Theatre Award for best play. *The Observer's* Michael Coveney described it as "one of the most exciting verbal concoctions of the modern theatre" (793). The American premiere, directed by Gregory Mosher, was on February 6, 1984, at the Goodman Theatre in Chicago, and soon after transferred to Broadway. The movie version, directed by James Foley, with an expanded and slightly altered screenplay by Mamet, was released in 1992.

Reviews of the play were mixed, partly because some felt a number of the actors' performances were below par, but most critics agreed that here was a theatrical talent who would do much to change the future of American theater. Rich viewed the play as "the most accomplished play its author has yet given us ... Mamet's command of dialogue has now reached its most dazzling pitch, so has his mastery of theatrical form" (334), and Howard Kissel called it "the most exciting American play in years" (336). *New York Post's* Clive Barnes declared, "This is a play to see, remember and cherish. Mamet holds up a mirror to America with accusatory clarity" (337). As with Douglas Watt's review for the *Daily News*, dislike of the play was mostly grounded in what they saw as Mamet's dark worldview, while others, such as Brendan Gill, found his language too "stunningly coarse" (114), warning playgoers they might take offense. Many critics showed admiration for the skillful way Mamet characterizes his salesmen as disgusting and contemptible, yet ultimately also sympathetic and attractive. Praise was also won for his development of a theatrical language that was simultaneously vital, memorable, poetic, and mockingly real. Barnes declared, "Mamet has a miraculous ear for the heightened music of American dialect—it makes poetry out of common usage," and compared Mamet's linguistic skill to that of Hemingway. Jack Kroll called the play "dazzling" and Mamet "the Aristophanes of the inarticulate" (109).

The David Mamet Society, an international society of scholars, students, and others, was set up shortly after the success of *Glengarry* to encourage further study of Mamet's work, and it has been publishing *DM: The David Mamet Review* on an annual basis since 1994, in which there have been a number of pieces on this play.

SUGGESTED READINGS

Barnes, Clive. "Mamet's *Glengarry*: A Play to See and Cherish." *New York Post,* March 26, 1984. *New York Theatre Critics' Review* 45 (1984): 336–37.

Bigsby, Christopher, ed. *Cambridge Companion to David Mamet.* Cambridge, UK: Cambridge University Press, 2004.

———. *David Mamet.* New York: Methuen, 1985.

Boon, Kevin Alexander. "Dialogue, Discourse and Dialectics: The Rhetoric of Capitalism in *Glengarry Glen Ross.*" *Creative Screenwriting* 5.3 (1998): 50–57.

Brewer, Gay. *David Mamet and Film: Illusion/Disillusion in a Wounded Land.* Jefferson, NC: McFarland, 1993.

Carroll, Dennis. *David Mamet.* New York: St. Martin's, 1987.

Coveney, Michael. "*Glengarry Glen Ross.*" *Theatre Record,* June 18–July 1, 1994: 793.

Cullick, Jonathan S. "'Always Be Closing': Competition and Discourse of Closure in David Mamet's *Glengarry Glen Ross.*" *Journal of Dramatic Theory and Criticism* 8.2 (spring 1994): 23–36.

Dean, Anne. *David Mamet: Language as Dramatic Action.* Rutherford, NJ: Fairleigh Dickinson University Press, 1990.

Gill, Brendan. "The Theatre: The Lower Depths." *New Yorker,* April 2, 1984: 114.

Greenbaum, Andrea. "Brass Balls: Masculine Communication and the Discourse of Capitalism." *Journal of Men's Studies* 8.1 (fall 1999): 33–43.

Gussow, Mel. "Real Estate World a Model for Mamet: His New Play Draws on Life." *New York Times,* March 28, 1984: 19.

Harriott, Esther. *American Voices: Five Contemporary Playwrights in Essays and Interviews.* New York: McFarland, 1988.

Hudgins, Christopher, and Leslie Kane, eds. *Gender and Genre: Essays on David Mamet.* New York: Palgrave, 2001.

Kane, Leslie, ed. *David Mamet: A Casebook*. New York: Garland, 1992.

———. *David Mamet in Conversation*. Ann Arbor: University of Michigan Press, 2001.

———. *David Mamet's* Glengarry Glen Ross: *Text and Performance*. New York: Garland, 1996.

Kissel, Howard. "Glengarry Glen Ross." *Women's Wear Daily*, March 27, 1984. *New York Theatre Critics' Review* 45 (1984): 335–36.

Kolin, Philip C., and Colby H. Kullman, eds. *Speaking on Stage: Interviews with Contemporary American Playwrights*. Tuscaloosa: University of Alabama Press, 1996.

———. *Weasels and Wisemen: Education, Ethics, and Ethnicity in the Work of David Mamet*. New York: St. Martin's Press, 1999.

Kroll, Jack. "Mamet's Jackals in Jackets." *Newsweek,* April 9, 1984: 109.

Lahr, John. "Fortress Mamet." *New Yorker,* November 17, 1997: 70–82.

London, Todd. "Mamet vs. Mamet." *American Theatre* 13.24 (July–August 1996): 18–21.

Lublin, Robert I. "Differing Dramatic Dynamics in the Stage and Screen Versions of *Glengarry Glen Ross*." *American Drama* 10.1 (winter 2001): 38–55.

Mamet, David. *American Buffalo: A Play*. New York: Grove, 1977.

———. *Edmond: A Play*. New York: Grove, 1983.

———. *Oleanna*. New York: Pantheon, 1993.

———. *Speed-the-Plow: A Play*. New York: Grove, 1987.

———. The Water Engine: An American Fable *and* Mr. Happiness: Two Plays. New York: Grove, 1978.

Nelson, Jeanne-Andrée. "So Close to Closure: The Selling of Desire in *Glengarry Glen Ross*." *Essays in Theatre* 14.2 (May 1996): 107–16.

Rich, Frank. "Theater: A Mamet Play, *Glengarry Glen Ross*." *New York Times*, March 26, 1984. *New York Theatre Critics' Review* 45 (1984): 334.

Roudané, Matthew C. "Public Issues, Private Tensions: David Mamet's *Glengarry Glen Ross*." *The South Carolina Review* 19.1 (fall 1986): 35–47.

Savran, David, ed. *In Their Own Words: Contemporary American Playwrights*. New York: Theatre Communications, 1988.

Showalter, Elaine. "Acts of Violence: David Mamet and the Language of Men." *Times Literary Supplement*, November 6, 1992: 16–17.

Storey, Robert. "The Making of David Mamet." *The Hollins Critic* 16.4 (October 1979): 1–11.

Watt, Douglas. "A 'Dearth' of Honest Salesmen." *Daily News*, March 26, 1984. *New York Theatre Critics' Review* 45 (1984): 335.

Weber, Myles. "David Mamet in Theory and Practice." *New England Review* 21.2 (spring 2000): 136–41.

Worster, David. "How to Do Things with Salesmen: David Mamet's Speech-Act Play." *Modern Drama* 37.3 (fall 1994): 375–90.

10

August Wilson
The Piano Lesson
1987

BIOGRAPHICAL CONTEXT

Born April 27, 1945, as Frederick August Kittell, after his father, Wilson later took his mother's maiden name of Wilson to show allegiance to her and his African American heritage. It also reflected disapproval of his white birth father, a German baker who lived apart from the family and eventually abandoned them. Growing up in the poor black neighborhood of Pittsburgh known as the Hill, which has since vanished through urban renewal, Wilson was the first son and the fourth of six children crammed into a two-room apartment above a grocery store. Working as a cleaner, their mother, Daisy, provided as best she could. In the late 1950s she married David Bedford, an ex-convict with whom Wilson had a conflicted relationship, and who moved the family to Hazelwood, a mostly white suburb, where they regularly faced racist taunts. Bedford died in 1969, and years later Wilson would base Troy Wilson, from *Fences* (1985), on his stepfather.

Encouraging her children to read, Daisy had fierce pride in her culture and ethnicity, which Wilson illustrates by her refusal to accept the secondhand washing machine she was offered from a radio station competition when they realized she was black; she should have been given a brand new one. Rather than be treated so unfairly, she continued to wash their clothes by hand. Wilson dropped out of high school at age 15 on a similar principle, refusing to defend himself against false charges of plagiarism on a paper he wrote about Napoleon Bonaparte. He spent the next few months in the library, discovering books by writers including Richard Wright, Ralph Ellison, Langston Hughes, and Amiri Baraka, as well as works on black anthropology and sociology. He also listened to the men at street-corner stores, telling stories he would later include in play scripts. Enlisting in the United States Army for three years in 1962, he was discharged the following year.

In 1965, the same year his birth father died, Wilson moved into a rooming house with fellow black intellectuals to become a writer. Buying a typewriter and a Victrola, he wrote poetry and listened to blues music. Although his poems won little attention, Wilson's expertise with metaphor was developed, just as was his love and understanding of the encoded messages of black culture he heard within the blues. Wilson published poems in several small periodicals, including *Black World, Negro Digest,* and *Black Lines,* and read his work at local art houses. The black power movement and Nation of Islam were very influential on this period of his life, with their emphasis on self-sufficiency, self-defense, and self-determination. Such concepts lie at the heart of his work.

In 1968, with writer and teacher Rob Penny, Wilson helped found the Black Horizons Theater in Pittsburgh. Here he gained some theatrical knowledge, directed plays, and produced fledgling dramas of his own. Black Horizons was created to provide a forum to celebrate black culture and aesthetics, particularly as espoused by Amiri Baraka, whose plays they produced. *Rite of Passage* was the first play Wilson wrote, but it remains unproduced and unpublished. In 1969 he married Brenda Burton, a Muslim, and briefly converted to Islam in an unsuccessful attempt to sustain the marriage. They had one daughter, Sakina Ansari, the following year, but were divorced by 1972. *Recycle* (1973), significantly about a troubled marriage breaking up, was briefly performed in a Pittsburgh community theater. Wilson continued working with poems and plays, of which the latter included one-acts *The Coldest Day of the Year* (1976), an allegorical love story reminiscent of works by Edward Albee and Baraka, and *The Homecoming* (1976), about the death of a fictional itinerant blues singer-guitarist, Blind Willie Johnson, which were locally produced.

In 1976, a friend, Claude Purdy, heard Wilson read from a series of poems about the stagecoach robber Black Bart and suggested they had dramatic possibilities. Four months later Wilson had turned them into a musical satire with 27 characters: *Black Bart and the Sacred Hills*. Purdy felt it needed further revision but invited Wilson to visit him in St. Paul, Minnesota, to work on it. While visiting, Wilson met Judy Oliver, a social worker, and they swiftly became close. Deciding to relocate permanently to St. Paul in 1978, Wilson got a job working for the Science Museum of Minnesota, writing plays about Margaret Mead and the Native American Coyote figure to enhance their exhibits. *Black Bart* was first performed in Los Angeles that same year. After three years he quit the Science Museum to concentrate on his own drama and just worked part time as a cook for Little Brothers of the Poor.

In 1979 Wilson wrote a play about the mixed-up lives of gypsy (jitney) taxicab drivers in 1970s Pittsburgh, *Jitney*, which he sent to the Playwrights' Center in Minneapolis. He also started another play, *Fullerton Street*, taking place the night of the Joe Louis–Billy Khan fight from the 1940s. Exploring the loss of values by blacks who migrated north, it depicts a couple falling apart under pressure from alcoholism and unemployment and remains unproduced, but provided material for the later *Seven Guitars* (1995).

In 1981 Wilson married Oliver and began submitting plays to the National Playwrights Conference of the Eugene O'Neill Theatre Center. *Jitney*, *Fullerton Street*, and *Black Bart* were all rejected. Meanwhile, the Playwrights' Center staged *Jitney* in 1982 to good reviews, and it was produced that same year at the Allegheny Repertory Theatre in Pittsburgh. After revision and an intervening 18 years, *Jitney* would run on Broadway in 2000 as one of the plays in a historical cycle of plays based on black experience during each decade of the twentieth century, which Wilson would promise the American public by 1984. In 1982 the National Playwrights Conference finally accepted *Ma Rainey's Black Bottom*, set during a 1920s Chicago recording session, depicting the frustrations and struggles of black musicians. After workshop revisions, it was produced to much acclaim at Yale Repertory Theatre in 1984, with Lloyd Richards as director, which began a long and fruitful relationship between Wilson and Richards. Sadly, Wilson's mother died in 1983, shortly before her son's first big success.

From 1984 through 1987, Yale Repertory Theatre produced a new Wilson play each year, which transferred to Broadway to growing success. *Ma Rainey's Black Bottom* opened on Broadway later that same year, ran for 275 performances, and won the New York Drama Critics' Circle Award. On the strength of this, Wilson won a series of prestigious fellowships, which allowed him to devote his attentions to full-time writing. *Fences*, Wilson's Pulitzer-winning family story set in 1957, premiered at Yale in 1985, moved to Broadway in 1987, and was still running when *Joe Turner's Come and Gone* (1986), set in a rooming house in the 1910s as Herald Loomis travels north to find his wife and child, reached Broadway in 1988.

Joe Turner had been partly inspired by a Romare Bearden painting called *Mill Hand's Lunch Bucket* (1978), and the paintings of Bearden, with their striking evocations of the black experience, would inspire Wilson's next play, *The Piano Lesson* (1987), in which family members argue about ownership of a family heirloom and come to reassess their cultural heritage. It won him another Pulitzer before it even opened on Broadway in 1990, and secured

Wilson's national reputation; a CBS Hallmark Hall of Fame presentation followed in 1995.

By the close of 1990, Wilson's marriage to Oliver was over, and he moved to Seattle. His next play, *Two Trains Running* (1990), took on urban black culture in the tumultuous 1960s and won him his fifth New York Drama Critics' Circle Award in 1992, although critical reaction was becoming less favorable. Wilson had met Constanza Romero, who was in charge of costume design, during production of *Two Trains*, and they married in 1994. *Seven Guitars* (1995), a murder mystery about the exploitation of black music and the lives of a group of people in the 1940s, was another moderate success.

Shortly after *Seven Guitars* opened in New York in 1996, Wilson gave a controversial keynote address to the Theatre Communications Group National Conference, titled "The Ground on Which I Stand." While he acknowledged an indebtedness to white dramatists, Wilson insisted he stands as an artist firmly in a black tradition that is substantially different from the white. He asked that colorblind casting (black actors playing traditionally white roles and vice versa) be stopped, and pointed out the need for regional black theaters. Publicly voicing his personal politics, aesthetics, and future vision, Wilson insisted his stance was not separatist, but insurance against the appropriation of black culture. He also attacked critics, including Robert Brustein, who had written a scathing review of *Piano Lesson*, as cultural elitists, sparking a firestorm of printed counterattacks and an unsatisfying and unresolved public debate between Wilson and Brustein in 1997.

In 1997 Wilson had another daughter, Azula Carmen. His next play, *King Hedley II* (1999), about an ex-con trying to rebuild his life in 1980s Pittsburgh, and using characters from the earlier *Seven Guitars*, had a lukewarm reception, but his historical cycle of plays was nearing completion. Aunt Esther, the elderly character from *Two Trains*, features in the remaining two plays: *Gem of the Ocean* (2004), is set in 1904 and depicts a spiritual quest to find a mystical city, and *Radio Golf*, scheduled to open at Los Angeles's Mark Taper Forum in 2005, tells the tale of real estate developers trying to tear down Esther's home in the 1990s.

PLOT DEVELOPMENT

In the early morning as a storm gathers, Boy Willie arrives at the home of his uncle Doaker and sister Berniece in Pittsburgh. Waking up the household, he enters with his friend Lymon. They have brought a truckload of watermelons up north to sell. Boy Willie plans to take his profits back south, but Lymon wants to stay in the city. Berniece is annoyed at the disturbance, asking them to quiet down. They talk about Sutter, a white landowner from their hometown, who has drowned in his well; the rumor is he was pushed in by the Ghosts of the Yellow Dog. They ask Doaker for a drink to celebrate. Berniece is worried they have stolen the truck, but they assure her Lymon bought it; however, Lymon is running from something. Boy Willie asks to see his niece, Maretha, but Berniece refuses to wake her and returns to bed.

The men discuss Wining Boy, an itinerant musician and Doaker's brother, whose wife, Cleotha, died. Lymon notices the piano. Boy Willie is raising cash to buy Sutter's land and wants to sell the family piano. Doaker explains how Avery Brown came north to ask Berniece to marry him a year after her husband, Crawley, died, and decided to start a church. He sent a white man to see if Berniece would sell the piano and give Avery the money to start his church. She refused to sell or marry, but Boy Willie plans to find out who the man was.

Interrupted by Berniece crying out, Boy Willie rushes to help. She has seen Sutter's ghost and accuses Boy Willie of killing him. He denies it, but she tells him to leave, blaming him also for Crawley's death. Suggesting Sutter was looking for the piano and she should get rid of it, he refuses to leave until he has sold his watermelons. Berniece goes to dress and Boy Willie teases Doaker about women. But Doaker has had no interest in women since his wife, Coreen, left him. He has worked 27 years for the railroad, currently as a cook, and offers his vision of the railroad.

Maretha enters, and Boy Willie warmly greets her. They play the piano for each other. Boy Willie is upset Maretha knows nothing of its history. Avery arrives for Berniece, as she is helping him get a bank loan. He works as an elevator operator and explains how he was called to be a preacher, in a dream of three hobos who take him to meet Christ. Boy Willie asks Berniece about selling the piano, but she refuses and leaves. Boy Willie and Lymon go to sell watermelons.

Three days later, Wining Boy arrives. He and Doaker catch up, drink, and discuss their ex-wives. Boy Willie and Lymon join them; their truck keeps breaking down and they have sold no melons. They talk about the Ghosts of the Yellow Dog, who have reputedly been killing a string of racist white men. Wining Boy claims he asked the Ghosts for advice and they gave him three lucky years. Boy Willie has found the white man who wanted to buy the piano, and his uncles discuss the likelihood of Boy Willie getting the land from Sutter.

Three years previously Boy Willie and Lymon had stolen some wood. Crawley was helping them move it when white men ambushed them. Crawley fought back and got killed, while they ran. Both were later caught and sent to Parchment Farm (a prison work farm). After release, Lymon was picked up for vagrancy, but his arrest was only a scam to get cheap labor. He was offered prison time or a fine. He chooses prison, but his fine is paid by Stovall, who now insists he must work it off. Lymon ran away and came north with Boy Willie. They discuss the difference between the North and the South and the way laws favor the whites; all have spent time on Parchment Farm and sing a work song together. Boy Willie asks Wining Boy to play the piano, and his uncle tells them about the burden of being a piano player. When Boy Willie talks again about selling the piano, Doaker tells Lymon the family history connected with it, which goes back to slavery times.

It was carved by Doaker's grandfather, Willie Boy, after Sutter's grandfather exchanged Willie Boy's wife and son (Mama Berniece and Papa Boy Walter) to get the piano for his wife, Ophelia. Ophelia missed her slaves and wanted them back, so Sutter told Willie Boy to carve their images into the piano, but he carved his whole family history. Doaker's older brother, Boy Charles, the father of Boy Willie and Berniece, decided his family should have that piano, and stole it with his brothers when the Sutters were on a July 4th picnic in 1911. Doaker and Wining Boy escaped with the piano, but Boy Charles got trapped in a boxcar with four hobos and they were all burned to death by angry whites. These hobos became the Ghosts of the Yellow Dog. Boy Willie insists his father, rather than sharecrop, would have traded the piano for land, just as he plans to do. Wining Boy plays his song about being a rambling, gambling man, as Berniece returns.

Boy Willie tries to lift the piano, and they hear Sutter's ghost. Berniece becomes angry, saying the piano is too precious to sell, but Boy Willie offers his vision of land ownership as being more important. He admits he would not sell the piano if she used it. She relates how her mother, Ola, polished it and asked her to play, pointing out that it has been the women who suffer most from the men's acts of defiance, left to raise their children alone. She accuses them of killing Crawley, though Boy Willie insists it was his own fault. Berniece hits him, Doaker pulls her off, and Maretha screams, having seen the ghost.

Act 2 begins the next day as Doaker prepares for work. Wining Boy returns from the pawnshop, unable to sell his old suit. Doaker admits he has seen Sutter's ghost before, thinks he is after the piano, and says Berniece should get rid of it. Wining Boy is broke and borrows money from Doaker. Boy Willie returns after a successful morning selling watermelons. He and Lymon sort their money, while Wining Boy sells his suit, shirt, and shoes to Lymon. Lymon wants to look for women and goes to change. While Lymon is gone, Wining Boy explains how he once slept with Lymon's mother and could be his father. Wining Boy offers Lymon advice on how to get women as they go out.

Later that evening, Berniece prepares a bath as Avery arrives to propose. She refuses, and he criticizes her for not letting Crawley go or allowing anyone to love her. She is angry at his sexist implication that she needs a man to be happy and tells him to wait until he has his church. Explaining Sutter's ghost, she asks him to bless the house. He suggests she move the piano to his church. She points out that there is a reason she does not play it; she thinks playing conjures its spirits, and does not want that. Avery asks her to play the piano for God, but she refuses, so he promises to return and try an exorcism.

Later that night, Boy Willie arrives home with Grace. As they fondle, they knock over a lamp and wake Berniece. Berniece tells Boy Willie he cannot do that in her house; upset, he and Grace leave. Lymon comes looking for Boy Willie. He likes Grace too, but Boy Willie got to her first. Lymon tells Berniece about his hopes to find a job and a good woman and asks why she is not married. She says she is not interested. Lymon gives her a bottle of perfume and, while putting some on, kisses her neck. The next kiss she returns, but then leaves, and Lymon happily sleeps on the couch.

The following morning Boy Willie rushes in to wake Lymon. He needs help to take the piano, but cannot move it. Doaker insists they wait until Berniece returns. Boy Willie leaves, promising to be back with moving equipment and saying he will give half the sale money to Berniece.

Later, Boy Willie continues preparations to move the piano while telling Maretha about the Ghosts of the Yellow Dog. Berniece returns and sends Maretha upstairs, and Boy Willie follows. Berniece tells Doaker she will threaten Boy Willie with Crawley's gun if he continues. She tells her brother to leave, but he points out that this is Doaker's house, and Doaker refuses to take sides. They argue, and Boy Willie says he is not scared of death. As Berniece straightens Maretha's hair, Boy Willie criticizes the way she treats her daughter, not telling her about the family's past and making her feel second best to whites. Boy Willie insists a positive attitude is what it takes, and criticizes Berniece for giving in.

Avery arrives, saying he will soon get his church. Lymon returns with a rope, telling Boy Willie he has Grace waiting outside, and they are going on a date. Only interested in the rope, when Boy Willie tries to move the piano, Berniece shows her gun. Lymon is uncertain about helping, but Boy Willie is unperturbed. Wining Boy barges in, drunk; breaking the tension, he plays a song for Cleotha. He joins Berniece saying Boy Willie cannot take the piano. Grace storms in looking for Lymon. They all sense Sutter's presence, and Grace runs off, with Lymon in pursuit. While Boy Willie mocks, Avery tries his exorcism. Boy Willie chases up the stairs after Sutter and is repeatedly thrown back. He begins a life-and-death struggle, refusing to give in, unlike Avery, who admits he can do nothing. Seeing her brother in trouble, Berniece plays the piano, calling on her ancestors for help. They chase Sutter away, and calm is restored as Berniece thanks them for their aid. Boy Willie appears, telling Berniece she can keep the piano if she and Maretha keep playing it, and prepares to leave.

CHARACTER DEVELOPMENT

Though 30, Boy Willie retains all the vitality his youthful name implies. His tremendous energy is precisely what his sleeping family needs. While Doaker and Berniece have withdrawn from the world, Boy Willie and his friend, Lymon, are in that world, striving to better themselves. While Boy Willie's ultimate goal is land, Lymon's is a good woman. Both goals suggest a positive future of connection and possible growth. These men have goals and a sense of direction, which have definite value in a world where so many live without either. Their way north has been a constant struggle as they keep breaking down, but they have not given in. Both men represent a celebratory force of life that is in marked contrast to the house in which they arrive.

Frustrated by his willingness to work and the lack of opportunity, Boy Willie's determination to own land is to ensure that he has work for the future, which will benefit him and not whites. He will not settle for the exploitative sharecropping into which his father had been forced. The play's epigraph makes clear Boy Willie's dream and plan for the future: "Gin my cotton / Sell my seed / Buy my baby / Everything she need." The lyric underlines the importance of tilling your own land. Owning Sutter's land will give him a firmer economic and social footing. Although he gets no money from the piano, and despite the uncertainty of the land still being for sale, the impression remains that Boy Willie has the energy and the desire to fulfill his dream.

Lymon has come north to escape the corruption of the South. He could end up a wanderer like Wining Boy—suggested by his buying and wearing Wining Boy's clothes, and the possibility Wining Boy could be his biological father—but Lymon is not as rootless as he at first seems. In his late-night discussion with Berniece, we learn he has firm goals and wants to settle. Strongly attracted to Grace, he wins her from Boy Willie and goes with her to pursue his dreams at the close.

Berniece is fearful of her heritage and her own color and transmits this self-effacing fear to her daughter, Maretha, encouraging her to conform to white expectations, teaching her to be quiet and unassuming, and greasing down her hair. She conveys no inkling of her true heritage to the girl, refusing to pass on the family history or any trait she associates with black life. Boy Willie sees this as stripping Maretha of a valid identity. He believes Maretha needs a sense of her family in order to build self-pride and become a viable and valuable member of the black community.

The repetition of names in the Charles family indicates a strong connection to past generations, but it is a connection Berniece ignores—her move north seems part of this effort. She does not want her quiet but essentially empty life messed up by her brother's noise and energy. She resists the life he brings, making him inhospitably unwelcome and trying to devalue and denigrate everything he does. Accusing him of crimes, from stealing their truck to killing Sutter, she is determined his presence can only bring trouble. She prefers to shut out life, mourning her husband, three years dead. Yet there is a flicker of life inside, waiting to be reawakened, which we see when she allows Lymon to kiss her, and kisses him back. She also takes up a gun to prevent Boy Willie from taking the piano. Having regained sufficient spirit to stand up to her brother, she is only a short step from finding the courage to face not only whites but her own heritage.

Next to Boy Willie, Doaker and Wining Boy seem directionless. Both start set apart from the others, observing and commenting rather than getting involved. While their brother, Boy Charles, had two children to continue his name, neither of their marriages produced offspring, reflecting the emptiness of their chosen lives. Their wives were noticeably dissatisfied by husbands who were constantly restless but had no sense of direction; Cleotha asked Wining Boy to leave, and Coreen simply left Doaker. Boy Charles's wife, Ola, in contrast, paid faithful tribute to her dead husband's memory for 17 years by polishing the piano for which he gave his life.

Doaker's apparent contentment is complacency, for he has largely switched off from life. After Coreen left, he refused to see any more women. While the idea of Sutter's ghost has Boy Willie bridling with rage, Doaker has seen the ghost and done nothing. Though comfortable at home (we see him cooking and ironing with ease and familiarity), Doaker has traveling in his blood and is unable to let go of his railroad life. He has spent his life constantly moving, but has made little progression, having worked for the railroad for 27 years.

Wining Boy's best-known song is of the "rambling gambling man," who lives a similar life of aimless wandering and hardship. His glories in music and gambling have been in the past, and he has become tired and outdated. We see a glimmer of his old vitality when he plays, but he is held back by a lack of direction. Having survived on the support of others, he has selfishly given little in return. Even his family is tiring of the way he turns up only when he needs something. It comforted him to know that even though she asked him to leave, his wife still loved him and insisted she would be there for him, but she is now dead.

Doaker and Wining Boy undergo a profound revitalization in the play, goaded into action by their nephew. Doaker starts by telling the family story, then we witness the increase of his stature as he finally asserts his authority against Boy Willie and it is accepted. The first sign of change in Wining Boy is his decision to return south once he has raised the necessary cash. Selling his old clothes to Lymon illustrates a willingness to shed his old way of life and start anew. His increase of stature comes when singing a newly composed song about Cleotha, which faces the past and allows him to move forward. The song, like the carvings on the piano, adds to the family history, so it is fitting he should play it on that same piano. At this point Wining Boy also finds the strength to stand up to his nephew and tell him not to take the piano.

Although Avery's religious intentions seem, like the man, honest enough, Wilson is wary of Christian preachers, finding their tendency toward passivity a troubling message for communities needing to take action. Just as Wining Boy's tale of the man from Spear tells of a preacher who could not follow through, Wilson's tendency is to portray all such figures as potentially hypocritical, self-serving, or at least too concerned with the realm beyond rather than the here and now. Avery tries to inspire Berniece to take up her life and face the piano through religion, but that is not a sufficient impetus. Nor will his religion be sufficient when it comes to combating Sutter's ghost. Berniece will finally face the piano out of family feeling, not religious compulsion, and she does so to aid her brother. This is clear in her choice of song: an evocation of family rather than a hymn.

Sutter represents the role of whites in black history. His great weight conveys the opulence and greed of a man who has fed off the labor of blacks for years. But Sutter has fallen, quite literally, as he tumbled down the well. Sutter's time is passing, he is dead, and although his ghostly presence objects, he cannot cover up the decline of his family's control. Of his heirs, his brother lives up north and is willing to sell his Southern heritage to the enemy, in the form of Boy Willie, and of his sons, one has moved north and the other is an idiot, indicating the decline of white power in the South.

The rise of the Ghosts of Yellow Dog shows the contrasting growth in power of blacks in the area. The demise of Sutter and other whites points to a black ability to wreak vengeance and acts as a warning to whites to behave better in the future. All this should make the way easier for blacks to take control of their lives in the South, if only they can build the motivation to do so, as Boy Willie intends. Boy Willie's family history has been one of resistance to white control, and it is unsurprising he chooses the same path; in the play, he teaches the others to do the same.

THEMES

All of the characters in this play have lessons to learn, and the content of the lesson varies, depending on the character. The lesson of the piano is rooted in the heritage of slavery. Slavery, to Wilson, is a key historical period in the African American sensibility and should neither be ignored nor forgotten. Wilson believes blacks should have an annual celebration to remind them of this part of their history, just as Boy Willie suggests an annual party to celebrate his father's liberation of the piano; both are about refusing white oppression.

Berniece and her two uncles, Doaker and Wining Boy, discover better self-worth and renew their spirits by reconnecting with their historical and cultural heritage. Wilson sees too many blacks as ready to accept negative white assessments of their culture and insists they need to define that culture for themselves. Integral to that definition is an embrace and an understanding of their own history in America. The catalyst for their learning is the central conflict between Boy Willie and Berniece over the piano, which represents an argument over whether to honor their slave ancestors or put the family's past enslavement behind them. Although Berniece ends with the piano, Wilson does not take sides; preserving one's heritage or using whatever it hands down to build a better future are both viable options.

Boy Willie's desire to sell the piano is his way of honoring his ancestors and building on their heritage. For him, selling the piano is not a denial of the past but a validation. Berniece, on the other hand, wants to keep the piano but refuses to pass on its full legacy to her daughter or accept it into her own life, which does no honor to her family ancestors. Berniece has become fearful of her family legacy, seeing the sadness it has brought to the women-folk, and is teaching her daughter, Maretha, white-community values rather than those values by which her own family has lived and died.

Berniece has played the piano for her mother because through its tones Ola could hear her late husband. Since her mother died, being scared by the piano's spirits rather than comforted, Berniece has silenced them by refusing to play. But these are her family spirits she rejects. Maretha's occasional playing is unable to release them because she has been kept ignorant of their presence and relevance to her life. Berniece feels that she is keeping Maretha free of a burden by not telling her about the piano, but it is a necessary burden.

The piano's history is a responsibility that should be borne, or the family will lose an important part of its identity and strength.

The piano symbolizes the Charleses' history of slavery and freedom, and this is something they need to own. Owning the piano strengthens the family; allowing someone else to own it will weaken them all. Boy Charles knew this, which was the reason he stole the piano in the first place: "Say it was the story of our whole family and as long as Sutter had it . . . he had us. Say we were still in slavery." For Boy Willie to sell the piano to a white man could be a metaphor for assimilation. To play the piano is to claim and possess it, and everything for which it stands: the blood and suffering of the Charles family as well as their strength and spirit. Boy Willie does not need the piano to connect him as he is quite literally a re-embodiment of his father, as Berniece herself recognizes. Also, Boy Willie has neither left the South nor tried to hide from the past.

The piano was first claimed by Boy Willie's great-grandfather, who, in defiance of its white owners, carved his entire family history into the wood. That claim was reaffirmed when the brothers stole it from the Sutters. They did this, significantly, on Independence Day, making the act a strong statement of the family's complete independence. Boy Willie takes this claim one step further by trying to claim the original family property from Sutter's heirs. But Boy Willie must learn that it is not always wise or necessary to sell off any part of your heritage, and better to progress by other means. Fortunately, Wilson presents him with the strength and the willpower to do so.

Rather than view his color as limiting, Boy Willie sees it as liberating. He uses his family history as a source of strength and pride, unlike Berniece, who can see that same past only as a source of shame and anguish. However, despite his strength, Boy Willie cannot win the battle against the ghost alone—he needs the help of his sister and the support of his family. A lesson the piano teaches them is that they must be united before they can turn their former bondage into a full sense of freedom. Who gets the piano is less important than the family's need to exorcise Sutter's ghost, which represents white dominance. The piano leads brother and sister to team together against their real enemy, Sutter, rather than fight each other. Berniece creates a song that draws on her past and her heritage to chase off the ghost. Her playing releases the piano's spirits, as it acknowledges and embraces their presence. Since Berniece has rediscovered how to use the piano, Boy Willie is content to leave it with her as he heads back south. The play closes triumphantly with Berniece singing "Thank you" in celebration of her reconnection to her past and her family, and through these, a stronger and more fulfilling life in the present.

HISTORICAL CONTEXT

On one level, all of Wilson's plays are individual history lessons, as each rewrites one particular decade of American history in terms of its black experience. Wilson purposefully places blacks into a history from which they have often been overlooked, and gives them prominence. This is to encourage blacks to stake claim to their own history, which can bring stronger identities and greater strength to face future challenges. Wilson tells the stories of ordinary people rather than the famous, within credible historical contexts. *Piano Lesson*, set in 1936, is centered in the period of the Great Depression, when the American economy seemed crippled. It was a time when people grabbed any chance they could to survive, and cities like Pittsburgh were filled with breadlines, unemployment, and housing shortages.

But Wilson is less concerned with the usual privations of the period and more with its effect on the black population. The 1930s also marked the height of the black migration north in search of jobs and a better life, even though the North held few more real opportunities than the South. Wilson wants to emphasize Boy Willie's decision to stay in the South as being a sensible choice. *Piano Lesson* is also unlike any Depression-era play set among white folk, the difference being that for blacks the Depression caused less of a change of circumstance. Even in the prosperous 1920s, Berniece's only work opportunity would have been to clean someone else's house or clothes. Doaker has been working for the railroad since 1909, which would have been an envied position among blacks for its stability, yet he has never risen above menial work. The fact that Sutter's brother is willing to sell his land to the proverbial enemy is a sign of the desperation of the times among the newly poverty-stricken whites.

Despite its Depression setting, the play reaches back to slavery times in its review of black history. As a self-declared "cultural nationalist," Wilson insists that "blacks have a culture ... our own mythology, our own history, our own social organizations, our own creative motif" (Moyers 54) which need to be taught and accepted. Without knowledge of one's past, Wilson would say, is to have no sense of one's own identity. Slavery, to Wilson, is a key historical period in the African American sensibility and should not be ignored or forgotten, and this is profoundly illustrated in *Piano Lesson*. The black experience of disinheritance, colonization, and oppression sanctions a resilience of spirit in those that survive and a courageous heart in those that do not. Men like Boy Charles, Crawley, and Boy Willie refuse to be treated like second-class citizens and will claim what they feel is rightfully theirs, be it a piano, wood, or land. Such lessons in resistance and resilience need repeating to encourage those blacks who continue to struggle against aspects of white oppression or their own feelings of inadequacy. As scholar Sandra Shannon has suggested, Wilson's strength lies less in inspiring people with greatness, but in making them realize the potential greatness in their own ordinary pasts.

LITERARY STYLE AND DEVICES

Despite layers of symbolism, the dominating metaphor of the title, and a ghost, Wilson's play seems largely realistic, drawing in its audience with detailed characterizations and gentle humor. Rather than the overt political propaganda of 1960s black writers like Baraka and Ed Bullins, Wilson offers a more internal examination of black life in America. Conflict with whites has not disappeared but occurs offstage. The focus is centered on how black people can help themselves.

The piano dominates the play, waiting for people to take heed of the lesson that is carved onto its surface and exuded through its physical and metaphorical presence. In an interview with John DiGaetani, Wilson pointed out, "It's not insignificant that the piano in the play is a European instrument, but carved with African mask-like figures. A European instrument is a perfect symbol for the combination of African and American cultures" (DiGaetani 284). When asked if the piano could be a symbol of a uniquely American combination of cultures, Wilson replies, "It has black and white keys. And you need both keys to make music" (DiGaetani 284). In the same way, Wilson acknowledges you need both whites and blacks to create a stronger America, and that elements of both white and African cultures can contribute to this development.

Boy Willie represents one of Wilson's "warrior spirits"—people who refuse to accept any restrictions on their potential—a character type he includes in each play to represent the potential strength of blacks. Every detail of the play has layered meaning. For example, though it begins with the potential of dawn time, there is still "something in the air that belongs to the night," because the house remains entrenched in the life-denying pall cast over it by its current occupants. Yet their stasis is soon to be threatened, and we are told that "something akin to a storm" is about to arrive to shake things up. That "storm" is embodied by Boy Willie, who arrives in a whirl of noise and activity. Boy Willie comes to wake the house up, literally and metaphorically. His hollering and bombast will force them to reengage with the world and the past from which they have set themselves apart.

Wilson often talks about the four Bs that have influenced his writing: Bearden, Baraka, Borges, and the Blues. He explains that he writes about the black experience in America in order to convey in terms of the life he knows best those things that are common to all cultures—a concept he credits to the painter Romare Bearden. Indeed, this play was inspired by a Bearden picture called *The Piano Lesson* (1983), of a young black girl sitting at a piano. While Baraka motivates him politically rather than artistically, and Argentinean writer Jorge Luis Borges has inspired Wilson's economy of writing and moving attention to detail, it is the Blues that seems the biggest influence.

Music is highly important to the dramatic flow of Wilson's work, and nowhere is this more evident than in *Piano Lesson*, with its five songs, used to alter the mood, teach a lesson, and to provide subtle commentary on the play's themes. When the men sing the Parchment Farm song together, we recognize the burden these men all share, and ways in which they have learned to survive. It is a moment of unity, anger, and strength. Wilson's characters frequently approach and define their lives through music, and the singing and playing of traditional songs becomes almost ritualistic. These blues encode much of their African American identity, and nearly every character sings at one point or another.

Wilson may seem largely realistic in presentation, but he is also highly inventive in his use of music and metaphor, and his presentation of so much American black cultural history has vastly expanded theatrical representations of black experience. The pictures he paints are at times as dark as those of Bearden, but they also contain the same degree of hope and possibility. He shows both the bitterness and the potential in the black American legacy, as he portrays characters seeking and sometimes finding justice, empowerment, spiritual enlightenment, freedom, and a sense of personal and/or social identity. He offers no easy answers, but possibilities.

SITUATION OF WORK

Wilson has insisted that in all of his plays, "I always point toward making that connection, toward reconnecting with the past. You have to know who you are, and understand your history in America over more than three hundred years, in order to know what your relation is to your society" (Rothstein 8). It is this historical aspect of Wilson's plays that is most striking. In 1984 Wilson declared his intention to write a play based on black experience for every decade of the twentieth century, and he did: 1900s *Gem of the Ocean*, 1910s *Joe Turner's Come and Gone*, 1920s *Ma Rainey's Black Bottom*, 1930s *The Piano Lesson*, 1940s *Seven Guitars*, 1950s *Fences*, 1960s *Two Trains Running*, 1970s *Jitney*, 1980s *King Hedley II*, and 1990s *Radio Golf*.

No other black dramatist has covered so broad a scope and put the black experience so centrally in public view, especially since most of these plays have also enjoyed solid Broadway runs. Also, no other black dramatist has been so commercially and critically successful, with as many awards, which offers an inspiration to others.

In some aspects, more complex than the multiple prizewinning *Fences*, *Piano Lesson* represents an accumulation of all of Wilson's techniques, beliefs, and themes. Containing nearly every major issue that Wilson has broached in his work—including the inequalities of the American social and legal systems, the ambivalent heritage of slavery and the past in general, his suspicion of Christianity, recognition of the need for economic viability, importance of community, and the advantages of the South over the North—in many ways, *Piano Lesson* offers an instant primer to Wilson's whole canon. As scholar Peter Wolfe insists, "Tone and theme dovetail perfectly in *Piano Lesson;* a fierce, wise, and gripping work that confirms the steady growth of a major American playwright" (108).

Wilson's success is predictable; the finely observed nature of his writing brings his characters to life with a compelling realism. Simultaneously ordinary and unique, his creations register deeply with both black and white audiences. His plays are ensemble pieces offering a vision of a whole community rather than just individuals. Wilson subtly exposes the inequities of the American social, legal, and political systems through characters' back stories and ambitions as much as by their current condition. If Boy Willie were not black, there would be no question over whether he would get his land; if Maretha were not black, Berniece would not spend hours straightening her hair. Through such nuanced details, we learn of a black experience filled with racial tension and troubling questions of identity and empowerment.

Gerald Berkowitz calls Wilson "the most important dramatist of the 1990s" (194), and many more critics would view him as the foremost black dramatist of the last quarter of the twentieth century. Rarely has any serious twentieth-century dramatist gained such critical acclaim and commercial success as Wilson's first four Broadway productions. It is little wonder that commentators have swiftly granted Wilson canonical status. As John Lahr, critic for the *New Yorker*, has stated, "No one else—not even O'Neill, has aimed so high and achieved so much" (101).

CRITICAL RECEPTION

Wilson's first Broadway play, *Ma Rainey's Black Bottom* (1984), had been an instant hit, and this success continued through to *Piano Lesson* (1987), which first played at the Yale Repertory Theatre, then opened on Broadway at the Walter Kerr Theatre in 1990. Wilson's subsequent plays, however, met with more muted success. Though a lesser theatrical commercial success than *Fences*, *Piano Lesson* encapsulates all of Wilson's art and politics, going beyond the simpler realism of *Fences* and offering within its single form a complete survey of black experience in America since slavery. Wilson has won the most New York Drama Critics' Circle Awards of any playwright, and a prior Pulitzer for *Fences*, but with its Pulitzer, New York Drama Critics' Circle Award, and subsequent Hallmark Hall of Fame television production in 1995, which was able to reach an even vaster audience than its 328 theater performances, *Piano Lesson* marks the pinnacle of Wilson's achievement.

Reviews of both play and film (for which Wilson wrote the screenplay) were predominantly positive, and Charles S. Dutton, who had previously played Levee in *Ma Rainey's Black Bottom*, was highly praised for his performance as Boy Willie in each. Critic Clive Barnes described the Broadway production as the "best and most immediate" (325) of Wilson's plays, with an "iron-firm and fascinating dramatic framework," and compared Wilson's skill to that of Shakespeare (326). While William Henry III declared Wilson "has transcended the categorization of 'black' playwright to demonstrate that his stories, although consistently about black families and communities, speak to the entire U.S. culture" (329). A few, however, felt the play had too many digressions, offered contradictory opinions, and did not convincingly convey its use of the supernatural. Robert Brustein was the most vociferous in attack, announcing the play "an overwritten exercise in a conventional style," which was misguidedly "locked in a perception of victimization" (28). He also criticized the use of the supernatural as a "contrived intrusion," inappropriate in a realist drama, and concluded that "Wilson is reaching a dead end in his examination of American racism" (29). This began a bitter feud between Wilson and Brustein over each one's perception of the future of the American theater.

Meanwhile, academic critics found the play far less flawed, especially in its use of the supernatural, which is seen as a valid aspect of Wilson's desire to reconnect contemporary blacks to their past, and an element endemic to black art, with its roots in African spirituality. Likewise, the digressions and contradictions are all part of black concepts of oral history and signifyin'. The term "signifyin'" is one used in black culture to denote a style of speech uniquely African American that is often used to create a more attractive reality. These factors confirm Wilson's importance as an artist equally able to speak to blacks and whites, within a predominantly white establishment. As critic Frank Rich surmises, Wilson is a playwright able to introduce "white audiences to black America without patronizing either whites or blacks" (8).

SUGGESTED READINGS

Baker, Houston A., Jr. *Blues, Ideology, and Afro-American Literature*. Chicago: Chicago University Press, 1984.

Baraka, Imamu Amiri. "Black (Art) Drama Is the Same as Black Life." *Ebony*, February 1971: 74–82.

Barnes, Clive. "*Piano Lesson* Hits All the Right Keys." *New York Post*, April 17, 1990. *New York Theatre Critics' Review* 51 (1990): 325–26.

Berkowitz, Gerald M. *American Drama of the Twentieth Century*. New York: Longman, 1992.

Bissiri, Amadov. "Aspects of Africanness in August Wilson's Drama: Reading *Piano Lesson* through Wole Soyinka's Drama." *African American Review* 30.1 (1996): 99–113.

Boguimil, Mary L. *Understanding August Wilson*. Columbia: University of South Carolina Press, 1999.

Bommer, Lawrence. "A Keeper of Dreams." *Chicago Tribune*, January 15, 1995: 16–21.

Brustein, Robert. "The Lesson of *The Piano Lesson*." *New Republic*, May 21, 1990: 28–30.

Ching, Mei-Lei. "Wrestling against History." *Theater* 20 (summer-fall 1988): 70–71.

DiGaetani, John. "August Wilson." *A Search for a Postmodern Theater: Interviews with Contemporary Playwrights*. New York: Greenwood, 1991. 275–84.

Elkins, Marilyn, ed. *August Wilson: A Casebook*. New York: Garland, 1994.

Ellison, Ralph. *Shadow and Act*. New York: Random, 1964.

Freedman, Samuel G. "A Voice from the Streets." *New York Times Magazine*, March 15, 1987: 36, 40, 49, 70.

Gates, Henry Louis, Jr. "Department of Disputation: The Chitlin' Circuit." *New Yorker*, February 3, 1997: 44–55.

Gussow, Mel. "Fine-Tuning *The Piano Lesson*." *New York Times Magazine*, September 10, 1989, part 2, sec. 6: 18–19, 58, 60.

Henry, William A., III. "Two-Timer." *Time*, April 23, 1990. *New York Theatre Critics' Review* 51 (1990): 329.

Herrington, Joan. *I Ain't Sorry for Nothin' I Done: August Wilson's Process of Playwriting*. New York: Limelight, 1998.

Kramer, Mimi. "Travelling Men and Hesitating Women." *New Yorker*, April 30, 1990: 82–83.

Lahr, John. "Black and Blues." *New Yorker*, April 15, 1996: 99–101.

Moyers, Bill. "August Wilson's America: A Conversation with Bill Moyers." *American Theatre*, June 1989: 12–17, 54–56.

Nadel, Alan, ed. *May All Your Fences Have Gates: Essays on the Drama of August Wilson*. Iowa City: University of Iowa Press, 1994.

Oshinsky, David M. "*Worse Than Slavery*": *Parchman Farm and the Ordeal of Jim Crow Justice*. New York: Free Press, 1996.

Pereira, Kim. *August Wilson and the African-American Odyssey*. Urbana: University of Illinois Press, 1995.

Plum, Jay. "Blues, History, and the Dramaturgy of August Wilson." *African American Review* 27 (winter 1993): 561–67.

Rich, Frank. "Broadway's Bounty: Dramas Brimming with Life." *New York Times,* June 3, 1990, sec. 2: 1, 8.

Rothstein, Mervyn. "Round Five for a Theatrical Heavyweight." *New York Times,* April 15, 1990, sec. 2: 1, 8.

Roudané, Matthew. *American Drama since 1960: A Critical History*. New York: Twayne, 1996.

Savran, David, ed. "August Wilson." *In Their Own Words: Contemporary American Playwrights*. New York: Theatre Communications Group, 1988. 288–305.

Shafer, Yvonne. *August Wilson: A Research and Production Sourcebook*. Westport, CT: Greenwood, 1998.

Shannon, Sandra G. *The Dramatic Vision of August Wilson*. Washington, D.C.: Howard University Press, 1995.

Wilson, August. *August Wilson: Three Plays*. Pittsburgh: University of Pittsburgh Press, 1991.

———. "The Ground on Which I Stand." *American Theatre,* September 1996: 14–16, 71–74.

———. "How to Write a Play Like August Wilson." *New York Times,* March 10, 1991, sec. 2: 5, 17.

———. *Seven Guitars*. New York: Dutton, 1996.

———. *Two Trains Running*. New York: Plume, 1993.

Wolfe, Peter. *August Wilson*. New York: Twayne, 1999.

Bibliography

Abbotson, Susan C. W. *Thematic Guide to Modern Drama*. Westport, CT: Greenwood, 2004.

Adam, Julie. *Versions of Heroism in Modern American Drama: Redefinitions by Miller, O'Neill, and Anderson*. New York: St. Martin's, 1991.

Aronson, Arnold. *American Avant-Garde Theatre: A History*. New York: Routledge, 2000.

Berkowitz, Gerald M. *American Drama of the Twentieth Century*. New York: Longman, 1992.

Berney, K. A., ed. *Contemporary American Dramatists*. Detroit: St. James, 1994.

Bernstein, Samuel J. *The Strands Entwined: A New Direction in American Drama*. Boston: Northeastern University Press, 1980.

Bigsby, Christopher. *Contemporary American Playwrights*. New York: Cambridge University Press, 1999.

———. *A Critical Introduction to Twentieth-Century American Drama*. New York: Cambridge University Press, 1982.

———. *Modern American Drama, 1945–2000*. New York: Cambridge University Press, 2000.

Bloom, Clive, ed. *American Drama*. New York: St. Martin's, 1995.

Bock, Hedwig, and Albert Wertheim, eds. *Essays on Contemporary American Drama*. Munich, Germany: Hueber, 1981.

Bonin, Jane F. *Major Themes in Prize-Winning American Drama*. Metuchen, NJ: Scarecrow, 1975.

Booker, Margaret. *Lillian Hellman and August Wilson: Dramatizing a New American Identity*. New York: Peter Lang, 2003.

Bottoms, Stephen J. *Playing Underground: A Critical History of the 1960s Off-Off-Broadway Movement*. Ann Arbor: University of Michigan Press, 2004.

Bronner, Edwin. *The Encyclopedia of the American Theatre: 1900–1975*. San Diego, CA: Barnes, 1980.

Broussard, Louis. *American Drama: Contemporary Allegory from Eugene O'Neill to Tennessee Williams*. Norman: University of Oklahoma Press, 1962.

Brustein, Robert. *Reimagining American Theatre*. Chicago: Dee, 1992.

Bryer, Jackson R., ed. *The Playwright's Art: Conversations with Contemporary American Dramatists*. New Brunswick, NJ: Rutgers University Press, 1995.

Bryer, Jackson R., and Mary L. Hartig, eds. *Companion to American Drama*. New York: Facts on File, 2004.

Cohn, Ruby. *New American Dramatists: 1960–1980*. New York: Grove, 1982.

Coven, Brenda. *American Women Dramatists of the Twentieth Century: A Bibliography*. Metuchen, NJ: Scarecrow, 1982.

Crespy, David A. *Off-Off-Broadway Explosion: How Provocative Playwrights of the 1960s Ignited a New American Theater*. New York: Back Stage, 2003.

Davis, Walter A. *Get the Guests: Psychoanalysis, Modern American Drama, and the Audience*. Madison: University of Wisconsin Press, 1994.

Demastes, William W. *Beyond Naturalism: A New Realism in American Theatre*. Westport, CT: Greenwood, 1988.

Downer, Alan S., ed. *The American Theater Today*. New York: Basic Books, 1967.

———. *American Drama and Its Critics: A Collection of Critical Essays*. Chicago: University of Chicago Press, 1965.

Fleche, Anne. *Mimetic Disillusion: Eugene O'Neill, Tennessee Williams, and U.S. Dramatic Realism*. Tuscaloosa: University of Alabama Press, 1997.

Freedman, Morris. *American Drama in Social Context*. Carbondale: Southern Illinois University Press, 1971.

Golden, Joseph. *The Death of Tinker Bell: The American Theatre in the 20th Century*. Syracuse, NY: Syracuse University Press, 1967.

Greenfield, Thomas Allen. *Work and the Work Ethic in American Drama, 1920–1970*. Columbia: University of Missouri Press, 1982.

Hall, Ann C. *"A Kind of Alaska": Women in the Plays of O'Neill, Pinter, and Shepard*. Carbondale: Southern Illinois University Press, 1993.

Harris, Andrew B. *Broadway Theatre*. New York: Routledge, 1994.

Herman, William. *Understanding Contemporary American Drama*. Columbia: University of South Carolina Press, 1987.

Herron, Ima Honaker. *The Small Town in American Drama*. Dallas, TX: Southern Methodist University Press, 1969.

King, Bruce, ed. *Contemporary American Theatre*. New York: St. Martin's, 1991.

King, Kimball. *Ten Modern American Playwrights: An Annotated Bibliography*. New York: Garland, 1982.

Kolin, Philip C., ed. *American Playwrights since 1945: A Guide to Scholarship, Criticism, and Performance*. Westport, CT: Greenwood, 1989.

Krutch, Joseph Wood. *The American Drama since 1918: An Informal History*. Rev. ed. New York: Braziller, 1967.

Laufe, Abe. *Anatomy of a Hit: Long Run Plays on Broadway from 1900 to the Present Day*. New York: Hawthorn Books, 1966.

Lewis, Allan. *American Plays and Playwrights of the Contemporary Theatre*. Rev. ed. New York: Crown, 1970.

Londré, Felicia Hardison, and Daniel J. Watermeier. *The History of North American Theater: The United States, Canada, and Mexico, from Pre-Columbian Times to the Present*. New York: Continuum, 1998.

McDonough, Carla J. *Staging Masculinity: Male Identity in Contemporary American Drama*. Jefferson, NC: McFarland, 1997.

MacNicholas, John, ed. *Twentieth-Century American Dramatists*. Detroit: Gale, 1981.

Mann, Emily, and David Roessel, eds. *Political Stages: Plays That Shaped a Century*. New York: Applause, 2002.

Marranca, Bonnie, and Gautam Dasgupta. *American Playwrights: A Critical Survey*. New York: Drama Book Specialists, 1981.

Marsh-Lockett, Carol P., ed. *Black Women Playwrights: Visions on the American Stage*. New York: Garland, 1999.

Maufort, Marc, ed. *Staging Difference: Cultural Pluralism in American Theatre and Drama*. New York: Lang, 1995.

Meserve, Walter J. *Discussions of American Drama*. Boston: Heath, 1965.

———. *An Outline History of American Drama*. Rev. ed. New York: Feedback Theatrebooks & Prospero, 1994.

Murphy, Brenda. *American Realism and American Drama, 1880–1940*. New York: Cambridge University Press, 1987.

———. *Congressional Theatre: Dramatizing McCarthyism on Stage, Film, and Television*. Cambridge: Cambridge University Press, 2002.

Nannes, Caspar H. *Politics in the American Drama*. Washington, DC: Catholic University of America Press, 1960.

Olauson, Judith. *The American Woman Playwright: A View of Criticism and Characterization*. Troy, NY: Whitston, 1981.

Parker, Dorothy, ed. *Essays on Modern American Drama: Williams, Miller, Albee, and Shepard*. Toronto: University of Toronto Press, 1987.

Poland, Albert, and Bruce Mailman, eds. *The Off, Off Broadway Book: The Plays, People, Theatre*. Indianapolis, IN: Bobbs-Merrill, 1972.

Porter, Thomas E. *Myth and Modern American Drama*. Detroit: Wayne State University Press, 1969.

Pradhan, N. S. *Modern American Drama: A Study in Myth and Tradition*. New Delhi: Arnold-Heinemann, 1978.

Price, Julia S. *The Off-Broadway Theater*. Westport, CT: Greenwood, 1974.

Roudané, Matthew C. *American Drama since 1960: A Critical History*. New York: Twayne, 1996.

———, ed. *Public Issues, Private Tensions: Contemporary American Drama*. New York: AMS Press, 1993.

Scanlan, Tom. *Family, Drama, and American Dreams*. Westport, CT: Greenwood, 1978.

Scharine, Richard G. *From Class to Caste in American Drama: Political and Social Themes since the 1930s*. Westport, CT: Greenwood, 1991.

Schlueter, June, ed. *Feminist Rereadings of Modern American Drama*. Rutherford, NJ: Fairleigh Dickinson University Press, 1989.

———. *Modern American Drama: The Female Canon*. Rutherford, NJ: Fairleigh Dickinson University Press, 1990.

Schroeder, Patricia R. *The Feminist Possibilities of Dramatic Realism*. Madison, NJ: Fairleigh Dickinson University Press, 1996.

———. *The Presence of the Past in Modern American Drama*. Rutherford, NJ: Fairleigh Dickinson University Press, 1989.

Shaland, Irene. *American Theater and Drama Research: An Annotated Guide to Information Sources, 1945–1990*. Jefferson, NC: McFarland, 1991.

Szilassy, Z. *American Theater of the 1960s*. Carbondale: Southern Illinois University Press, 1986.

Taylor, William E., ed. *Modern American Drama: Essays in Criticism*. DeLand, FL: Everett/Edwards, 1968.

Vorlicky, Robert. *Act Like a Man: Challenging Masculinities in American Drama*. Ann Arbor: University of Michigan Press, 1995.

Wainscott, Ronald H. *The Emergence of the Modern American Theater, 1914–1929*. New Haven, CT: Yale University Press, 1997.

Weales, Gerald. *American Drama since World War II*. New York: Harcourt, Brace & World, 1962.

———. *The Jumping-Off Place: American Drama in the 1960's*. New York: Macmillan, 1969.

Wilmeth, Don B., and Christopher Bigsby. *The Cambridge History of American Theatre*. 3 vols. New York: Cambridge University Press, 1998–2000.

Wilson, Garff B. *Three Hundred Years of American Drama and Theatre: From Ye Bear and Ye Cubb to Chorus Line*. Englewood Cliffs, NJ: Prentice-Hall, 1982.

Index

About the Author

SUSAN C. W. ABBOTSON has taught English for more than 15 years, first at the high school level and now at Rhode Island College. Her previous books include *Thematic Guide to Modern Drama* (2003), *Student Companion to Arthur Miller* (2000), and *Understanding* Death of a Salesman (1999), all available from Greenwood Press.